What is to Be Done About Crime and Punishment?

Roger Matthews
Editor

What is to Be Done About Crime and Punishment?

Towards a 'Public Criminology'

palgrave
macmillan

Editor
Roger Matthews
University of Kent
Canterbury, United Kingdom

ISBN 978-1-137-57227-1   ISBN 978-1-137-57228-8   (eBook)
DOI 10.1057/978-1-137-57228-8

Library of Congress Control Number: 2016936722

© The Editor(s) (if applicable) and The Author(s) 2016
The author(s) has/have asserted their right(s) to be identifi ed as the author(s) of this work in accordance with the Copyright, Designs and Patents Act 1988.
This work is subject to copyright. All rights are solely and exclusively licensed by the Publisher, whether the whole or part of the material is concerned, specifically the rights of translation, reprinting, reuse of illustrations, recitation, broadcasting, reproduction on microfilms or in any other physical way, and transmission or information storage and retrieval, electronic adaptation, computer software, or by similar or dissimilar methodology now known or hereafter developed.
The use of general descriptive names, registered names, trademarks, service marks, etc. in this publication does not imply, even in the absence of a specific statement, that such names are exempt from the relevant protective laws and regulations and therefore free for general use.
The publisher, the authors and the editors are safe to assume that the advice and information in this book are believed to be true and accurate at the date of publication. Neither the publisher nor the authors or the editors give a warranty, express or implied, with respect to the material contained herein or for any errors or omissions that may have been made.

Cover illustration: © Photocase Addicts GmbH / Alamy Stock Photo

Printed on acid-free paper

This Palgrave Macmillan imprint is published by Springer Nature
The registered company is Macmillan Publishers Ltd. London

Contents

Notes on Contributors

Ben Bowling is Professor of Criminology & Criminal Justice and Deputy Dean of the Dickson Poon School of Law, King's College London. His books include *Violent Racism* (OUP 1999), *Racism, Crime and Justice* (with Coretta Phillips, Longman 2004), *Policing the Caribbean* (OUP 2010), *Global Policing* (with James Sheptycki, Sage 2012), *Stop & Search: Police Power in Global Context* (with Leanne Weber, Routledge 2012) and the four-volume *Global Policing and Transnational Law Enforcement* (with James Sheptycki, Sage 2015). He has been an adviser to the UK Parliament, Foreign and Commonwealth Office, Equality and Human Rights Commission, the European Commission, Interpol and the United Nations.

Caroline Chatwin is Senior Lecturer in Criminology at the University of Kent, where she runs third year and master's level courses on 'drugs, culture and control'. She is a leading international scholar in the field of European drug policy, and has a single author research monograph, *Drug Policy harmonization and the European Union*, published with Palgrave Macmillan. She has also researched cannabis markets in the UK, internet research methods, older cannabis users and policy responses to new psychoactive substances.

Francis T. Cullen is Distinguished Research Professor Emeritus and a Senior Research Associate in the School of Criminal Justice at the University of Cincinnati. His recent works include *Environmental Corrections: A New Paradigm for Supervising Offenders in the Community*, *Correctional Theory: Context and Consequences*, and *Reaffirming Rehabilitation* (30th anniversary edition). His current research interests are in correctional policy, theoretical criminology, and the organisation of criminological knowledge. He is a past president of both the American Society of Criminology and the Academy of Criminal Justice Sciences.

Elliott Currie is Professor of Criminology, Law and Society at the University of California, Irvine, and Adjunct Professor in the Faculty of Law, School of Justice, Queensland University of Technology. He is the author of *Confronting Crime: an American Challenge, Reckoning: Drugs, the Cities, and the American Future*, Crime and *Punishment in America, The Road to Whatever: Middle Class Culture and the Crisis of Adolescence* and *The Roots of Danger: Violent Crime in Global Perspective*, and co-author of *Whitewashing Race: the Myth of a Colorblind Society*.

Fiona Haines is Professor of Criminology at the University of Melbourne and Adjunct Professorial Fellow at the Australian National University. She has extensive expertise in white collar and corporate crime, globalisation and regulation. Her current projects include research in Indonesia and India, analysing local grievances against multinational enterprises for human rights abuse, and research in Australia analysing community protests against coal seam gas. Her most recent book is *Regulatory Transformations: Rethinking Economy Society Interactions*, Hart Publishing, 2015, co-edited with Bettina Lange and Dania Thomas.

Shruti Iyer is an undergraduate research fellow at King's College London, currently pursuing a degree in politics, philosophy and law.

Helen Johnson is a consultant researcher and lecturer with a PhD in criminology on emotions and desistance. She specialises in the use of innovative qualitative methods and her research interests include emotions, role transition, desistance, gender, repertory grid technique, personal construct theory and prostitution. She has over ten years of experience and is involved in a number of research (and related) projects on improving service provision for vulnerable populations, in particular exiting prostitution.

Liz Kelly is Professor of Sexualised Violence at London Metropolitan University, UK, where she is also director of the Child and Woman Abuse Studies Unit (CWASU). She has been active in the field of violence against women and children for almost thirty years. She is the author of *Surviving Sexual Violence* (1988), which established the concept of a 'continuum of violence' and over seventy book chapters and journal articles. In 2000 she was awarded a CBE in the New Year's Honours List for 'services combating violence against women and children'.

Cheryl Lero Jonson is Assistant Professor in the Department of Criminal Justice at Xavier University, Cincinnati. Her recent works include *Correctional*

Theory: Context and Consequences and *The American Prison: Imagining a Different Future*. Her current research interests are the effects of imprisonment, the use of incentives to downsize prison populations and the effectiveness of active shooter responses.

Michael R. McGuire has developed an international profile in the critical study of technology, crime and the justice system, in particular issues around cyberoffending and cybercrime. His first book *Hypercrime: The New Geometry of Harm* (Glasshouse, 2008), involved a critique of the notion of cybercrime as a way of modelling computer-enabled offending and was awarded the 2008 British Society of Criminology runners-up Book Prize. His most recent publication, *Technology, Crime & Justice: The Question Concerning Technomia* (Routledge, 2012) was the first book in the field of Criminology and Criminal Justice to provide an overview of the implication of technology for the justice system and complements a range of applied studies in this area, including the comprehensive UK Review of Cybercrime conducted for the Home Office. He is currently preparing the *Handbook of Technology, Crime and Justice* (Taylor Francis 2016) together with a monograph *The Organisation of Cybercrime*, which will provide one of the first detailed studies of the use of digital technologies by organised crime groups.

Roger Matthews is Professor of Criminology at the University of Kent. He is author of *Realist Criminology* (Palgrave Macmillan 2014) and *Exiting Prostitution; A Study in Female Desistance* (with He. Easton, L. Young and J. Bindel, Palgrave Macmillan 2014). He was also an advisor to the All-Party Parliamentary Group on Prostitution and the Global Sex Trade in 2014 and co-author of *Shifting The Burden: Inquiry to Assess the Operation of the Current Legal Settlement on Prostitution in England and Wales* (London: HMSO).

Daniel P. Mears is the Mark C. Stafford Professor of Criminology at the College of Criminology and Criminal Justice, Florida State University, USA. He conducts research on a range of crime and justice topics, including studies of offending, juvenile justice, supermax prisons, sentencing and prisoner reentry. His work has appeared in *Criminology, the Journal of Research in Crime and Delinquency*, and other crime and policy journals and in *American Criminal Justice Policy* (Cambridge University Press), which won the Academy of Criminal Justice Sciences Outstanding Book Award, and, with Joshua C. Cochran, *Prisoner Reentry in the Era of Mass Incarceration* (Sage Publications).

John Pitts is Vauxhall Professor of Socio-Legal Studies at the University of Bedfordshire. He has worked as: a school teacher; a street and club-based youth worker; a group worker in a Young Offender Institution; and as a consultant on youth crime and youth justice to the police and youth justice and legal professionals in the UK, mainland Europe, the Russian Federation and China. In the last decade, he has undertaken research on violent youth gangs and acted as a consultant and researcher on gangs to central and local government, police authorities and think tanks. He is currently researching young peoples' pathways into organised crime in a northern city.

Robert Reiner is Emeritus Professor of Criminology, Law Department, London School of Economics. His recent publications include: *Law and Order Polity*, 2007; *The Politics of the Police,* 4th ed. Oxford University Press 2010; *Policing, Popular Culture and Political Economy: Towards a Social Democratic Criminology*, Ashgate 2011; *Crime Polity*, 2016.

James Sheptycki is Professor of Criminology, McLaughlin College, York University. He has written on a variety of substantive topics in criminology, including domestic violence, serial killers, money laundering, drugs, public order policing, organised crime, police accountability, intelligence-led policing, witness protection, transnational crime, risk and insecurity. He is currently engaged in research concerning guns, crime and social order.

Angela J. Thielo is Assistant Professor in the Department of Criminal Justice at the University of Louisville. She is currently completing her PhD in criminal justice at the University of Cincinnati. She co-edited a special issue on 'Downsizing Prisons' that appeared in *Victims & Offenders*. Her recent publications focus on attitudes toward correctional policy, with a special focus on public support for the rehabilitation and redemption of convicted offenders.

Nick Tilley is a member of University College London's Jill Dando Institute. He is also an Adjunct Professor in the Griffith Criminology Institute, Brisbane. His long-term research interests concern theoretically informed applied social science. He has focused mainly on policing, crime prevention and realist research methods. Current projects relate to the international crime drop, what works in crime reduction and the prevention of youth related sexual abuse and violence.

Nicole Westmarland is Professor of Criminology and Director of the Durham University Centre for Research into Violence and Abuse. She has researched various forms of violence against women and her book *Violence Against Women— Criminological perspectives on men's violences* (Routledge, 2015) brings together different forms to look at the overlaps between them. Her ongoing work includes a project aimed at increasing police understanding of and responses to coercive control.

List of Tables

List of Boxes

1

Introduction: Towards a Public Criminology

Roger Matthews

There has been a recent shift of emphasis towards making social scientific investigation more policy relevant. University departments and funding bodies are increasingly using terms like 'impact', 'deliverables' and 'outputs' and more frequently aim to identify the beneficiaries of research studies. There has also been an important and timely debate in the social sciences about developing a 'public criminology' that is able to contribute to contemporary policy debates (Burawoy 2005; Currie 2007). Some leading criminologists have argued that the criminological industry is becoming increasingly socially and politically irrelevant and has little to contribute to the major debates on crime and justice (Austin 2003; Cullen 2011). Others have put the case for making criminology more policy oriented by asking 'What is to be done?' (Burawoy 2005, 2008). This debate raises important questions about the role of the academic researcher.

In line with this renewed emphasis on linking theory to policy this collection aims to encourage academics, researchers and students at all

R. Matthews (✉)
University of Kent, Canterbury, UK

© The Editor(s) (if applicable) and The Author(s) 2016   **1**
R. Matthews (ed.), *What is to Be Done About Crime and Punishment?*,
DOI 10.1057/978-1-137-57228-8_1

levels to think about the policy implications of their work. Considering questions of policy, it is suggested, moves investigation from a purely descriptive or detached stance and encourages researchers to engage more directly with the issues that interest them. This often results in the production of more satisfying and useful forms of investigation and analysis.

Despite the recent shift in emphasis towards policy relevance there still remains a large body of professional criminologists who are reluctant to engage in the policy process, either because they feel it is not their role or they fear that their suggested reforms will fail and that this will compromise their credibility. The major barrier, however, to making a significant contribution the policy process comes not so much from a fear of failure or co-option but the reality that a great deal of criminological investigation is poorly conceived and researched. Indeed, there is a growing body of criminological material that has been described as 'So What?' criminology (Matthews 2009). This material tends to be theoretically weak, methodologically inadequate and has little or no policy relevance.

One of the most notable developments in criminology in recent years has been the demise of theory and an increase in weak forms of conceptualisation. Key terms are often taken at face value and are not disaggregated, with the consequence that concepts like 'crime' and 'race' remain broad generic categories that lack specificity. Operating with these taken for granted, common sense categories results in the object of study remaining vague and undifferentiated with the consequence that it becomes difficult to formulate clear and detailed forms of analysis and, by implication, sound policy options. The main problem, however, is that weak forms of conceptualisation result in a lack of direction and focus to the research. In addition, the use of inconsistent and inappropriate categories serves to construct a blurred conceptual grid through which the social world is apprehended. Unfortunately, no amount of methodological manipulation can overcome these conceptual deficits (Sayer 2000). Thus there is a need to link theory, method and policy to produce forms of 'joined up' criminology that can combine theoretical sophistication and methodological rigour with policy relevance.

There is also a significant body of self-styled 'critical' or 'radical' criminology that does not feel it necessary to engage in detailed empirical investigation. Instead, evidence is used selectively and sparingly. This results, as Elliott Currie points out in Chap. 2 in this book, is a form of 'liberal idealism' that produces speculative forms of expose criminology and generally refuses to take crime and victimisation seriously (see also Zedner 2011). As Currie suggests we are, however, at a crossroads both socially and politically, as well as criminologically. If criminology is to have any purchase on pressing contemporary issues it needs to develop a global response that is able to address the structural roots of crime and associated forms of suffering. In particular, the continuing level of violence around the world, especially in its more hidden forms, continues to present a major challenge to criminologists.

Nicole Westmarland and Liz Kelly develop a similar theme in their examination of domestic violence. As the authors point out in Chap. 3 domestic violence is one of those hidden 'private' forms of violence which surveys repeatedly show is endemic and highly gendered. Despite the widespread nature of domestic violence the rate of prosecutions and convictions remains remarkably low. Moreover, the strategies that have been employed to date to address this issue have proved to have a limited effect. Westmarland and Kelly argue that there is a need to move beyond current conceptions and policies on domestic violence and focus greater attention on the perpetrators.

Another area of violent activity is gang rivalries. This form of interpersonal violence and intimidation often remains hidden but can have a significant impact on the quality of life of people living in affected neighbourhoods. As John Pitts argues there are liberal idealists who try to deny the existence of gangs or claim that the media somehow 'construct' the notion of 'the gang'. In contrast, Pitts suggests in Chap. 4 that gangs are a serious problem in certain areas and their activities impact disproportionately upon the poorest and most vulnerable sections of society. Addressing this issue, he argues, requires a multi-agency and multi-faced sustainable strategy.

A consistent theme that runs through the chapters in this book is that positive and progressive reforms are not only possible but that there are numerous examples of specific reforms being beneficial in the past. In pursuing this theme Nick Tilley argues we should acknowledge that, in relation to crime prevention, there have been a number of ethical and effective gains in recent years. A key element in developing effective crime control policies, he suggests in Chap. 5 following Robert Merton (1949), is to develop middle range theories. That is, move away from a preoccupation with finding the root causes of crime to forms of explanation involving lower-level forms of theorising that can be tested through empirical research. This form of 'radical realism' challenges many of our preconceptions about the nature of theorising and also the relation between theory and policy formation.

For many the immediate response to crime and interpersonal violence is to summon the police. However, in recent years the role of the police and their effectiveness has been increasingly called into question. Some commentators see the police as part of the problem rather than the solution. Benjamin Bowling, Shruti Iyer, Robert Reiner and James Sheptycki ask the critical questions of what exactly do the police do and what type of police force do we want. In a world in which the uniformed police are only part of the wider policing process the authors argue in Chap. 6 that: the remit of the uniformed public police should be broader than crime control; their powers should be restricted in terms of the use of force and intrusive surveillance; and that the police need to develop new technologies, more transparent modes of accountability, improved data gathering techniques and more sophisticated forms of intelligence-led policing.

Alongside the police most people think about imprisonment as a 'natural' response to serious crime. However, the problems facing the prison system are such that it is increasingly seen as being in a state of 'crisis'. Hundreds, if not thousands, of publications over the years have pointed to the detrimental effects of imprisonment, on prisoners, their families, their neighbourhoods and society in general. In fact, it is difficult these days to find anyone defending incarceration. However, there is a real paucity of studies that seriously discuss penal reform. For those who do engage in penal reform there is call amongst liberal idealists for the abolition of prisons and the suggestion that they should be replaced by community-based penalties, although researchers have shown that these options are equally ineffective in reducing recidivism and costs. Unfortunately, the alternatives which are suggested by the abolitionists to deal with serious and persistent offenders are not seen as appropriate in the eyes of the general public, while criminologists warn about the dangers of 'net widening'. Thus, in contrast to this apparently 'radical' approach, Francis Cullen, Daniel Mears, Cheryl Jonson and Angela Thielo argue in Chap. 7 that a range of realistic and practical steps can be taken to make prisons less damaging and improve the quality of outcomes. With over two million people incarcerated in the USA and the steady increase in the prison population in the UK the time has come for a serious rethink of the use and purpose of imprisonment.

One of the most difficult issues in relation to policy development has been that of drugs. In fact, the drugs debate appears to be bogged down by hyperbole and an apparently endless stream of circular arguments. The rhetoric of the 'war on drugs' is now wearing thin and, as Caroline Chatwin argues in Chap. 8, there is an urgent need to broaden the debate and take into account harm minimisation strategies, while upholding human rights and giving public health a more prominent role in the formation of policy.

An equally challenging issue, which has received limited attention from criminologists over the years, is developing a consistent and effective response to white-collar and corporate crime. In addressing this issue in Chap. 9 Fiona Haines notes that the harms caused by white-collar and corporate crime have to be considered in a context in which these activities are embedded in a system of material and ideological benefits that condition the way in which both governments and the general public view these transgressions. Consequently, she suggests that there are three basic options to consider when addressing the issue of white-collar and corporate crime. The first involves better regulation of activities, such as introducing anti-trust measures. Second, the development of forms of responsive regulation and problem solving. Third, the development of a more fundamental reordering of how businesses ply their trade and a corresponding shift in the modes of regulation.

In many respects the criminological landscape appears to be changing. As some forms of recorded crime are decreasing in some locations new forms of transgression are becoming more prominent. In Chap. 10 Mike McGuire, like Fiona Haines, identifies a range of responses that are available for limiting the extent and impact of cyber crime. This can involve technical responses, criminal justice interventions and the development of a more informed and engaged public. However, McGuire argues that the game is changing and a more connected and increasingly intelligent network of operators are emerging, such that the provisions that have been put in place to date are looking increasingly inadequate. The response to this changing situation requires, he argues, more than a technical fix and he calls for a more nuanced social and political strategy that holds transgressors to account.

Finally, Helen Johnson and Roger Matthews address the deeply divided issue of prostitution or 'sex work'. They argue that there is an identifiable link between the form of conceptualisation of this issue and the policy choices. On one side the 'abolitionists' support the Nordic model that criminalises buyers and decriminalises the women involved in prostitution, who are seen as victims. This policy position follows from the premise that prostitution is a form of violence against women. The liberal 'sex-work' lobby, on the other hand, favours a policy of decriminalisation or legalisation and do not think that sanctioning buyers is appropriate. In Chap. 11 Johnson and Matthews outline the Nordic model and identify the critique presented by the liberal 'sex-work' group. They argue that, while the arguments against the Nordic model are unconvincing, in countries like the UK an effective policy on prostitution needs to incorporate a version of the Nordic model while also going beyond it.

Overall, it is anticipated that although each of these chapters focuses on a specific issue this collection will encourage readers to think more seriously about the relation between theory and practice and to develop an approach to criminological issues that is more engaged and more useful.

References

Austin, J. (2003). Why criminology is irrelevant. *Criminology and Public Policy, 2*, 557–564.

Burawoy, M. (2005). For public sociology. *The British Journal of Sociology, 56*(2), 259–294.

Burawoy, M. (2008). What is to be done? Theses on the degradation of social existence in a globalised world. *Current Sociology, 56*(3), 351–359.

Cullen, F. (2011). Beyond adolescence-limited criminology: Choosing our future. *Criminology, 49*, 287–330.

Currie, E. (2007). Against marginality: Arguments for a public criminology. *Theoretical Criminology, 11*(2), 175–190.

Matthews, R. (2009). Beyond 'so what?' Criminology: Rediscovering realism. *Theoretical Criminology, 13*(3), 341–362.

Merton, R. (1949). *Social theory and social structure.* New York: Free Press.

Sayer, A. (2000). *Realism and social science.* London: Sage.

Zedner, L. (2011). Putting crime back on the criminological agenda. In M. Bosworth & C. Hoyle (Eds.), *What is criminology?* Oxford: Oxford University Press.

2

The Violence Divide: Taking "Ordinary" Crime Seriously in a Volatile World

Elliott Currie

Introduction

Almost twenty-five years ago Jock Young described crime as a "moral barometer" of society—a "key indictor as to whether we are getting things right, achieving the sort of society in which people can live with dignity and without fear" (Young 1992, p. 34). Today, the pattern of violent crime around the world provides a particularly troubling reading of how far we are from "getting things right" in our contemporary global society, and it cries out for serious attention and action. But whether we will see that sustained attention, much less social action, on the scale we need in the coming years is by no means certain.

There are strong forces operating both within and beyond the discipline of criminology that place formidable obstacles in the path of tackling global violence with the seriousness it deserves. But, at the same time, there are glimmers of hope that the field may be deepening and maturing

E. Currie (✉)
Department of Criminology Law and Society, University of California, Irvine, CA, USA

© The Editor(s) (if applicable) and The Author(s) 2016
R. Matthews (ed.), *What is to Be Done About Crime and Punishment?*,
DOI 10.1057/978-1-137-57228-8_2

in encouraging ways. There are several possible futures for criminology in an increasingly volatile world: and which of those futures we get will depend a lot on us; and what kind of future we get is not just an abstract academic question. It is important—not just for those of us who are in the business of studying crime, but for the lives of great numbers of people outside our ranks, and for the fate of values that we cherish, or ought to—that values include social justice and the reduction of needless human suffering and insecurity.

In fact I will go so far as to say that we are at a point when the choices we make about what our field really stands for, what it is really about, may be more important than they have ever been. We are at a moment in global history where the potential for the erosion of many of those core values is very real and is, in some ways, accelerating—a time when the consequences of some of our most problematic social and economic choices are becoming more and more visible, when a great many global chickens are coming home to roost.

I want to sketch out some aspects of where I think we are, and then ask whether criminology will be capable of stepping up to do the job that's needed. I suggest several possible scenarios, good and bad, for what criminology could look like down the road; and suggest some elements of the kind of criminology that can most usefully grapple with the global trends that are now upon us.

"Lidless" Capitalism and the Violence Divide

The overarching context for understanding global violence in the twenty-first century is the rise and spread of what we might call "capitalism with the lid off" (or what I sometimes call "hit the fan" capitalism). We have now been through several decades of that remarkably unrestrained version of global capitalism, which has changed the world in ways that are profoundly relevant for those of us who study crime and justice. It has relentlessly widened social and economic inequalities, both within countries and between them. It has transformed the nature of work in ways that have exacerbated a spreading crisis of economic insecurity in advanced and developing countries alike. It has forced the movement of vast numbers of people both within and between countries on a scale that has very few precedents in recent history. And it has done all of that with startling speed.

What economists call the 90–10 ratio—the disparity between the incomes of the most affluent 10 percent and the poorest 10 percent of households—has risen in the OECD countries from about 7–1 in the 1980s to roughly 10–1 now. Increasing fortunes at the top have gone along with declining economic conditions for the bottom two-fifths of the population (OECD 2015). In the United States, long the most unequal of advanced industrial countries, the incomes of the bottom tenth of the population have fallen by roughly 17 percent since the start of the century, while those of the top five percent have rapidly increased (Greenstein 2015).

Around the world, one key reason for the rise in inequality is the decline in stable work. The International Labour Organization reports that only one-quarter of workers globally now enjoy a "stable employment relationship," with the great majority—particularly in less developed countries— working in informal jobs, in individual self-employment or unpaid family employment, or in temporary contracts (ILO 2015). The proportion of poor youth who are "disconnected" from both legitimate work and school, which was already at crisis levels before the recent global recession, is now arguably higher than it has been for seventy-five years. In some countries of what we, still rather euphemistically, call the developing world–and in some American neighborhoods–those "disconnected" youth are now the majority. And though in many countries the belated recovery from the most recent global economic slowdown has improved things a little, by most measures the state of lower-income people in much of the world is more perilous than before the "great recession" began. Despite significant increases in employment, for example, and faster overall economic growth, the number of Americans officially in poverty—universally understood to be a misleadingly low measure of the extent of real deprivation—remains higher than it was before the recession began, at roughly 15 percent of the population (Greenstein 2015).

That even a return to a degree of economic growth has barely dented the growing trends toward insecurity, deprivation, and inequality suggests that—short of genuinely transformative social policies–we are in for a long period of social and economic volatility and widespread insecurity, in the midst of unprecedented technological capacity. And in most countries—certainly in my own—no such transformative policies are on the horizon, and indeed proposals to do anything serious about the changes that are now undermining well-being, opportunity, and security on a global scale are nowhere to be found in mainstream political debate. Indeed, the suffusion of global political discourse with the language of austerity and rejection of public investment and public responsibility for the consequences of "lidless" capitalism means that, with rare but interesting exceptions, serious confrontation with these issues is simply not on the table. No one now takes responsibility for mitigating the multiple crises brought on by "lidless" capitalism, much less pressing for genuine alternatives.

To be sure, painting these overarching trends with such a broad brush obscures important differences in the experience of particular countries—both in the impact of economic and social changes and in the political responses to them. But it is safe to say that this is the broad context that has predominantly shaped the global pattern of violent crime and responses to it in the twenty-first century, and that is likely to do so for some time to come.

One of the least surprising results of those deepening social disparities and insecurities is the corollary divide in the risks of violence. In what follows I focus entirely on what I call "ordinary" violence—street crimes and domestic violence behind closed doors—even though, as I show, there is really nothing "ordinary" about the pattern of these crimes around the world. I will not talk here about the often parallel issues raised with respect to state or corporate crime, nor speak to the ways in which decades of unrestrained global capitalism have helped to create conditions that breed groups given to mass atrocities. Not because these are, in any sense, of secondary importance, but because "ordinary" violence is what I know most about, and because I believe that ordinary violence in the twenty-first century is a human crisis of devastating proportions, one which, like many other contemporary human disasters, is savagely unequal in its impact.

I have been immersed lately in figures on the distribution on violent death around the world and, even though I already knew something about these realities, it has been a mind-boggling experience to look really hard at those numbers, and to think about their implications. The world is increasingly divided into places that are relatively peaceful and where people can generally feel pretty secure personally; and places where the specter of violence is at least as pervasive as it has ever been and is often more so—sometimes *much* more so.

Close to half of the world's homicides each year take place in countries that comprise just 11 percent of the world's population (UNODC 2015a, p. 22). And all of those places fall squarely into the category of the "usual suspects." They are places that are predictably wracked by the defining ills of "lidless" capitalism: widening income and wealth inequalities; high levels of absolute and relative poverty; weak, underfunded, and sometimes crumbling public support systems; ineffective and often corrupt criminal justice agencies that were never reliable providers of community safety and are now crippled by the combination of a sustained onslaught of unprecedented levels of violence and decades of public underinvestment; and, more often than not, a lethal flow of guns and a booming drug trade. Some of those places have gotten a little better lately, some have gotten a lot worse, but all of them remain in terrible shape—and it's hard to see what will change that reality in the foreseeable future barring, again, epochal changes in fundamental social and economic policies that are not now live subjects of discussion in the political sphere.

If you look long enough at the statistics on the plague of violence in these places, you can start to get numb to their human meaning. But that would be a terrible disservice to the hundreds of millions of people caught in the lower and more desperate reaches of "lidless" capitalism. The cold numbers represent nothing less than a global massacre inflicted on precisely those people who are also most predictably assaulted by the multiple burdens of living at the bottom of an unforgiving and neglectful global social order.

If you live in Honduras you are more than: two hundred and fifty times more likely to die by violence than if you live in Japan; a hundred times more likely to die by violence than if you live in the Netherlands; ninety times more likely than if you live in the UK. (Currie 2015a; UNODC 2015b). In the Honduran city of San Pedro Sula, which has been frequently described in recent years as the most violent place in the world, a report in the *Guardian* newspaper quoted a local mortician as saying that "people here kill people like they were chickens" (Brodzinsky 2013). You are a hundred times more likely to be murdered in Guatemala City or Tegucigalpa than in Copenhagen or Berlin (UNODC 2015b).

In the United States, as in some other countries, we are much given to celebrating the "crime drop" since the early 1990s. And the decline in violent crime from its peak in the late 1980s and early 1990s is certainly real—but much more so for some places and people than for others. It is far more uneven and fragile than our usual public discussion assumes, and has left parts of the country still in the grip of a profound violence and fear. And, as in the world as a whole, the violence divide in the United States falls along thoroughly predictable lines.

At last count, the city of Gary, Indiana, just a stone's throw from where I grew up, racked up a homicide death rate far in excess of that in Kingston, Jamaica, the most violent city in one of the world's perennially most violent countries. Detroit, New Orleans, and Newark (New Jersey) all suffer homicide rates that top the rate in Port-au-Prince, Haiti. More people die by violence in the city of Baltimore, Maryland, than in the countries of Sweden, Norway, and Denmark combined (Daley 2015).

Newark is also one of several American cities that, as I write in 2015, are suffering a dramatic rise in homicide (Davey and Smith 2015)—including six killings in as many days during one week in the month of August (Coleman 2015). Baltimore is another, suffering "a wave of killings the like of which hasn't been seen in four decades" during 2015 (Campbell and Jedra 2015). My home town of Chicago, which a columnist (Ehrenfreund 2015) for one of the country's most respected newspapers recently described as a "very safe" city, witnessed eight homicides in less than two days in July (Yan and Holland 2015).

Unsurprisingly, the global split between places where violence is a routine fact of life and those where it is a small and sometimes dwindling possibility is deeply entwined with race. It is no accident that the places that routinely show up at the top of the lists of the world's most violent are places like South Africa, parts of Latin America and the Caribbean, and the urban ghettoes of the United States. And it's important to understand just how closely these places now resemble one another. The homicide death rate among black men in the state of Indiana is higher than the rate for men in South Africa or Brazil. If black Americans had enjoyed the same risk of homicide as white Americans in 2013, we would have saved nearly seven thousand black American lives (Currie 2015b). Of the 233 homicides in Baltimore from the start of 2015 to mid-September, where the race of the victim is known, 218 were African-American—205 of them African-American men (*Baltimore Sun* 2015).

The news is not all bad, and it is important, again, to recognize the ways in which specific countries and specific places within them have been impacted—and have responded—differently. There are some countries where violence has dropped considerably from a peak—including very volatile ones, like Brazil and South Africa, and much of the United States. But what is blindingly obvious in the age of hit-the-fan capitalism is the stark bifurcation of violent death in the world—and the reality that, in the hardest-hit communities, even significant declines have left violent crime at levels that constitute a human emergency.

These widening disparities in violence are paralleled by widening disparities between those countries that are locking more and more people behind bars and those where incarceration is decreasing—many of which are places where rates of imprisonment were low to begin with. Finland and Germany, among others, generally shrank their prison population in recent years; Brazil added almost half a million prisoners since the early nineties—and looks to be on the verge of adding a lot more (ICPS 2015).

I think it is not too much to say that these global disparities—in the risks of violence and in the risks of incarceration—represent both a public health emergency and a human-rights catastrophe. Yet one of the most striking aspects of that emergency is that it is only rarely called out as such. Indeed, just as the impact of "ordinary" violence is stunningly uneven across the world, so too is the perception, even the awareness, of it. What strikes me as an intolerable violation of human rights, security, and dignity—and a powerful indictment of the social order of "lidless" capitalism—is well-nigh invisible to many observers, and explicitly denied by others—including a surprising number of people whose job it is to understand these issues. And, to the extent that this remains true, it obviously undercuts our ability to do much about the violence divide—either on the level of social policy and social action, or of education and analysis. And that means in turn that the routine infliction of preventable violence and suffering on some of the world's most vulnerable people will surely continue. We cannot predict with any precision what "ordinary" violence will look like ten or twenty or thirty years down the road, but we can be pretty sure of that much.

What accounts for that surprising invisibility? I think it's a mix of several different things—some social, some technical, some ideological. On the simplest level, as I have argued before (Currie 2009), the tendency for the plague of "ordinary" violence to fall off the social and political radar screen is a natural consequence of its concentration among people who have little voice and little visibility *most* of the time, and less than a little political influence. In that sense the absence of sustained awareness or concern about the impact of violence on poor communities, whether in Detroit or Guatemala City, is not very surprising, since we don't hear much about *other* pervasive social disasters in those places either: high levels of death from infant mortality and accidents; outsized levels of easily preventable communicable diseases and exposure to environmental toxins; of substance abuse and untreated mental illness. If white American youth died of homicide at the same rate as their black counterparts, and the United States had lost roughly 13,000 young white men to violence in 2013 (instead of 836), I think it can be confidently said that there would have been a massive public outcry (Currie 2015b). It is not that we saw *no* expression of outrage over the comparable loss of young African-American lives, it is just that it was mainly confined to the communities where they lived—communities where street memorials to the fallen and virtually endless funeral services are an expected part of the landscape.

The social invisibility of the marginalized victims of violence is compounded by some aspects of the way we conventionally measure violent crime. Honest criminologists have been saying for a long time that many of our conventional crime statistics systematically obscure the extent of violence among the most marginal and thus most vulnerable populations—but we use them anyway, usually without careful acknowledgement of their limits. This is not a big problem for our understanding of homicide, but it has crippled our understanding of the severity and social distribution of other forms of "ordinary" violence. We know that conventional victim surveys fail to capture a large proportion of the routine violence that afflicts poor communities, in the United States and elsewhere, just as police statistics do; we know that we get a far better estimate of the problem from data on hospital admissions for violent injuries, which, in the United States, consistently reveal more than double the number of serious assaults that have shown up in national victim surveys in recent years.

Yet much of the discussion of American violence in both the criminological profession and the mass media proceeds as if victimization survey data were an accurate reflection of the problem—effectively "disappearing" a large fraction of the people most routinely victimized.

More subtly, we have difficulty grasping the degree to which the fundamental processes of "lidless" capitalism breed "ordinary" violence because mass incarceration has swept a good part of the evidence for that connection out of sight. This is a consequence of the rather peculiar way in which we measure what we call the crime rate. We count the crimes committed by offenders still on the street—but we consider neither the crimes they commit (or suffer) while behind bars nor the theoretical implications of the fact that we have swept great numbers of the people at highest risk—more than two million in the United States at any given point—off the street. As I have argued before (Currie 2003, 2015a), looking at crime this way is like measuring the extent of some major illness without counting the people we've hospitalized. Understanding the depth and spread of violence in our time—and its links to the depriving and disrupting forces of "lidless" capitalism—calls for measures that look simultaneously at levels of violence and levels of incarceration, especially in those countries—like the USA, Brazil, or El Salvador—where the growth of incarceration in recent decades has been massive. Seen in this way, the crime "drop" also falls into a more accurate perspective; we may have shrunk, up to a point, the official number of street crimes, but that does not mean we have seriously blunted the tendency of our social order to produce criminals.

For all of these reasons—along with some related developments in contemporary criminology I will return to in a moment—both the extent of the ongoing social disaster of "ordinary" violence and its close connections to the perfusion of a particularly destructive socio-economic order are often obscured. But that doesn't make the disaster any less real, or any less urgent.

Some Possible Futures

I think that addressing that disaster is an essential task for criminology in the modern world—one of the most basic reasons why we have criminology at all. The question is whether criminology in the coming years will even be capable of confronting these developments analytically, much less of addressing them in the world of policy and social action. And on that score I think there's bad news and good news.

The bad news is that there are some powerful forces both within and outside the universities that work against our ability to tackle those critical global issues with the attention and seriousness they deserve. The good news is that there is also more good, socially engaged, and creative criminology being done around the world today than at any time I can remember. And, if we put our minds to it, we can build on that work to transform the relevance and social significance of the discipline.

We're at a point in our discipline, in other words, that is messy and not easy to characterize. And so there are actually several very different futures that seem possible from where we stand now and—with a nod to one of the most influential of American criminological voices to whom I frequently refer, Clint Eastwood—I'll call them the good, the bad, and the ugly.

Let's start with the ugly. In my least optimistic moments, I see us operating in a world where the impacts of predatory capitalism get even rougher than they are now—and in which criminology increasingly takes on the role of helpless bystander, or at worst accomplice, in containing the social and personal consequences. Much of organized criminology, by default or by design, takes on the job of helping to manage the volatility and disorder that will continue to be generated by growing inequality, economic marginalization, and social disruption (and fed by an over-the-top culture of consumption that adds fuel to the fire—see Treadwell et al. 2013).

In this scenario I see continuing policies of austerity in social spending and a level of political gridlock and obstruction that will ensure we do not tackle the roots of the endemic long-term economic marginalization and communal insecurity that are so deeply entwined with high levels of violent crime. I see the inward-turning self-destruction of the most devastated communities around the world continuing as a result.

In the United States that stagnating, or even deepening, crisis—that permanent emergency—may co-exist with some real, but crucially limited, strategies to reduce the unsustainable costs of our traditional response to social disintegration—mass incarceration. I see us very likely continuing to move toward reducing the extremes of incarceration for minor offenders. Picking off this low-hanging fruit will satisfy some critics while keeping our overall reliance on mass incarceration largely intact. And we will not put up the money to do much with the people we keep out of prison, so we will continue to, mostly, abandon them—as we've been mostly doing all along. And if our abandoned and marginalized communities should heat up again, we could see a return of even more punitive practices—and possibly the growth of strategies of social control that may be even scarier.

In this scenario, we can expect to see dwindling public resources for the kinds of criminological work that do not directly articulate with the pressing and immediate goal of the social control of disadvantaged and dispossessed populations. In the context of an ongoing fiscal crisis, criminologists will be asked more and more to come up with strategies to control those populations that are both effective and inexpensive. In the context of spreading policies of austerity and assaults on the public sector, in some countries criminology will do its best just to hang on. And where it hangs on successfully, it does so by making itself a docile partner to increasingly mean-spirited or desperate governments in the service of social control.

Criminology that pushes boundaries, that raises questions critically about the larger trajectory of the economy and society, that insists on exploring a more equitable spread of the fruits of economic growth to everyone as a better response to crime, that insists on linking issues of violence with larger global social forces, gets increasingly marginalized. It becomes harder to make a living doing that kind of engaged and critical criminological work, and the harder it gets the fewer the people who are willing to put their futures on the line to do it. Graduate school advisors steer their students away from that kind of work because it probably will not get them published, almost certainly will not get them a grant, and likely will not get them a job. Then those students become the next generation of advisors, and they pass on the same message, to a steadily dwindling number of the sort of students who feel passionately about launching a more dynamic and humanly engaged career.

In a climate of perennial fiscal constraint and entrenched pessimism about the possibility of structural change, the focus of criminology narrows to strategies targeted at the individual level or, at the most, to narrowly drawn interventions at the micro community level. We see a resurgence of interest in pharmacological approaches to preventing crime and controlling offender populations—partly because they fit the developing zeitgeist, partly because they're cheap—in an age where even parts of the far right recognize that mass incarceration is a fiscally unsustainable way to control stubbornly persistent marginalized populations.

That's the ugly future. Most of the time I do not actually think it's going to happen, at least not as starkly as I have drawn it. But that does not mean it is not a possibility. Elements of that scenario already exist in some places. Notably in the United States, where we have a combination of developments pushing in that direction: continuing (if largely ignored) social crisis on the one hand; sharply constrained public resources on the other; the drift (or gallop) toward a sort of visceral and impatient Darwinism as our default approach to social policy; the growing demand that universities justify themselves according to how seamlessly they contribute to corporate and governmental imperatives.

A more likely criminological scenario in response to the multiple and reinforcing crises of "lidless" capitalism is essentially business as usual; the perpetuation of a criminology, or criminologies, mainly doing the kind of work that, however technically adroit, by and large ignores the larger structural context in which both crime and punishment are now unfolding. A lot of good and important work will get done, to be sure, but much of it will be relegated to the margins of academia and even more thoroughly relegated to the sidelines of public discourse and social policy. Meanwhile, the global forces march on that predictably generate both violence and harsh responses to it in the name of public safety. Too many of us, as a result, practice a kind of "as if" criminology, to borrow Pat Carlen's (2008) phrase, focusing on the investigation of small questions of delinquent motivation or the precise evaluation of minor interventions, when large parts of the world are coming apart, with entirely predictable consequences.

The third scenario—the "good" one that I had hoped to see unfold in my lifetime—is pretty clear from the failings of the first two. The most promising future for criminology involves the maturing and spreading of a truly structural and globally engaged work that not only puts the larger developments in world society at the forefront of analysis, but also works to create new and more effective ways of linking that intellectual work with movements for social change—which includes a concerted effort to move out beyond our usual academic and governmental constituencies to build stronger working relationships with people who are trying to make change from the ground up.

There are formidable obstacles to achieving that kind of future for criminology. Some of them have to do with pressures within the world of academia that many of us have been talking about for a long time but which, oddly enough, have not gotten any better as a result, and in some places have surely gotten worse. In an academic environment that in many countries is increasingly one of perennially scarce resources and competition for funding, the pressure to win at that game by doing more of the same old, same old is ever-present. In my own university, which I continue to regard as generally a good place that does a lot of things well and serves a lot of important and progressive social functions, the talk is more and more about the need to look good on very conventional measures of productivity and excellence. But excellence is defined as publishing in the journals that embody the status quo and landing grants that incentivize research into questions that have already been thoroughly explored, using concepts and methods that are careful not to deviate much from what has gotten funded in the past.

And this shapes the kind of intellectual climate that we produce on the ground. Too many of my students are smart, capable, and socially concerned—but also scared. They agonize over whether it's better to put their head down and just do what they believe they have to do to move ahead in the field, or stick their neck out and face the very real possibility of being an unemployed and indebted PhD. They have heard their professors telling them that the aim of their education is to train for the field—meaning, in essence, that we should train them to do the kind of research that people are already doing, and to shun like the plague work that smacks of being outside that mainstream. They may have heard an editor, of what was once one of our most probing and important journals, tell students, without irony, that when it comes to submitting articles for publication "innovation is deviation." It would be hard to overstate how much that mentality contributes to undermining the capacity of academic criminology to grapple effectively with the global trends that are shaping (and mis-shaping) the lives of real people around us.

Another contribution comes from a somewhat unexpected source, the stubborn persistence of a brand of "progressive" criminology that is distinguished by its claim that violence really isn't much of a problem—a stance that deflects attention both from the global public health disaster that violence represents and from the larger structural forces that cause it. I suspect that this may be a lesser issue in many countries than it is in the United States, where there has been a really remarkable resurgence in the last several years of a particularly strident version of what the British Left Realists famously called "left idealism" (Lea and Young 1984), but which in its current form is probably better captured by Roger Matthews' term "liberal realism," or what I have sometimes called "liberal minimalism" (Currie 1992; Matthews 2014).

The key characteristic of the contemporary variant of liberal idealism is that it is very concerned with the over-reach of the criminal justice system but not very concerned about crime. On one level, this perspective has produced some important and lasting contributions to our understanding of issues of punishment and social control. But on another level, it is hard not to see it as a puzzling and ultimately destructive example of a criminological perspective that violates the fundamental realist principle of taking crime seriously. Liberal idealism is likely, at the very least, to downplay the seriousness of ordinary violence as a social ill, and at the extreme to claim that it's all just a matter of social construction.

Liberal idealism has often been unusually prominent in the American debate about crime. I think part of the reason is that we lack much of a social democratic tradition—that is, a tradition of left thinking that both understands the damage that rampant capitalism can do to people and communities, and believes that public action can help to mitigate or, better yet, prevent that damage. Instead, much progressive thinking in America, not least within criminology, has been deeply libertarian, individualist, and anti-government. Its individualism makes it relatively blind to the human impact of adverse social forces. Its distrust of anything smacking of the state makes it wary of claims that public authority or public resources might be used in progressive and emancipatory ways. An excessive concern about the ravages of serious crime, accordingly, comes to seem suspiciously like a Trojan horse opening the way for repressive governmental intrusion. And in a country where fears of victimization and anger at criminals have indeed often been deployed for authoritarian and repressive purposes, that concern can't be entirely wrong. But it is tragically incomplete, in ways that feed into our national complacency about violence and its unfairly divided impact on human lives.

Liberal idealism was an especially powerful force in American criminology in the 1960s and 1970s. It began to lose luster in the 1980s and 1990s, partly because of the "in your face" reality of violence that was hard for even the most committed social constructionist to deny. Violent crime was virtually impossible to ignore, and it was getting rougher: there was more deadly weaponry involved; more highly visible social devastation; and more ruined lives. And it was so heavily and so obviously concentrated among certain kinds of people in certain communities that it was no longer possible to deny the close connection between the larger structural crisis of growing social disadvantage and the catastrophic levels of street crime in the cities. Moreover, the increasingly successful effort by feminists to put violence against women onto the public and academic agenda made it hard to appear both progressive and oblivious to the reality of women's victimization.

But liberal idealism is now coming back, with a vengeance. That may be, in part, because the "crime drop" has made some people at least, including some academic criminologists, less concerned personally about violent crime—an outlook not generally shared by people who live in the kinds of places where violence is still an inescapable fact of life. You don't find much complacency about violence in places like East Oakland, or Baltimore, or the South Side of Chicago (not to mention Guerrero, Capetown, or San Salvador). But it's the native outlook, the default position, for a certain kind of academic criminologist.

And so I have been reading, much to my astonishment, a number of widely reviewed accounts of crime and punishment in the United States that bring back the tropes of earlier liberal idealism without so much as a nod toward self-criticism. I have read recently, for example, that America may finally be relinquishing what one author calls its "senseless fear of crime." I have heard the USA described as our "so-called high crime society"—this in a country where the chance of violent death among young black men in some states is roughly equal to that of young men in El Salvador. The message is barely changed from a generation ago, that crime is basically a bugaboo thrust upon a panicky and incipiently racist public by manipulative politicians and by media ever on the lookout for a good story.

At the same time, the newly resurgent liberal idealism exaggerates the positive shifts that have taken place in the American criminal justice system. There is a genre of writing now that looks at the tapering off in the rise of prison populations—and at state-level measures that have taken some nonviolent and nonserious offenders out of prison—and concludes that we have moved "beyond the punitive era" or, at the extreme, that "mass incarceration is dead." Again, what makes these statements so frustrating is that they are almost comically extreme. To be sure, there are real and significant shifts in the way many American states are approaching lower-level crimes, especially drug offenses; and the slowing of our nearly four decades of growth in prison and jail populations is both important and welcome. But these trends need to be put in perspective. In California, after several important moves to downsize our state prison population, we still incarcerate about as many people as Germany, France, and Japan combined. If mass incarceration is dead, somebody forgot to tell the people who run the prisons and jails.

Most of the recent shifts, moreover, both in rhetoric and in policy, are directed at the "low-hanging fruit" of the offender population. Most partisans of getting nonserious offenders out of state or federal institutions, up to and including the President of the United States, are generally silent about the need to adopt a less draconian approach to more serious offenders, and often hasten to express a zero tolerance stance toward violent crime. And without softening the way we sentence more serious offenders we will never relinquish our place at the top of the list of international incarceration rates. After several years now of what some are ready to call a revolution in our approach to penal policy, the United States imprisons people at a rate ten times that of Germany and fourteen times that of Japan (ICPS 2015).

The new brand of idealist complacency is peculiarly out of sync with the global reality of violence and repression in the twenty-first century—and startlingly tone-deaf to the reality of the deep suffering on the other side of the violence divide. But the degree to which this perspective has suffused the liberal wing of academic criminology in the United States is downright startling. Not long ago, in a graduate seminar that I teach at Irvine, we were discussing a recent book about gang violence in Southern California and El Salvador and the structural and historical links between the two places. In the course of the discussion one student declared that crime wasn't a problem in American cities. Pressed a little on this, he allowed that violent crime might indeed be a problem in El Salvador, but that it certainly was not a problem in, say, Los Angeles or Oakland. This in a country where—again—some of our cities rank among the most violent places on the planet. In the same class this year we read a widely discussed recent book that argues that American liberals—not American conservatives—were responsible for creating our exploding prison system, because they essentially *invented* the problem of black crime in America's inner cities; they "constructed" a problem of criminality in African-American communities that really did not exist, and therefore provided cover for a massive prison expansion to contain it (Murakawa 2014). This in a country where we lose eight thousand black lives a year to homicide.

Many Americans have been understandably outraged by the spate of highly visible police shootings of black men in the last few years. But when it comes to the routine and ongoing disaster of communal violence in our cities—a disaster with a cruelly disproportionate impact on black Americans—there is a stunning silence, not just on the part of the technocratic center or the complacent right, but from much of the left. The reasons for that silence are surely complex, and well worth studying in themselves. But what is clear is that it results in the ceding of concern about American violence to others whose agendas are usually a lot less progressive, and the implicit tolerance of a level of human suffering and of inequality in the likelihood of violent death that no one should accept—least of all people who purport to be in the business of studying crime.

This level of denial represents an abdication. It means that some of the people we might most expect to take on the job of forthrightly confronting the structural roots of violence, in America and around the globe, are looking the other way, at best; and, at worst, are colluding in the creation of a "story" about the nature of social life in the twenty-first century that bears little resemblance to reality and that trivializes the suffering of large numbers of our most vulnerable and dispossessed people.

And to the extent that it displaces a more grounded perspective from the left of center, this stance contributes to a sharp narrowing of the dialogue about crime—a constriction of focus that renders us increasingly unable to grapple seriously with the state of crime and punishment in the contemporary world. We have the liberal idealists on one side. We have the still very powerful voices of the authoritarian and punitive right on another side, both in the United States and in many other countries—and we may get more of them as mass joblessness and a tide of desperate immigration intensify fears of disorder and decline in many countries. We have legions of administrative criminologists in the middle—criminologists who, as Roger Matthews puts it, don't have much interest in "understanding the wider social context that shapes and produces crime" (2014, p. 13). What is missing in the dialogue is a perspective that unflinchingly confronts the perilous state of so many communities today and the continuing tragedy that afflicts the people who live in them. A tragedy that many find easy to ignore because the people it hits hardest are mostly marginal, young, and expendable.

Put in another way, a serious discussion about *causes* of "ordinary" violence has become all too rare. And that leaves us, in turn, poorly equipped to talk about remedies. You cannot, after all, say much about how to fix a problem that you do not agree actually exists. The result is that, in the face of stubbornly entrenched suffering, we are failing at one of criminology's most central and necessary tasks; coming up with credible solutions that attack these ills at their root and helping to mobilize the kind of political response that can begin to put those solutions into practice.

Toward Globally Engaged Criminology

In the face of these forces that operate to undercut the best kind of criminological work, what can we do to build a better future for our enterprise? In the interest of space, let me just quickly put a few things on the table that I think are important.

One of the most crucial requisites for that better future is to strengthen the infrastructure that supports a globally engaged criminology that openly and effectively strives to maximize justice and minimize suffering.

In other words, we need to build more and better institutions that support this work and that diminish the sense of frustration and even marginality that can afflict those who engage in it.

We need to build stronger international networks of scholars who are committed to that kind of criminology. In that vein, I want to give a shout-out to the work of my colleagues who have created the International Conferences on Crime, Justice, and Social Democracy at the School of Justice at Queensland University of Technology in Australia—a dynamic and exciting model of the kind of global networking and sharing of perspectives and experience that we need more of.

We need, within our own national criminological organizations, to bring this work into the mainstream—indeed to *make* it the mainstream—of the discipline. I am often struck by how many of my colleagues who go to meetings of the American Society of Criminology actually think a lot like I do. And yet many have a persistent sense that the kind of work they most want to do is considered marginal to the field, and vaguely disreputable. Maybe it was once, it is not any more. But our sense of who we are has not caught up to the more complex, and more encouraging, reality. We need to develop the confidence to recognize that shift and to cease feeling overpowered by an imagined consensus we feel outside of. There's an interesting movement afoot in the ASC that, I am happy to say, is being mobilized by some of my former students, among others, to do just that; to create a new American criminology that puts the quest for social justice front and center—and that insists on regarding that kind of work as a new mainstream in the field.

Let me be clear, by the way, that I am not suggesting that everyone needs to do this kind of work. There's plenty of room in this field for all kinds of research and for a lot of divergent conceptions of what's important. But I am saying that I think the balance needs to shift. It needs to be less hard to do critical and socially engaged criminological work, and it needs to be easier to bridge the gap between that work and the levers of social action and social policy.

In pursuit of building that new mainstream, we need new, and bolder, and more innovative avenues for publication. We need more journals that are willing to go beyond the formulaic presentation of cookie-cutter research reports—journals that foster energetic debate and push the boundaries of the field. We do have some now, we need more. We need more programs within our university departments that explicitly train students to think in a more holistic and more global fashion about violence and social injustice, and that do not shy away from actually teaching them something about history and political economy.

The best and most relevant criminologies in the future will be criminologies that are both rooted in deep and fine-grained analyses of the social and economic trajectories of specific societies, and able to understand how an increasingly integrated global economic order impacts communities, cultures, and personalities (for some steps in this direction, see Carrington et al. 2015). Yet it is fair to say that very few emerging criminologists today are being given the tools to work on those levels or to understand those connections. In the United States today we have great numbers of students leaving our PhD programs who could describe the intricacies of hierarchical linear modeling at great length and in great detail, but who have been taught virtually nothing about the social and economic structure and historical trajectory of their own country, much less anyone else's (I hasten to add that there's nothing wrong with students knowing a good deal about hierarchical linear modeling, but that cannot be *all* they know).

We also need to rethink not only what we teach and what we regard as essential in the intellectual toolkit of criminologists but also our sense of who our audience and our allies should be. It is hardly news to say that much of contemporary criminology is work done mainly for consumption by other criminologists—and only some of *them*. When we do go beyond that insular audience, it is most often to address our work to criminal justice practitioners or other government entities. And, up to a point, that is surely a good thing. But it can't be our only orientation. We need to build much stronger relationships with movements outside the universities working for social justice and social change, and to make working with—and for—those movements a viable career option for students. Some of us recently called a meeting for graduate students in my department to talk about the possibilities of nonacademic careers working with nonprofit organizations. The good news was that there was an extraordinary degree of interest. The bad news was that nearly everyone felt a little furtive about the meeting, as if this was a taboo and possibly dangerous subject for people who were supposed to be aspiring to a career in a place exactly like the one they were in.

We need, in short, to develop ways of fostering a criminology that is more than a relatively passive witness to the destruction wrought by contemporary global forces—much less an accomplice—and instead vigorously steps up to take on the job of combating those forces and dedicating itself unapologetically to the reduction of needless pain, fear, and injustice around the world. That is the kind of criminology I want to be doing for as long as I'm capable of doing it. And the more people who join me, the happier I will be.

References

Baltimore Sun. (2015). *Baltimore Homicides.* www.data.baltimoresun.com. Accessed September 2015.

Brodzinsky, S. (2013). Inside San Pedro Sula—The most violent city in the world. *Guardian,* May 15.

Campbell, C., & Jedra, C. (2015). Man killed in Northeast Baltimore, in city's 200th homicide of 2015. *Baltimore Sun,* August 10.

Carlen, P. (2008). Imaginary penalties and risk-crazed governance. In P. Carlen (Ed.), *Imaginary penalties.* Cullompton: Willan.

Carrington, K., Hogg, R., & Sozzo, M. (2015). Southern criminology. *British Journal of Criminology,* advance access, August 20.

Coleman, V. (2015). How Newark is responding to summer homicide surge. *NJ.com,* August 31.

Currie, E. (1992). Retreatism, minimalism, realism: Three styles of reasoning on crime and drugs in the United States. In J. Lowman & B. D. MacLean (Eds.), *Realist criminology: Crime control and policing in the 1990s* (pp. 88–97). Toronto: University of Toronto Press.

Currie, E. (2003). Of punishment and crime rates: Some theoretical and methodological consequences of mass incarceration. In T. G. Blomberg & S. Cohen (Eds.), *Punishment and social control* (2nd ed., pp. 483–494). New York: Aldine de Gruyter.

Currie, E. (2009). An unchallenged crisis: The curious disappearance of crime as a public issue in the United States. *Criminal Justice Matters, 75*(March), 22–23.

Currie, E. (2015a). *The roots of danger: violent crime in global perspective* (Second revised ed.). Oxford/New York: Oxford University Press.

Currie, E. (2015b). Shouldn't black lives matter all the time? *Contexts, 14*(3), 17–18.

Daley, K. (2015). 100: New Orleans hits triple digits in murders 55 days sooner than last year. *NOLA.com*, July 16.

Davey, M., & Smith, M. (2015). Murder rates rising sharply in many cities. *New York Times*, September 1.

Ehrenfreund, M. (2015). I went looking for the uptick in murders in U.S. cities. Here's what I found. *Washington Post*, September 4.

Greenstein, R. (2015, September 17). *New census data show historical health coverage gains, though disappointing results in poverty and income*. Washington, DC: Center on Budget and Policy Priorities.

International Centre for Prison Studies (ICPS). (2015). *World Prison Brief University of London*.

International Labour Organization (ILO). (2015). *World employment social outlook*: *The changing nature of jobs, Executive summary*, Geneva.

Matthews, R. (2014). Realist Criminology. *Palgrave Macmillan*.

Murakawa, N. (2014). *The first civil right: How liberals built prison America*. Oxford/New York: Oxford University Press.

Organization for Economic Cooperation and Development (OECD). (2015). *In it together: Why less inequality benefits all*. Paris: OECD Publishing.

Treadwell, J., Briggs, D., Winlow, S., & Hall, S. (2013). Shopocalypse now: Consumer culture and the riots of 2011. *British Journal of Criminology, 53*(1), 1–17.

United Nations Office on Drugs and Crime (UNODC). (2015a). *Intentional homicide counts and rates per 100,000 Population, 2000–2013*.

United Nations Office on Drugs and Crime (UNODC). (2015b). *Global study on homicide*. www.unodc.org/gsh

Yan, H., & Holland, L. (2015). Gruesome weekend for Chicago leaves city, police chief reeling. *CNN.com*, July 6.

Young, J. (1992). Realist research as a basis for local criminal justice policy. In J. Lowman & B. D. MacLean (Eds.), *Realist criminology: Crime control and policing in the 1990s* (pp. 33–72). Toronto: University of Toronto Press.

3

Domestic Violence: The Increasing Tensions Between Experience, Theory, Research, Policy and Practice

Nicole Westmarland and Liz Kelly

Introduction

For most of the twentieth century domestic violence was dismissed as a private, personal issue; it is now recognised globally as a significant social issue faced by up to one in three women in their lifetimes (WHO 2013). It acts as a barrier to women realising their rights and achieving their full potential and it intersects with other forms of inequality, including ethnicity, class and (dis)ability (Westmarland 2015). Feminists have located it within the wider concept of violence against women and girls, identifying commonalities and connections between the many forms, including: low reporting rates; low conviction rates; a range of myths and stereotypes that serve to justify abuse; and a historic failure of the state to prevent, prosecute and protect (Coy et al. 2008). In 2012/13 in England and Wales, 91 people were recorded as being killed by their partner or

N. Westmarland (✉)
Centre for Research into Violence and Abuse, Durham University, Durham, UK

L. Kelly
London Metropolitan University, London, UK

ex-partner, of these, 76 were female and 15 were male (Office for National Statistics 2014). These figures should be considered a starting point since an unknown number of women die because of partner violence in other ways, for example through suicide, drug or alcohol misuse, or the effects that long term physical violence has on their bodies (Westmarland 2015).

Despite the seriousness of the issue, and the shift in recognition, we only know a limited amount about the nature and extent of domestic violence and, crucially, effective methods of primary and secondary prevention. Half a century since the first women's refuges were established, there remains not only disagreement about how much domestic violence there is and how best to reduce it, but also what it is and how it should be defined.

This chapter considers the emergence of new responses, including: legal and institutional reforms; current debates around the naming of domestic violence; its connections with other forms of violence against women; and related problems with its measurement. We argue that we are now at a point of confusion in how domestic violence and abuse are responded to, and explore this through examining current responses and juxtaposing them with the accounts of survivors. We draw on data from a recently completed study (Westmarland and Kelly 2016) to illustrate some of the key issues. We use this data to highlight the inadequacies of current policies and to make the case for bolder approaches that are grounded within the everyday inequalities women face today. Current government policy and statutory interventions are clustered around the opposite of what we know; they are focused on a minority of women who experience repeated physical assaults such that they reach a 'high' category on a risk assessment form, those reporting to the police and those with social services involvement. This is shift away from previous framings which sought to reach and support all victims. We suggest an alternative framing which recognises the central role of gender (Jakobson 2014) and other inequalities, and begins from the experiences of the majority.

Developing Responses

The 1970s saw the first refuges/shelters open to provide sanctuary for women and children escaping domestic violence in the USA and then the UK. Networks of safe houses now exist across the globe, and are linked to helplines, advocacy and counselling services. The women's organisations which began these services have been the prime change makers in local and national communities, arguing for institutional responses that support women and hold abusive men to account. Alongside this they have built what is termed the empowerment approach to work on domestic violence, standing alongside women as they seek to rebuild their lives in the aftermath of abuse (Kelly and Sharp 2014). This approach seeks to offer holistic responses, tailored to the needs of individual women and where they are in the process of ending violence. Within such specialist services are those which offer support to women from minority communities, where racism and immigration issues may create additional support needs. For several decades women's organisations held the issue of domestic violence and refuges were considered a core response, financed through local authority grants and other funding streams. As other players came into the field the focus has shifted to, in the case of the UK and other countries, criminal justice and multi-agency responses. This has combined with a commissioning process that places the network of refuges and the empowerment approach they use under intense pressure,[1] with services for black and ethnic minority women the most affected.

Law reform and law enforcement have become key elements in efforts to address domestic violence, to transform it from private family concern outside the ambit of the state to a public matter in which the rights of individuals to personal safety are paramount. This is the outcome of a historic process, initiated by women's groups and feminist scholars in the 1970s (Dobash and Dobash 1992). The call to respond to domestic violence as a crime was both substantive and symbolic. When physical and sexual assaults took place in the family, they were not considered criminal assaults, but 'domestic disputes/disturbances', best dealt with by delicate negotiation, calming down and mediation. The tolerance of violence towards wives has been documented historically (Dobash and Dobash 1979), including the martial rape exemption that remained the case in many European countries until the 1980s/1990s. Even where the crime was one of murder, it was often treated differently, as a 'crime of passion' or reduced to manslaughter on the grounds of 'provocation'—that the

---

[1] See this briefing from Women's Aid England on the loss of specialist services http://www.women-said.org.uk/page.asp?section=0001000100100022&sectionTitle=SOS

victim had 'nagged' or had an affair. The gendered way in which crime was defined, understood and, on occasions, excused became a key focus in the emergent field of feminist jurisprudence, with domestic violence one of the paradigmatic exemplars (Schulhofer 1995).

Two decades later, at the level of rhetoric at least, a profound shift has gathered momentum across the globe, aided by the UN which placed violence against women within its terms of reference. Alongside the move to de-privatise domestic violence has been a parallel campaign to have it treated as a crime, through changes in both statute law and procedural implementation. The forms that legal changes have taken are diverse globally, although a number of common threads are evident: creating specific or new offences; making assaults within the home an aggravating factor in sentencing; developing specialist responses in police, prosecutors and courts; the creation of civil law protection orders. At the procedural level mandatory or positive arrest and prosecution policies have also been introduced in various jurisdictions.

The argument for criminalisation was that assaults inside the home should be treated in the same way as crime outside it. The reality, however, is rather more complex—since domestic violence is not a crime like any other. Historically, constructions of law on assaults have presumed one or more of the following: that the parties are strangers; that both parties are male; that the event is taking place in public; that this is a one-off event. None of these presumptions hold for domestic violence, which takes place in the context of an intimate relationship (even if no longer the case), most commonly involves a male aggressor and a female victim, and is an incident within an ongoing pattern of coercive control. There are also differences in why victims have recourse to law: and that women and the criminal justice system (CJS) do not necessarily share the same 'justice goals' (Ferraro 1993; Holder and Mayo 2003). Women are often motivated by short-term instrumental goals, the immediate cessation of the violence and for their partner to be held to account. The police and courts, on the other hand, are more interested in whether the evidence 'proves' a crime has been committed and can be prosecuted. A further question that has emerged is whether all women have the same interests, with many in the USA asking profound questions about the differential implementation of law, meaning that it is disproportionately black men who are criminalised (Erez et al. 2008; Sokoloff and Dupont 2005).

Very limited research has been undertaken on how diverse groups of abused women understand justice. One such study—a consultation following publication of *Safety and Justice* by the then Westminster government in the UK (Home Office 2003)—was undertaken by the Women's National Commission (2003). Overall, women strongly supported pro-active interventions, including by the police, and had an expectation that government and agencies ought to be able to deliver protection and safety. There was also extremely strong support for policies that enabled women and children to stay safely in their own homes (see also Kelly and Humphreys 2001; Mullender et al. 2002). One legal reform which meets this challenge is the 'removal law', originally introduced in the late 1990s in Austria, whereby police can remove a perpetrator from the home, although it took until 2013 for a similar provision to be introduced in England and Wales.

Multi-agency Work

From the 1990s more emphasis was placed on inter- and later multi-agency work, a process which, at its best, was intended to be a co-ordinated community response within which victims are supported and perpetrators held to account (Shepard and Pence 1999). Over the three decades a range of models have been in evidence, and most government and international policy has supported this approach. Some critical issues have been voiced, such as, the role of the lead agency as a central concern: who initiates co-operative links; who sets the overall agenda; and who (if anyone) maintains the vision and drive over time. These have all been identified as significant in determining the forms, content and outcome of initiatives. That leadership may also involve the exercise of power and control has been avoided in all but a few commentaries, and who occupies these locations has seldom been the subject of intense scrutiny. Two early Home Office crime prevention papers (Liddle and Gelsthorpe 1994; Sampson et al. 1988), however, point to the importance of status, resources and confidence in the emergence of leaders, and to the salience of gender and race. Each of these factors puts women's organisations at a disadvantage, their cumulative and compounding impacts make it extremely unlikely that the position of lead agency will go to local refuges and campaigning groups. This inequality, combined with a feminist analysis of domestic violence, means that many women's organisations and individual feminists come to inter-agency work with an immense amount of knowledge and expertise, but with minimal formal and/or institutional power and with an acute discomfort with the ways power is routinely exercised by powerful agencies and individuals.

> When reform efforts focus on coordinating the system rather than on building safety considerations into the infrastructure, the system could actually become more harmful to victims than the previously unexamined system. (Shepard and Pence 1999, p. 41)

One more recent development exemplifies these misgivings. Multi-Agency Risk Assessment Conferences (MARACs) began over a decade ago in Cardiff and have become one of the core required responses in England and Wales. Cases which reach 'high' on risk assessment measures, which privilege physical assault, are referred into MARAC, where a range of professionals share what they know about the case and decide on a course of action. Critics have noted that: women are not present; they may not have given consent for all the information to be shared; and that the lever of threatening to remove children is often used to 'steer' women into making 'the right decision', i.e. separating from the abusive man (Coy and Kelly 2011). The functioning of MARACs has also been seen as a form of surveillance, rather than support, of women (Davies 2015). Rather than the process being led by women's own process of ending violence, more recent responses expect women to be able to move to strong self and child protective action when they may still believe themselves to be at fault, or want to believe the man's promises to change, or have not yet named what is happening as violence.

These developments sit in tension with what women have said makes a difference for them, enabling them to consider what paths to tread. In several evaluations (Burton et al. 1998; Kelly 1999) what women talked about was not positive arrest, integrated responses, advice or referrals, but the clear messages that they received from caring workers: naming violence; being told it was not their fault; and especially that they deserved something better. What children have told us (Mullender et al. 2002) is that they want to be noticed, told what is happening and listened to. Unfortunately, these basics of practice seldom appear these days in guidelines or policy.

Defining Domestic Violence and Abuse

In the 1990s many local authorities began developing localised approaches to domestic violence, but even domestic violence forums lacked agreed definitions. This was, in some sense problematic; how could informed discussions on a topic happen in a multi-agency setting if people were not talking about the same thing? Adopting a common understanding was therefore deemed an important building block in developing effective partnership working (Hester and Westmarland 2005).

Today there is a common policy definition and it is broader than it has ever been, having been through at least three iterations. The current Westminster government definition has been adopted across government departments and by many other statutory and voluntary sector organisations and is presented in Box 1.

> **Box 1: Current Westminster Government Definition of Domestic Violence and Abuse**
>
> Any incident or pattern of incidents of controlling, coercive or threatening behaviour, violence or abuse between those aged 16 or over who are or have been intimate partners or family members regardless of gender or sexuality. This can encompass, but is not limited to, the following types of abuse: psychological; physical; sexual; financial; emotional.
>
> * Controlling behaviour is: a range of acts designed to make a person subordinate and/or dependent by isolating them from sources of support, exploiting their resources and capacities for personal gain, depriving them of the means needed for independence, resistance and escape and regulating their everyday behaviour.
> * Coercive behaviour is: an act or a pattern of acts of assault, threats, humiliation and intimidation or other abuse that is used to harm, punish, or frighten their victim.
>
> *This definition, which is not a legal definition, includes, so called, honour based violence, female genital mutilation (FGM) and forced marriage, and is clear that victims are not confined to one gender or ethnic group.

Whilst a shared understanding is important, this definition confuses more than it clarifies; it conflates family and domestic violence and refers to a broad range of forms of violence, many if not all of which are gendered, but with this aspect invisible within the text. We have argued elsewhere that as a consequence it functions to disguise, dilute and distort the reality of domestic violence (Kelly and Westmarland 2014).

It obscures at best, and denies at worst, a gendered analysis of men's violence against women. Whilst we do not dispute that violence is also perpetrated against men, this definition is disconnected from the Westminster government's own violence against women and girls strategy which, following the UN in General Recommendation 19 with respect to CEDAW, defines violence as that which takes place 'because she is a woman or happens disproportionally to women'. By placing FGM, forced marriage and honour based violence in the equivalent of a footnote, it both minimises forms of violence that are disproportionately experienced by minority women and fails to recognise the specific dynamics involved in them.

In conflating family and domestic violence the definition assumes that the dynamics in intimate partner violence are the same as those between siblings, or between parents and adult children. In particular, coercive control is a concept developed to make sense of the ways in which men impose their will in heterosexual relationships, drawing on cultural norms about masculinity and femininity. It is extremely unlikely that these function in the same way in other familial relationships. The reality of intimate partner violence is obscured by reference to it being *either* an 'incident' or a 'pattern'—it is precisely the repetition, the web of forms of power and control and cumulative impacts, that make domestic violence so harmful and difficult to extricate oneself from.

These issues may seem like academic semantics, but they have very real consequences in terms of what gets measured—the questions that are asked in prevalence studies, how official statistics are compiled—and ultimately the shape, nature and extent of service provision. Continuing to include 'any incident' in the definition has meant that prevalence findings from the Crime Survey England and Wales (previously the British

Crime Survey) show a significant number of male victims. But further analysis reveals that women are disproportionately those who report multiple incidents, sustaining injury and living in fear—all aspects of what most people understand as being part of defining domestic violence. We suggest that the definition of domestic violence should be limited to current or ex partnerships, and centre on it being 'a pattern of coercive control' (Stark 2007) and that its gendered nature should be explicitly noted.

Problems with Legal and Policy Responses to Domestic Violence

The fact that a minority of reported rape cases progress all the way through the CJS and result in a conviction is now widely recognised (Angiolini 2015). That this is also the case for domestic violence related offences is less well known. The process by which cases drop out, fall out or are pushed out of the CJS is known as attrition. Hence, crimes with a low conviction rate have a high rate of attrition. The reason why so little is known about attrition in domestic violence cases is because, unlike rape, domestic violence is not a single, standalone offence; a perpetrator could be charged with harassment, criminal damage, actual bodily harm, grievous bodily harm, rape or murder. Whilst police are supposed to flag domestic violence cases, so that they can be identified, successive audits by HMIC (HM Inspectorate of Constabulary) reveal that this is not consistent across force areas (see HMIC 2014 for the latest report) and, following the government definition discussed earlier, conflate who is doing what to whom.

In the 2000s, Hester analysed intimate partner violence cases reported across the Northumbria police force area to explore what happened between initial report to final court outcome (Hester 2006). The study trawled police case files and identified 869 incidents recorded across three police command areas, finding a conviction rate of 4 %, lower than the conviction rate for rape in the same time period. A detailed breakdown of the attrition process is presented in Box 2.

Box 2: Pattern of Attrition in Recorded Domestic Violence Cases, Taken from Hester (2006)

- 869 recorded domestic violence incidents
- 222 resulted in arrest (26 % of those recorded)
- 60 charges for criminal offences (27 % of those arrested, 7 % of incidents recorded)
- 31 convictions (52 % of those charged, 14 % of arrests, 4 % of incidents recorded)
- 4 convictions were custodial sentences (13 % of convictions, 0.5 % of incidents recorded)

This pattern has been found to be 'depressingly similar' or even higher in other areas (Hester 2006). The police were found to be overly reliant on the willingness of victims to support prosecution; officers both understood and empathised with the many reasons women might have to do this, whilst being simultaneously frustrated at the number of victims who withdrew support for a prosecution.

> Many of them are sensible and have weighed it up. They don't want to go through with it in case they split up etc. I am sympathetic to this, they don't want to go to court which could be three months down the line if they are trying to rebuild the relationship. (Police Officer, cited in Hester 2006, p. 82)

Crown Prosecutors interviewed in the study were also of the opinion that it was the victims themselves who were the main source of attrition, though attrition was particularly marked in relation to the courts. That said, some prosecutors had continued cases without the victim giving evidence in court, and there were no instances in the sample of victims being compelled to give evidence. Hester concludes that there is a 'complex relationship' in the CJS process between the balancing of victim safety and the interest of CJS agencies in increasing court outcomes.

> For victimized women, attrition might be either positive or negative depending on the extent to which the criminal justice system enabled positive management of their safety. (Hester 2006, p. 89)

Drawing on this study, and a further longitudinal analysis, Hester and Westmarland (2006) considered the nature of convictions, and repeat offending by perpetrators over a number of years, both against the original partner they reported to the police and against new partners. This analysis concluded that the criminal justice framework is poorly suited to respond to domestic violence because of its focus on individual incidents.

> Domestic violence involves patterns of violent and abusive behaviour over time rather than individual acts. However, the criminal justice system is primarily concerned with specific incidents and it can therefore be difficult to apply criminal justice approaches in relation to domestic violence. (Hester and Westmarland 2006, p. 35)

Writing from a US perspective, Stark goes further, arguing that incident based frameworks are not only inefficient, but function to conceal men's control of women.

> Viewing woman abuse through the prism of the incident specific and injury-based definition of violence has concealed its major components, dynamics, and effects, including the fact that it is neither 'domestic' nor primarily about 'violence'. (Stark 2007, p. 10)

This analysis connects to Hearn's (1998) notion of 'incidentalism'. Drawing on in-depth interviews with abusive men he argues that they seek to represent their use of violence as being 'out of character' and 'incidental' to their lives and relationship. Thus the CJS focus on incidents coheres with the convenient reduction that perpetrators use and allows individual acts of violence to be disconnected from their context, for the incident to be exceptional.

What Is Coercive Control and Why Is It Important?

Evan Stark's (2007) influential book *Coercive Control* challenged not only institutional responses but also the direction taken by the US women's movement. Somewhat controversially, he posited that the revolution in responses to abused women had stalled; that despite the decades of energy and other resources that had been put into ending domestic violence, the end was still nowhere in sight. The new approach he proposes is evident in the sub-title of the book, 'the entrapment of women in personal life'.

> The main means used to establish control is the micro-regulation of everyday behaviours associated with stereotypic female roles, such as how women dress, cook, clean, socialize, care for their children, or perform sexually. (Stark 2007, p. 5)

Coercive control therefore involves the micro-regulation of gender, through which women are censured for failing to perform the man's expectation of appropriate and expected femininity (Stark 2007). This setting of limits to women's behaviour serves to limit her 'space for action' (Kelly 2013). Since this micro-regulation takes hold over time, and women become 'entrapped' in personal life, their lives became analogous to being held hostage.

> victims of coercive control are frequently deprived of money, food, access to communication or transportation, and other survival resources even as they are cut off from family, friends and other supports. (Stark 2007, p. 5)

For Stark, the misstep for women's services and the state has been to focus only on safety, thus failing to see that domestic violence should be understood as a 'liberty crime', that it is intended to limit women's freedom to think, act and feel without fear of censure or abuse. Interventions must, therefore, also be concerned with enhancing women's freedom.

Listening to the Voices of Survivors

When we listen to the voices of women who are experiencing or have survived domestic violence, we see that patterns of coercive and controlling behaviour are not just an 'add on' (as in the Westminster government definition), rather they are absolutely at the heart of what this violence is and its consequences. We have recently written on how the current definition, legal framework and criminal justice processes reflect, and arguably reinforce, domestic violence perpetrators' own descriptions of their use of violence and abuse (Kelly and Westmarland 2016). The language men used (particularly before they attended a domestic violence perpetrator programme) echoes the way the criminal justice system and MARACs centre on 'occasional', 'physical' and 'serious' violence rather than the ways women's everyday lives are regulated to the extent that they speak of constantly 'walking on eggshells'.

In the next section we focus on women's accounts, and show how much of the abuse they experienced bore little or no resemblance to conventional notions of crime.

Findings from Project Mirabal

Project Mirabal was a mixed-method study of the contribution perpetrator programmes make to co-ordinated community responses to domestic violence (Kelly and Westmarland 2015). The quantitative findings showed that physical and sexual violence reduced almost completely following men's attendance on a programme and women's access to specialist support. Whilst acts of harassment, abuse, coercion, control—the micro-regulation of women's everyday lives—reduced, they did so to a far lesser extent.

In terms of the indicators for physical and sexual violence for 'made you do something sexual that you did not want to do', 30 % of women said that this happened before the programme, but after the programme (measured 12 months after start date) this was measured at zero. The same pattern was evident for 'used a weapon against you', which changed from 29 % to 0 %. More common forms of violence such as 'slapped you, pushed you, or thrown something at you' also saw dramatic reductions— from 87 % before the programme to 7 % after. Similar decreases were seen for 'tried to strangle, choke, drown, or smother you (50 % down to 2 %) and 'punched, kicked, burnt or beaten you' (43 % down to 2 %).

In contrast, the use of harassment and abuse remained in the lives of around half of the women. Nearly all of the women (90 %) reported that before the programme their partner or ex-partner did things that scared or intimidated them, this reduced to 41 % after the programme. Similarly, 91 % said that he insulted them or made them feel bad about themselves before the programme—by the end this reduced to 48 %. Around half continued to say that their partner 'insists on knowing where I am or what I am doing' (80 % before the programme compared to 48 % afterwards) and around a quarter continued to try to look at her messages and contacts (62 % before the programme compared to 22 % afterwards). The same was true for other micro-regulation techniques, such as: preventing the woman from seeing friends and family; suggesting she change her appearance; and using money/finances as a form of control. We concluded that programmes were more effective at reducing physical and sexual violence than coercive control (Kelly and Westmarland 2015), the experiences which were most common in women's lives.

'Walking on eggshells'

Alongside the survey data, qualitative interviews were undertaken with women and men—at Time 1 near the beginning of a man's involvement on a programme and at Time 2 near the end. These confirmed the survey findings that little of the domestic abuse women were experiencing maps on to a conventional crime based framework, as the three case studies of Sophie, Dianne, and Suzanne[2] show.

'He can control the situation—and me, like a robot. Just needs a remote control.'

Sophie had been with her partner for three years, both had children from previous relationships. Sophie described how the emotional abuse increased to the point it was 'really bad' when the police were called. Her recollection is of the police asking whether she wanted to 'press charges', which placed her in the invidious position of deciding whether or not he

---

[2] We are using different pseudonyms to other publications, since here we give names to the woman and man in relationship with each other. Previous publications have not done this and we are ensuring that we protect anonymity of participants.

might be prosecuted. The impetus for calling the police on this occasion was that Sophie thought he was going to kill her. She was physically injured to the extent he was able to drag her round with one hand as she had no balance and could not walk—she described it as being 'almost a dancing partner for him'. The police called paramedics, though she also recalled fearing they would not believe her as Paul was acting 'as calm as a cucumber' and she could hear him laughing and joking with a police officer.

When we asked Sophie what sort of woman Paul was expecting her to be in the relationship she replied 'obedient', passive, to not have much of a personality of her own, not to argue, to be subservient. On the other hand, she perceived him as being forceful, controlling, holding the power—as she put it, having the 'upper hand', such that he could dictate what was going to happen and how their relationship would be. Her perception was that he had a 'fixed fantasy' of how he wanted life to be, but even when he got his way he still wasn't happy—the 'goalposts kept moving'. Sophie talked of how she felt she had become a 'nodding dog', always saying 'that's all right' and 'yes whatever'—constantly having to jump through hoops. However, she came to recognise that the more she did this, the more abusive he would become. Sophie knew that her partner had experienced trauma in his own life, and initially hoped that if she did everything for him, as he wanted it, and gave him enough of her love, this would nurture him and enable him to feel secure. Instead, he became more and more abusive.

When asked how free she felt to make her own choices, Sophie replied 'Not at all', providing a litany of examples of micro-regulation. Even for routine health appointments, if one was on a day Paul was not working he would insist on driving her there, waiting for her, being there when she came out of the door. He insisted on driving her places so that he could ensure she could not go anywhere else—to the extent that even buying a cup of coffee would be impossible. The only time Sophie experienced any kind of freedom was when he was at work and she was taking her child to sports clubs.

Sophie explicitly used the phrase 'walking on eggshells', meaning that she could not express or really 'be' herself because of fears of what might happen. She talked of a hyper vigilance, being alert to how Paul put his keys down, the tone of his voice, and adjusting her behaviour accordingly.

Whilst there were several incidents of injurious violence, what Sophie recounts is a life dominated by the whims of a controlling man, a man who exercised this control through behaviours that are unlikely to qualify as criminal offences. He was imposing what Anne Morris (2009) has termed 'an abusive household gender regime', in ways that were particular to what he knew about Sophie.

'I think he wanted me to be like a performer—if that makes sense?'

Dianne had been separated from her partner for two years, after a ten-year relationship. She was younger than Jake, and she described him as having 'control over me that I couldn't break. He had this utter and complete control over me, my whole self as a person'. This extended to limiting herself in terms of education and employment, even attending an exercise class or joining a gym, as his jealous surveillance was too overpowering to face on a daily basis. Just being late by five minutes was enough to provoke intense questioning. Jake's primary technique was financial control, of Dianne and others, her perception being that he used his money as a weapon.

Jake made a common threat—that Dianne would never get away from him—even after an injunction had been put in place when she had not felt safe when they were together; two years after the separation she still did not feel safe. As with Sophie, the only time that Dianne was able to make any choices, her only freedom, was where she took the children.

> It sounds silly and it was so restrictive but that's the only thing that I had a free choice about was if I wanted to take the kids out somewhere … take the kids to the park, taking the kids to me dads, taking the kids on a day out and he was okay about that … always okay about that because he knew I had the kids with me and in his mind I couldn't meet a man … nobody would talk to me so he never had a problem with that but I didn't have freedom of choice in anything else. I mean literally anything else.

Meals out with friends were 'forbidden', as were visits to her sister and mother. If she tried to step outside of his control there were consequences, including attempted murder—on one occasion by repeatedly trying to snap her neck and on another shooting a gun at the ceiling whilst threatening to shoot her. His surveillance persisted after separation through a range of tactics.

Physical and sexual violence became routine, but perpetrated in devious ways. For example, in front of the kids Jake would lean on her, making it look as if he was being affectionate, whilst pushing his knuckles into her thigh, in a way that she felt was 'daring her' to say that it hurt.

In Dianne's case there is more physical and sexual violence that fits a crime framing, but what was debilitating—and continued to be so two years after separation—was the way Jake had succeeded in intimidating her and constricting her space for thought and action. Jealous surveillance and undermining someone's sense of self and efficacy are unlikely to qualify as either a criminal offence or sufficient to qualify for a MARAC referral.

'That's what they do, that's why they get you pregnant'

Suzanne had children from a previous relationship and a baby with Phil, from whom she had just separated. Suzanne had had a prior relationship in which the man was violent, and Phil had perpetrated and been imprisoned for domestic violence against a previous partner. Suzanne occasionally used to feel scared when he was angry, but did not fear him the way that Sophie and Dianne feared their partners. However, Suzanne recognised that her children felt scared when they heard them arguing and feared Phil would hit her as her previous partner had done, although he never did assault her. However, he sought to control her and monitored her movements. She described feeling like she couldn't breathe.

> If I did go out he used to question who I was with and where we went. Then if I said I went to somewhere he would say 'What did yous go there for?' Like he would phone me friend that I was supposed to be with just to make sure I was with her—and then if he text us and asked where I was and I said where I was he would come to make sure I was there.

Suzanne felt that the reason both Phil and her previous partners had wanted her to have their children was as a way of increasing their control over her—that she could not go out as much if she had young children to look after. Phil expected a woman to be a housewife, clean the house, do the cooking and look after the children. Whilst she didn't think that being a woman meant there was anything she couldn't or shouldn't do, she acknowledged that that was difficult in practice because of the expectation that she manage the household. She described the man's role as being like 'the boss'—able to do what they want to do, go out whenever they want, have their own opinions, and care for children only when they wanted to.

Here again the issue of gendered expectations, which are imposed by men on the women they are in relationships with, emerges as a clear theme, partly because our methodology involved asking both women and men about their perceptions and views on gender and how these played out in the relationship. Very little of Suzanne's experience would fit into most perceptions of domestic violence.

The New Law on Coercive and Controlling Behaviour

As we write a new law is about to come into force in England and Wales, creating an offence of coercive and controlling behaviour. At first sight it ought to be possible to fit the experiences of the majority, as illustrated by our case studies, into its parameters. Clause 76 of the Serious Crime Bill creates the offence of 'Controlling or coercive behaviour in an intimate or family relationship'—again we see the conflation of intimate partner and family violence. For our purposes here though, the issue is whether experiences like those we outlined above would be actionable under this new law. The law requires that the behaviour be repeated and/or continuous, and that it cause fear on at least two occasions that violence is used, or causes 'distress with substantive adverse effect' on day to day activities. Whether it will be possible to fit the subtle forms of control into this legal framework remains to be seen, including the ways in which it threads through normative gender expectations of men and women in relationships. That the available defence of believing that they were acting in the best interests of the other person and that the behaviour can be considered reasonable in the circumstances adds further concerns about whether it is possible to police abusive gender relations through the criminal law.

Moving Forward, Making Connections

The three case studies reveal that the everyday micro-regulation of women's lives takes place, as Stark argues, through the policing of gender by abusive men. Rather than domestic violence being gender neutral it is fundamentally inflected by gender and power. Based on this we argue that there are three moves which would signal a different approach and start to shift definitional, policy and criminal justice practices closer to the theoretical insights outlined earlier and women's lived experiences. These are: a serious political commitment to gender equality and the gendering of domestic violence; greater focus on, attention to and knowledge of perpetrators; a truly integrated, human-rights based approach to ending all forms of violence against women and girls.

Gender Equality and Gendered Violence

The gender-neutral definition of domestic violence, its broadness and lack of integration with the violence against women and girls strategy, is completely at odds with theoretical understandings of men's violence against women. Stark shows how domestic violence has at its heart not physical violence but gendered control. The case studies all show that although the violence or threat of it played an important role, it was deployed as one amongst many control strategies—many of which were more common in women's lives. It was one element in the creation of abusive household gender regimes, regimes that were crafted around the particulars of each woman. The behaviours women found most debilitating and difficult to counter/resist (although at some points all of them did) were not criminal acts, and arguably would not even be such in the recent law reform. Bringing gender back in is also essential to linking in with the international human-rights framing of violence against women and girls—that gender based violence is both a cause and a consequence of gender inequality.

Burman (2012) reflects on a Swedish law embedded within a package of reforms—Women's Peace (*Kvinnofrid*)—the offence of 'gross violation of a woman's integrity'. She maintains that this was a turning point, since the entire package is rooted in recognition that men's violence against women in Sweden was one of the most serious obstacles to the achievement of gender equality, with its explicit links to power and women's human rights.

> This meant that the law became an instrument for promoting gender equality, and gender equality was simultaneously formulated as a relevant aspect of criminal policy. (Burman 2012, p. 6)

This specific offence was intended to chime more closely with what was known about violence against women in intimate relationships from feminist research; acts other than those that were already criminalised (assault, harassment) could be charged together as a course of conduct so long as they formed an aspect of repeated violation of the victim's integrity. There was also no requirement, as with an incident based focus, of specifying the exact time and place of each act. It also reflects Starks' argument that domestic violence is a liberty crime.

Whilst Burman (2012) notes a series of implementation gaps with the Women's Peace reforms (some forms of psychological violence remain excluded, the needs of migrant women are not met, and the ways in which race and ethnicity intersect with gender is poorly recognised) as a way forward, re-centering gender in understandings of and responses to domestic violence would be a foundation for a clearer and closer connection between theory, policy and practice; it would be able to encompass the experiences of the women in the case studies, to link safety and freedom.

Focus On, Attention To and Knowledge Of Perpetrators

To start to reduce domestic violence there needs to be a greater focus on domestic violence perpetrators. At the moment, the only mention of domestic violence perpetrators in multi-agency strategies is if there is a domestic violence perpetrator programme (DVPP), and many areas still do not have this most basic provision. Even if DVPPs are successful in helping men choose to make changes, it is important to remember that not all men who perpetrate violence choose to attend such a programme, and many are assessed as not being appropriate to attend. Moreover, Project Mirabal has shown that there are challenges for programmes in reducing coercive control.

The principle of holding perpetrators to account cannot only be addressed through DVPPs and/or the criminal justice system, although there are undoubted improvements that could be made here in ensuring that more cases are investigated and prosecuted. But many agencies encounter men who are controlling the women and children they live with—social workers, doctors and other health professionals, employers. Yet, when these men are designated 'perpetrators' there is tendency to freeze and withdraw, to fail to hold them to account. One key recent example is the Troubled Families initiative, where domestic violence has been recognised as a key feature, but little if any clarity has been provided on how men are addressed about this. Potential new ways to make violent men visible and a target of intervention include the engagement of GPs through the Hermes project (Williamson et al. 2015) and the co-location of workers from DVPPs in social work teams (Philips 2013). Both involve upskilling practitioners to address men as perpetrators of abuse, to challenge their behaviour explicitly, and we argue that this needs to be consistently integrated into all professional responses.

A Truly Integrated, Human-rights Based Approach to Ending All Forms of Violence Against Women and Girls

Understanding violence against women as a continuum (Kelly 1987) requires a recognition of the many forms of coercion, abuse and assault that are used to control women. Women learn to discount and minimise aspects of the continuum because so much of it is normalised within gender orders. This understanding sits at the heart of the calls made by women's organisations for an integrated approach to violence against women (VAW), which has prevention at its heart. Box 3 shows what a minimal approach to 'integrated' should mean.

Box 3: What the Term 'Integrated', as a Minimum, Refers to (from Coy et al. 2008)

- Working to an overarching definition that is compliant with UN obligations
- Addressing all forms of VAW simultaneously
- Working with connections between forms of violence, not least in terms of their underlying causes, short- and long-term impacts
- Mainstreaming VAW across all relevant policy areas at national, regional and local levels
- Encouraging and enabling integration of all forms of VAW into specific policy areas, like prevention and public awareness, and activities such as inter-agency co-ordination
- Recognition of the critical importance of, and inter-reliance on, the statutory and voluntary sector, including acknowledgement of the historic and ongoing contribution of specialised women's organisations.

In 2008 the End Violence Against Women coalition published a template for an integrated strategy on violence against women for the UK, *Realising Rights, Fulfilling Obligations* (Coy et al. 2008). The template was organised around the Six Ps—perspective, policy, prevention, provision, protection and prosecution. Current responses were found to place too much emphasis on prosecution, that there were overlapping and uncoordinated policies, and that prevention was often just an 'add on'. An integrated approach required a different balance across the six Ps: that perspective should come first, rooted in human rights and gender equality; prevention should be placed at the centre; followed by provision and protection; prosecution was placed at the end, in recognition that the majority of women and girls never reach this point. For the last decade, however, prosecution has been at the centre of government policy responses and has been re-emphasised through the appointment of Police and Crime Commissioners. The *Realising Rights* framework, therefore, remains as a challenge for national and local governments; a challenge which has a range of implications for policy and practice, not least being the critical importance of provision of community based specialised support services that work closely with women's experiences, using an empowerment model.

Conclusions

Drawing on recent theory and research findings we have argued that current policy framings fail to recognise the centrality of gender to domestic violence, through an overemphasis on incidents of crime. This reflects how abusive men describe their behaviour whilst being far distant from the lived realities of women and children experiencing domestic violence. So long as law and policy fail to recognise that domestic violence *is* coercive control, and that coercive control is rooted in the policing of gender in the household, this will remain the case.

References

Angiolini, E. (2015). *Report of the independent review into the investigation and prosecution of rape in London.* London: Metropolitan Police.

Burman, M. (2012). Immigrant women facing male partner violence—Gender, race and power in Swedish Alien and criminal law. *Feminists@law, 2,* 1. https://journals.kent.ac.uk/index.php/feministsatlaw/article/view/55. Accessed 23 Sept 2015.

Burton, S., Regan, L., & Kelly, L. (1998). *Supporting women and challenging men: Lessons from the domestic violence intervention project.* Bristol: Policy Press.

Coy, M., & Kelly, L. (2011). *Islands in the stream: An evaluation of four London independent domestic violence advocacy schemes.* London: CWASU, London Metropolitan University.

Coy, M., Lovett, J., & Kelly, L. (2008). *Realising rights, fulfilling obligations.* London: End Violence Against Women Coalition.

Davies, E. (2015). *Survivor led ethics in multi-agency work.* http://www.dvrcv.org.au/sites/default/files/Survivor-led_ethics_in_multi-agency_work_DVRCV_AUTWIN2015_davis.pdf. Accessed 3 Oct 2015.

Dobash, R., & Dobash, R. (1992). *Women, violence and social change.* Abingdon: Routledge.

Erez, E., Adelman, M., & Gregory, C. (2008). Intersections of immigration and domestic violence: Voices of battered immigrant women. *Feminist Criminology, 4,* 32–46.

Ferraro, K. (1993). Irreconcilable differences: Police, battered women, and the law. In N. Z. Hilton (Ed.), *The legal response to battering* (pp. 96–126). Newbury Park: Sage.

Hearn, J. (1998). *The violences of men*. London: Sage.

Hester, M. (2006). Making it through the criminal justice system: Attrition and domestic violence. *Social Policy and Society, 5*(1), 79–90.

Hester, M., & Westmarland, N. (2006). Domestic violence perpetrators. *Criminal Justice Matters, 66*(1), 34–35.

Hester, M., & Westmarland, N. (2005). *Tackling domestic violence: Effective interventions and approaches (Home Office Research Study 290)*. London: Home Office Research, Development and Statistics Directorate.

HMIC. (2014). *Everyone's business: Improving the police response to domestic abuse*. London: HMIC. Available at http://www.justiceinspectorates.gov.uk/hmic/wp-content/uploads/2014/04/improving-the-police-response-to-domestic-abuse.pdf

Home Office (2003). Safety and Justice. The government's proposals on domestic violence. London, Home Office.

Holder, R., & Mayo, S. (2003). What do women want?: Prosecuting family violence in the ACT. *Current Issues in Criminal Justice, 15*(1), 5–25.

Jakobson, H. (2014). What's gendered about gender-based violence? An empirically grounded theoretical exploration from Tanzania. *Gender and Society, 28*(4), 537–561.

Kelly, L., & Humphreys, C. (2001). Supporting women and children in their communities: Outreach and advocacy approaches to domestic violence. In J. T. Brown (Ed.), *What Works in Reducing Domestic Violence? A comprehensive guide for professionals* . London: Whiting and Birch.

Kelly, L. (1987). *Surviving sexual violence*. Cambridge: Polity Press.

Kelly, L. (1999). *Domestic violence matters: An evaluation*. London: Home Office.

Kelly, L. (2013). Standing the test of time? Reflections on the concept of the continuum of sexual violence. In J. Brown & M. Horvath (Eds.), *Handbook of sexual violence* (pp. xvii–xxvi). London: Routledge.

Kelly, L., & Sharp, N. (2014). Finding the cost of freedom: How women rebuild their lives after domestic violence. http://solacewomensaid.org/wp-content/uploads/2014/06/SWA-Finding-Costs-of-Freedom-Report.pdf

Kelly, L., & Westmarland, N. (2014). *Time for a rethink—Why the current government definition of domestic violence is a problem*. Trouble & Strife. http://www.troubleandstrife.org/2014/04/time-for-a-rethink-why-the-current-government-definition-of-domestic-violence-is-a-problem/

Kelly, L., & Westmarland, N. (2015). *Domestic violence perpetrator programmes: Steps towards change (Project Mirabal Final Report)*. London/Durham: London Metropolitan University and Durham University. Available at https://www.dur.ac.uk/resources/criva/ProjectMirabalfinalreport.pdf

Liddle, M., & Gelsthorpe, L. (1994). Crime prevention and inter-agency co-operation. Home Office Police Research Group, Crime Prevention Unit Series, Paper 53.

Morris, A. (2009). Gendered dynamics of abuse and violence in families: Considering the abusive household gender regime. *Child Abuse Review, 18*(6), 414–427.

Mullender, A., et al. (2002). *Children's perspectives on domestic violence.* London: Sage.

Office for National Statistics. (2014). *Crime statistics, focus on violence crime and sexual offences, 2012/13.* London: Office for National Statistics.

Philips, R. (2013). Dvip's co-location in Hackney children's services: A process evaluation. http://www.dvip.org/assets/files/downloads/DVIP%20Co-Location%20In%20Hackney%20Children%20Services%20-%20 A%20 Process%20Evaluation.pdf

Sampson, A., et al. (1988). Crime, localities and the multi-agency approach. *British Journal of Criminology, 28*(4), 478–493.

Schulhofer, S. (1995). The feminist challenge in criminal law. *University Of Pennsylvania Law Review, 143,* 2151–2207.

Shepard, M., & Pence, E. (1999). *Coordinating community responses to domestic violence: Lessons from Duluth and beyond.* London: Sage.

Sokoloff, N., & Dupont, I. (2005). Domestic violence at the intersections of race, class, and gender: Challenges and contributions to understanding violence against marginalized women in diverse communities. *Violence Against Women, 11*(1), 38–64.

Stark, E. (2007). *Coercive control: The entrapment of women in personal life (Interpersonal violence).* Oxford/New York: Oxford University Press.

Westmarland, N. (2015). *Violence against women: Criminological perspectives on men's violences.* London: Routledge.

Westmarland, N., & Kelly, L. (2016). Naming and defining 'Domestic violence': Lessons from research with violent men. *Feminist Review,*112, 113-127.

WHO. (2013). *Global and regional estimates of violence against women: Prevalence and health effects of intimate partner violence and non-partner sexual violence.* Geneva: WHO.

Williamson, E., Jones, S. K., Ferrari, G., Debbonaire, T., Feder, G., & Hester, M. (2015). Health professionals responding to men for safety (HERMES): Feasibility of a general practice training intervention to improve the response to male patients who have experienced or perpetrated domestic violence and abuse. *Primary Health Care Research & Development, 16*(3), 281–288.

Women's National Commission. (2003). *Unlocking the secret.* London: WNC.

4

Critical Realism and Gang Violence

John Pitts

The Mythical Gang

Although police officers, health, welfare and educational professionals, local residents and their children in gang-affected neighbourhoods are familiar with the effects of gangs and gang crime (Pitts 2008; Palmer 2009; Harding 2014), some academics remain sceptical (Brotherton and Barrios 2004; Hallsworth and Young 2008). They argue that notwithstanding the stylistic differences between contemporary youth cultures and those of the past, the contemporary furore surrounding violent youth gangs is akin to the demonising discourses—the 'moral panics'—which attended the Teddy boys in the 1950s, the mods and rockers in the 1960s, the punks in the 1970s, the lager louts in the 1980s and so on. They argue that these periodic expressions of popular outrage tell us more about the anxieties of an adult public, opinion formers and the media than the behaviour of young people (Hallsworth and Duffy 2011), for example, claims that; *the problem of the 'gang' is not the gang itself but the media driven moral panic and 'gang control industry' that surrounds it.*

J. Pitts (✉)
Vauxhall Centre for the Study of Crime, University of Bedfordshire, Bedfordshire, UK

© The Editor(s) (if applicable) and The Author(s) 2016   **57**
R. Matthews (ed.), *What is to Be Done About Crime and Punishment?*,
DOI 10.1057/978-1-137-57228-8_4

Some academics believe that this demonisation, or othering, has a more sinister purpose and argue that current concerns about violent youth gangs are orchestrated by the state, its agencies and the media, who generate 'imaginaries' to justify ever deeper incursions into our freedoms and ever greater control over our lives (Rose 2000; Muncie and Hughes 2002; Simon 2007; Hallsworth 2014).

In *The Criminologists Gang* Katz and Jackson-Jacobs (2004) take the next illogical step by arguing that the 'gang' is, in fact, a complete fabrication, because both popular and scholarly understandings of the 'gang' arise from the interplay of the self-aggrandising 'myths' generated by alleged 'gang members', the spurious targets identified by agents of the justice system and the theoretical prejudices of gang researchers. This 'myth-making' Katz and Jackson-Jacobs maintain, is akin to the practices of religious acolytes, because the central myth they foster is that the gang actually exists.

In many settings gang life consists in history-making events celebrating resonant symbols and posturing defiance against morally hostile forces. Fervent rituals professing commitments may be necessary because of the lack of any independent, objective reality of the gang. (p. 92)

That gang-involved young people generate myths about themselves is wholly unsurprising. Indeed, as Levi-Strauss (1966) observes, everybody creates myths—even social scientists, although they tend to call them theories—because myths enable us to make sense of our lives and, in the process, make them more manageable. In the case of crime, we have only to think of Bonnie and Clyde Barrow, or Butch Cassidy, the Sundance Kid and the Hole in the Wall gang—rapacious myth makers and self-publicists all—to recognise that myth making and the infliction of lethal violence upon the innocent are not mutually exclusive.

The contention that gang violence is a fabrication of the gang control industry and the media it feeds, and that the telling of tall tales by gang members demonstrates that gangs do not actually exist both duck the demonstrable reality that, all over the world, there are groups of socially disadvantaged young people who claim an affiliation to a named group whose raison d'être is crime and violence (see for example, van Gemert et al. 2008; Balasunderham 2009; Hagedorn 2012 and Harding forthcoming).

A gang of masked and hooded youths unleashed dogs on a 16-year-old boy before stabbing him to death, a court heard today. Seyi Ogunyemi died in a gang attack in Larkhall Park, south London, after being stabbed six times in April last year, the Old Bailey was told. His friend, then 17, was also attacked when the pair were confronted by up to a dozen youths with two dogs, jurors heard. 'At the time of the attack both dogs were unleashed, and chased and then brought down and savaged their victims, giving their human masters an advantage, enabling them then to access their victims in order to stab them with knives' he told the court. The gang of around 12 attackers, alleged to be from the Otre gang, otherwise called the Otre or G-Street gang, were 'patrolling' their 'home turf' of the Larkhill Park Estate, off Wandsworth Road in south London at around 7pm on April 27 last year, said Altman. Having spotted a group of six youths who they believed to belong to the rival ABM (All About Money) gang, from the nearby Stockwell gardens estate, they unleashed their dogs, with 'devastating effects', said Altman. 'It was described by one shocked observer as 'vicious' and as mirroring the behaviour of a pack of wild animals,' he said. Ogunyemi was brought down by the gangs' dogs before being stabbed six times in Larkhill Park. Two blows fatally pierced his aorta, and despite having emergency surgery he died at the scene. Two other men were stabbed in the attack. (Alexandra Topping, *The Guardian* 2010)

Cognitive Dissonance

Many political progressives find this reality deeply problematic. How can it be, they wonder, that socially disadvantaged young people, living on the social margins and denied access to all that makes life worth living, far from expressing class and ethnic solidarity with their similarly oppressed brothers and sisters, are prepared to inflict such vicious, sometimes lethal, violence upon them? And how, if we reject the brute determinism of traditional positivism and acknowledge the subject's capacity for agency and self-invention, can we sidestep the conclusion that this renders them responsible for their actions. These are problems that cannot be wished away by trite faux sociological generalisations like *the legacy of racial oppression* or *the embodied consequence of capitalist exploitation*, to which unreflective radicals are particularly prone. Ultimately, to paraphrase

E. M. Forster, in their fervent desire to see life steadily, they studiously avoid seeing it whole.

The introduction of a socially disadvantaged victim into the oppressed/oppressor binary creates a profound cognitive dissonance for those who need a clear-cut side to join (Festinger 1957; Becker 1966). This can be extremely distressing because it can disrupt a person's psychological equilibrium, prompting them to find ways of neutralising the contradiction. Gresham Sykes and David Matza (1957) suggest that in these circumstances people may adopt one or more of the following 'techniques of neutralisation':

1. *Denial of the victim*: in which the 'alleged' criminal victimisation is reframed as a 'normal', albeit robust, part of 'growing up' within a particular (sub-)cultural milieu. (Katz and Jackson-Jacobs 2004; Hallsworth and Young 2008).
2. *Denial of injury*: in which the severity and impact of the crime is denied or dismissed as a gross media exaggeration. (Aldridge et al. 2008).
3. *Denial of responsibility*: in which, because the nature, volume, severity and impact of the crime and its consequences is denied or minimised, the academic concludes that there is nothing for them to explain or justify. (Katz and Jackson-Jacobs 2004)
4. *Condemnation of the condemners*: in which those denying the severity and impact of the victimisation maintain that social scientists who highlight it are doing so because they are in the thrall, if not the pay, of the apparatus of social control (the police, the courts, the government etc.) which has an interest in orchestrating a moral panic about youth gangs. (Katz and Jackson-Jacobs 2004; Hallsworth 2013).
5. *Appeal to higher loyalties*: in which, although there is evidence of harm, academics maintain that the primary responsibility of the radical criminologist is to struggle against the demonisation of socially disadvantaged, allegedly gang-involved young people by agents of the state and their academic lackeys. (Becker 1966; Katz 1988; Simon 2007)

These neutralisations may insulate the naive social scientist from the brute realities of gang crime but they also militate against the development of a plausible analysis, and this condemns them to perpetual irrelevance.

Roger Matthews (2014) suggests that the antidote to such irrelevance is a 'Post Adolescent Criminology' which sees gang crime in the round and understands that, in W. H. Auden's phrase, *those to whom evil is done* (may sometimes) *do evil in return*. Elsewhere Matthews describes this as *Critical Realism*.

Critical Realism and Gang Violence

Critical realism is an approach to the study of social phenomena which poses a challenge to more conventional ways of doing social science. A critical realist approach to the issue of violent gang crime would be based on the following seven propositions:

1. There is a real, knowable, world 'out there'; not just a random collection of correlates, subjective personal experiences, 'imaginaries' or discourses.
2. 'Gangs' are real because both those who claim affiliation to them and those affected by them are aware of the gang as a discrete social grouping with a recognised soubriquet, an identifiable structure, distinct norms and values and an unambiguous raison d'être, namely the perpetration of crime and violence. Gangs may meet other needs and perform other functions but their existence is predicated upon crime and violence and if these characteristics are absent, they are not gangs.
3. Violent gang crime—not just criminalisation, demonisation or the depredations of the 'apparatus of social control'—is a serious problem, which bears disproportionately upon the poorest and most vulnerable young people, their friends, families and neighbours. Any criminology that denies or equivocates about this fact is doomed to political and practical irrelevance.
4. The nature of violent gangs, the neighbourhoods and networks in which they are embedded and the destinies of their affiliates are shaped in crucial ways by the interplay of social structure, culture and biography (Mills 1957; Young 2011), and it is the role of social research to reveal the nature of this interplay because social reality may be very different from its empirically observable surface appearance (Bhaskar and Callinicos 2003).

5. Nonetheless, the gang-involved and gang-affected young people who live within these 'social fields' (Bourdieu 1990) have a capacity for reflexivity and are capable of comprehending, reflecting upon and acting to change their predicament (Giddens 1984; Unger 1987; Archer 1995).
6. This capacity for reflexivity can be both prompted and facilitated by social scientific theory and participative social research (Adorno and Horkheimer 1944; Bhaskar 1989).
7. Critical realism does not stand outside, or above, the world of politics and policy; recognising that, for gang-involved and gang-affected young people, gaining an understanding of the real nature of their social predicament, through the development of reflexivity, is the first step towards changing that predicament.

Explaining Gang Violence

Explanations of gang violence in both the USA and the UK take a variety of forms. As we have noted, some liberal academics lay the 'gang problem' at the door of the 'apparatus of social control' which, through a process of projective identification, generates 'imaginaries' that become the focus of intervention (Katz and Jackson-Jacobs 2004; Hallsworth 2008, 2014). For others, 'labeling' or 'social reaction' theory is the favoured explanatory schema (Aldridge et al. 2008, 2011) but although labeling theorists' antipathy towards 'the state' is less vehement, they also suggest that, ultimately, 'gangs' are spoken into being by the 'control apparatus'.

Unlike their radical colleagues, mainstream criminologists in the UK accept that gangs are real. However, whereas the gang and gang violence are central concerns in North American criminology, in the UK they are treated as secondary issues and explained in the same way as other forms of crime; in terms of the moral character, proclivities or deficiencies of criminal individuals. This view finds its fullest expression in the 'risk factor paradigm' (Farrington et al. 2009), the logic of which dictates that the gang can never be more than an incidental repository for the aggregated risk factors besetting its affiliates.

Some social theorists have invoked the underclass thesis to explain gang violence. This takes two distinct forms. On the one hand there are what

Cornell West (1993) calls the Liberal Structuralists who, like William Julius Wilson (2012), point to the social and economic constraints on the life chances of, usually ethnic minority, citizens living in high crime, low income, neighbourhoods. On the other hand, there are the Conservative Behaviourists who, like Charles Murray (1984), maintain that, Black criminality is the product of an overweening welfare state that rewards fecklessness, undermines individual responsibility and discourages parental propriety, thus producing a culture of dependency and entitlement wherein sexual profligacy and criminality become the norm. Liberal structuralists tend to call for greater state intervention and progressive welfare reform, while conservative behaviourists support the inculcation of mainstream values, attitudes and behaviours, fiscal frugality and vigorous free market policies that drive the feckless back into work.

It is a short step from here to Iain Duncan Smith's 'Broken Britain' (Centre for Social Justice 2009) which explores 'pathways into poverty', (some of which, his critics claim, have been created by Mr. Duncan Smith himself). Pre-eminent amongst these pathways he argues, is a 'culture of worklessness and dependency'. As to the origins of this reprehensible sub-cultural mutation, he writes:

> Most significantly however, a catalyst and consequence of these pathways to poverty, is the breakdown of the family. Marriage, far more stable than cohabitation, has rapidly declined in recent decades; 15 per cent of babies in Britain are now born without a resident biological father; and we have the highest rate of teenage pregnancy in Europe. Without strong families violent and lawless street gangs, whose leaders are often school age, offer a deadly alternative.

This is obviously a caricature. Leaving to one side the perverse conflation of 'single' and 'unmarried' parenthood (the latter represented 44 % of live births in the UK in 2007), it holds that single parenthood has an 'independent effect' upon gang involvement. Definitions of the gang remain vague and 'guestimates' of gang involvement even vaguer, but the data presented in Duncan Smith's Centre for Social Justice report on youth gangs, Dying to Belong (2009), suggests that fewer than 20,000 young people in the UK are gang involved. If we set this figure against the 2,000,000, or so, single parents believed to be bringing up children in the UK (Gingerbread 2010), and when we recognise that many of the young people identified as gang members do not come from single parent families (Pitts 2008; Centre for Social Justice 2009), it appears that, at worst, single parent families could have generated only around 0.01 % of the young people involved in violent youth gangs.

Nihilism and Gang Violence

However, what many radical social scientists miss is that the recognition of cultural problems does not necessarily lead automatically to a Duncan Smith-style neo-liberal response. In *The Cultural Matrix: Understanding Black Youth* (2015) Orlando Patterson and Ethan Fosse argue that in the wake of the Moynihan Report (1965) on the Black Family from 50 years ago, social scientists, as a body, have shied away from cultural studies of the poor, particularly if they are Black, for fear that they might be seen to be pathologising them. They have, they argue, therefore shifted their focus from cultural to structural problems and Patterson and Fosse (2015) believe that this has been a serious mistake because: *The social problems [black youth] face are too great and too important not to take culture seriously.* In a similar vein Cornell West (1993) has argued that although right wing conservative behaviourists, focusing only upon moral values, have misunderstood both the origins and nature of the predicament of the urban underclass, then so have liberal structuralists, by focusing exclusively upon external economic structures. Their reluctance to confront the internal, psycho-cultural processes that are a consequence of life in the ghetto mean that they fail to recognise the nihilism that pervades the ghetto because it appears to be supportive of the Conservative case. West writes:

> this failure by liberals leaves the existential and psychological realities of black people in the lurch (because) the lived experience of coping with a life of horrifying meaninglessness, hopelessness and (most important) lovelessness … results in a numbing detachment from others and a self-destructive disposition toward the world. Life without meaning, hope and love breeds a coldhearted, mean-spirited outlook that destroys both the individual and others.

Ken Pryce (1979), a Jamaican sociologist who undertook an ethnographic study of the Caribbean community in the St. Paul's area of Bristol in the early 1970s, makes a similar point; seeing that people who are subject to the *Endless Pressure* of racism and economic exploitation:

> become the victims of their own unrestrained irascibility. In their day-to-day interaction with each other they inflict much damage on themselves and on each other, in much the same way that the environment brutalises them socially and economically.

Similarly, Bowling and Phillips (2006) argue that social and economic exclusion and the undeserved injustices experienced historically by members of the Black community can generate frustration and rage amongst Black young people which, as David Kennedy (2007) argues, help to promote norms and narratives supportive of gang violence.

The steady retrenchment of state welfare, educational and criminal justice services in the past three decades means that what Detlef Baum (1996) calls 'discredited neighbourhoods' are gradually floating free from the socio-cultural and political mainstream. In consequence, traditional modes of informal social control and informal social support, rooted in common values and an expectation of local solidarity, have become untenable (Wilson 1988/2012). The enforced estrangement of these neighbourhoods from the mainstream also calls into question the validity of those who populate them, not only in the eyes of others but also in their own eyes. As John Rodger (2008) concludes:

> Where marginality, social exclusion or sectarianism emerges, the sense of empathy for the other and the mutual restraint on behaviour which are built by frequent social interaction are absent. This tendency should be understood as a structural property of social systems where social polarization and inequality are present or deepening and not as a property of pathological individuals.

Here Rodger echoes Norbert Elias (2000), who believes that 'civilising processes' may co-exist with, or in certain circumstances be supplanted by, tendencies towards 'de-civilisation'. This happens when the actual or perceived weakening of the state's capacity to protect its citizens places pressure upon individuals to assume responsibility for managing the risks and threats previously dealt with by the state. The incalculability of the threats they face lead to heightened anxiety coupled with a pressing need to find ways to alleviate it. For those who lack the wherewithal to ensure their personal security this can lead to an erosion of reality congruence, a process in which potential threats become exaggerated, coupled with the diminution of mutual identification and tolerance. In these circumstances, young people may conclude that if the authorities are either unwilling or unable to protect them, they must 'take care of business' for themselves.

As veteran gang researcher James Short (1997) argues, over time these norms and narratives foster 'alternative cognitive landscapes', developing what is sometimes called a soldier mentality, characterised by a heightened sensitivity to threat and a constant preparedness for action (Sampson and Lauritsen 1994) if the young people come to believe that those around them are 'disrespecting' them.

Katz's more recent scepticism about the existence of gangs notwithstanding, in his earlier writings he argues that the central myth of the gang is that it is under constant threat of attack (Katz 1988). But, all too often, this myth turns out to be a self-fulfilling portent; one which is swiftly fulfilled as the anxiety it generates flows like an electrical surge through the intertwined networks in which these young people are enmeshed because, as Thomas and Thomas (1928) remind us, 'If men define situations as real, they are real in their consequences'.

The Social Field of the Violent Gang

Although Pierre Bourdieu never wrote about youth gangs, his work on social field theory has become a key point of reference in the academic debate (c.f. Hagedorn 2012; Pitts 2008; Wacquant 2008; Harding 2014). Bourdieu eschews individualising explanations, arguing that because human behaviour is primarily the product of the social fields in which they are embedded, they must be analysed independently of the personal characteristics of their inhabitants.

Bourdieu's social field is a competitive system of social relations, composed of individual 'agents' who are vying for the same stake. What is at stake is the attainment of the degree of dominance that allows them to confer, or withdraw, legitimacy from other 'agents' within the social field. He speaks of 'an ensemble of relationships between "agents" antagonistically oriented to the same prizes or values' or alternatively 'fields of organized striving' (Bourdieu 1990).

Action is explained in terms of position and trajectory. According to Bourdieu (1990) every position in a social field is seen to induce a set of motivations that are subjectively experienced as a 'chain of objective requirements ... what' should be done. Meanwhile, the actor's trajectory, their direction of movement through, and status within, the social field, determines the 'social fate' that propels them towards the places to which their socially constituted dispositions predestine them.

Although Bourdieu describes this process as 'agency' it bears little resemblance to the notion of 'free will' underpinning the agency/structure debate in conventional sociology (Giddens 1992). And this is because, for Bourdieu, agency is deeply imbued with, and patterned by, 'habitus; a socially constituted system of dispositions that orient thoughts, perceptions, expressions, and actions' (Bourdieu 1990). As one of Simon Harding's Lambeth respondents says:

> You learn it just by hanging around. … You know what you are supposed to do and not supposed to do really. Just like what you are allowed to do at school. They don't even need to explain it'. (Harding 2014)

The boundaries of social fields are demarcated by the points beyond which their effects and influence cease; the points at which the hostility loops back into the network. This explains why people living in gang-affected neighbourhoods report being unaffected by them and, in some cases, even being unaware of their existence (Harding 2014).

While Bourdieu provides an important perspective from which to understand how social relationships and status hierarchies operate within the social field of the gang, he presents us with a closed system. Put another way, if the habitus of the social field effectively constitutes the actors within it, how can they ever do anything differently, or indeed, anything different. But of course they do. As Simon Harding (2014) observes, only 10–20 % of young people affiliated to gangs in their early teenage years are still involved by their early twenties. This finding echoes those of the Edinburgh Study of Youth Transitions (Smith 2005) which found that in a sample of over 4,000 school students, self-nominated gang affiliates constituted 20 % of the cohort at age 13, but just 5 % by the age of 17. And, in line with what we know about the criminal careers of young women in general, the involvement of girls in gangs is of even briefer duration. Whereas in Edinburgh at age 13, the numbers of boys and girls claiming to be gang affiliated were similar, by 17 three times as many boys as girls claimed affiliation (Bjerregaard and Smith 1993). Moreover, when girls do leave the gang they are more likely to pursue conventional routes to academic and vocational success; suggesting that their involvement is both briefer and less embedded.

It would follow from this that if we are to stem gang violence, the social field in which gang-involved young people are embedded and the culture of nihilism and despair it can ferment, should be the primary targets for any intervention. But a major impetus for such change must be the capacity for reflexivity, change and growth exhibited by the young people who move on and move out of these toxic social fields.

Realistic Interventions to Stem Gang Violence

> I've got role models … Nelson Mandela … Martin Luther King … All that … But they don't have to live round here do they? (Jackson, 17-year-old gun owner, N.W. London)

The *Ending Gang and Youth Violence* (EGYV) report, published in November 2011, was the government's response to the riots in August of that year. It was based, in part, upon the deliberations of a rapidly convened International Forum on Gangs chaired by Theresa May and Iain Duncan Smith, which concluded, erroneously, that the riots had been fermented by youth gangs whose members were drawn from dysfunctional families. The report provided the blueprint for the government's national gang strategy; a three-year programme launched in January

2012, which eventually targeted 33 gang 'hot spots' in England, a further ten were added in 2014.

In most of these gang-affected areas the interventions targeted the families of gang-involved young people and/or supported programmes that aimed to change the attitudes and enhance the employability or the mental health of actual or potential gang members. However, the EGYV programme was launched at a time of severe cuts to youth services and its resources were distributed largely on the basis of the recipients' own estimations of whether or not their interventions did or could 'work'. As a result EGYV-funded provision has tended to be determined as much by local professional and political interests as by objective assessments of the nature and dimensions of the gang problem.

An evaluation of the first two years of the programme (Disley and Liddle 2015) found little sign of an 'evidence-based strategy' or a coherent model of gang intervention. This meant that no systematic baseline measures of gang involvement and gang activity could be put in place and, as a result, it remains unclear whether more young people are becoming involved in gangs, whether gangs are becoming more or less numerous and whether gang crime is becoming more or less serious.

Time and Change

It was not simply problems of conceptualisation, funding and implementation that hampered the EGYV programme however. While there was talk at the outset of the programme being a catalyst for a 'sustainable' 'step change' that would leave a 'lasting legacy', little serious consideration was given to the conditions under which experimental initiatives like EGYV might thrive.

Microsoft founder Bill Gates could have been talking about the EGYV programme, or indeed London Mayor Boris Johnson's 2015 Operation Shield, discussed below, when he observed that 'We always overestimate the change that will occur in the next two years and underestimate the change that will occur in the next ten' (Cummings 2013). In both the UK and the USA, the most effective gang violence reduction strategies have demonstrated a commitment to the long-term participation of those groups with a significant interest in the problem, the willingness and the capacity to do something about it and the resilience to keep at it until the job is done, which may mean that the initiative becomes a permanent feature of local service provision.

Factors found to facilitate effective partnership working of this type are: 'strategic oversight' (McGarrell 2009); the presence of scheme champions ensuring buy-in and mutual benefit across agencies (Davison et al. 2010); and good communication between partner organisations (McGarrell 2009).

In their *Gangs at the Grass Roots: Community Solutions to Street Violence* Brand and Ollerenshaw (2009) suggest that integrated multi-agency gang strategies are successful to the extent that those commissioning them are able to exert control or influence over:

- The commissioning of the strategy
- The integration of community members into the strategy
- The targeting of local interventions
- The co-ordination of the strategy
- The credibility and capacity of the strategy
- The review of the strategy

A study of 'commissioning' or 'public service purchasing' in education, health and/or social welfare undertaken by the Social Science Research Unit at the Institute for Education, London (Social Science Research Unit 2009) concluded that joint commissioning is successful where:

- There are trusting relationships between the commissioners and commissioned services
- This is built up over time by continuity of staff
- There is clarity about responsibilities and legal frameworks, particularly in relation to shared or pooled finances
- There is co-terminosity between organisational and geographical boundaries;
- There are clear structures, information systems and communications between stakeholders.

This resonates with the US experience. In the 1990s Spergel and Grossman (1998) produced a summary of the evidence of the effectiveness of the Comprehensive Gang Strategy developed by the US Department of Justice Office of Juvenile Justice and Delinquency Prevention (OJJDP) on five sites. They concluded that the most successful programmes had five main components:

- Community mobilisation
- Social intervention
- Provision of social opportunities
- Suppression
- Organisational change and development of local agencies and groups

Spergel and his colleagues (1994) also observed that the impact of these partnerships was maximised if they were underpinned by:

- proactive leadership by significant representatives of criminal justice and community-based agencies, which helped to mobilise political and community interests.

This mobilisation of 'political interests', drawing down political support from the places where real change can be effected is, as William Julius Wilson (1988/2012) has observed, central to effecting change in the, invariably impoverished, neighbourhoods where violent gangs are active.

Co-ordinated Enforcement and Social Action

In the late 1980s Boston Massachusetts experienced an epidemic of gang-related firearms homicides in some poor inner-city neighbourhoods. Between 1987 and 1990 gang-related murders rose from 22 per annum to 73. From then until 1995 they averaged 44 a year.

Launched in 1996, Operation Ceasefire drew upon Spergel and Goldman's Comprehensive Gang Model, to bring together practitioners, researchers and local people, including gang members, in gang-affected neighbourhoods to undertake an assessment of the youth homicide problem. Having recognised the suspicion and hostility that many local people felt towards the police, intervention officers spent months work-ing with community groups prior to the launch to improve local services and enhance youth provision. They then proceeded to implement what David Kennedy (2007) describes as a 'focused deterrence strategy, har-nessing a multitude of different agencies plus resources from within the community'. The objective of Operation Ceasefire was simple enough, it aimed to save lives and reduce serious injury. It did not aim to 'smash' gangs, although defection from gangs was a side effect of the initiative.

The strategy had three elements:

- *Enhancing community relations* to get local support for targeted crack-downs, stimulate community 'collective efficacy' in the development of informal social control and the reduction of incivilities.
- *Engagement with gang members* to elicit information, transmit consis-tent messages about targeted crackdowns and provide diversionary services for gang-involved young people.
- *Co-ordinated leverage on gangs* through highly publicised multi-agency crackdowns on certain specified behaviours, i.e. possession or use of knives and firearms, harassment and serious assaults.

This approach involved deterring chronic gang offenders violence by reach-ing out directly to gangs, saying explicitly that violence would no longer be tolerated, and backing that message by pulling every lever legally available when violence occurred … When gang violence occurred, a direct message (was sent) to gang members that they were under the microscope because of their violent behaviour. (Braga et al. 2001)

An analysis of the impact of Operation Ceasefire by the John F. Kennedy School of Government at Harvard, which began in 1996, concluded that the programme had been responsible for a fall in youth homicides from an average of 44 per annum between 1991 and 1995, to 26 in 1996 and 15 in 1997; a downward trend which continued until 1999.

However, with a change in project staff, and project philosophy, which resulted in the social intervention elements of the programme being abandoned, gang-related youth homicides began to climb again, reaching 37 in 2005 and peaking at 52 in 2010.

Ceasefire UK

Not Learning the Lessons of Ceasefire

Below, I shall argue that adaptations of the Ceasefire model have met with considerable success in two major UK cities. However, Operation Shield—piloted by Mayor Boris Johnson and the Metropolitan Police in three London boroughs in 2015, at a cost of only £66,666 per borough—was a resounding failure because it adopted some of Ceasefire's techniques while ignoring most of its underlying principles.

In Boston Ceasefire ran for three years, while in Glasgow and Manchester interventions based on the Ceasefire model have been in operation for well over a decade. In London the Operation Shield pilot was supposed to last for one year but voluntary sector agencies and community groups in two boroughs withdrew after six months because they regarded as draconian the apprehension en masse of 'gang nominals' logged on the borough's Gangs Matrix.

Gang nominals are people the police suspect of involvement in gang crime. Inclusion on the Gangs Matrix is based upon arrest and conviction data, on corroborated and uncorroborated intelligence, as well as material from YouTube and other social networking sites, CCTV footage and telephone traces. However, as the police acknowledge, identifying 'gang nominals' is not a precise science because the Matrix captures both active gang members and their non-offending associates and siblings who are on the system by dint of their proximity to, and the frequency of their association with, gang members rather than crimes they have committed.

However, for many of the young people in gang-affected neighbourhoods, relatively few of whom are involved in gang crime, association with gang members is pragmatic, a means of securing some degree of safety in a high-risk situation. This 'strategic positioning' was one of the main findings of research undertaken in London boroughs between 2006 and 2009 (Pitts 2008) and of other contemporaneous studies (Youth Justice Board 2007; Centre for Social Justice 2009). This close association between gang-involved and non-gang-involved children and young people is also evident in the 180 interviews undertaken in recent research for the Children's Commissioner on six sites across England (Beckett et al. 2013). This inevitably creates difficulties for the police.

Nonetheless, Operation Shield based its strategy on the premise that since gang crime is an act of a group, the authorities should target 'the group as a whole'—i.e. the offender and his or her known associates. Thus, all these associates, whether guilty of an offence or not, could be made subject to gang injunctions, mandatory employment training or eviction from social housing.

In the run-up to implementation most of those elements that research and experience indicate are central to successful gang crime reduction were either neglected or ignored: community involvement in goal-setting did not happen; relevant agencies and organisations were ill equipped and unprepared to deliver on the promises made at gang call-ins; and little attempt was made to develop positive relationships with gang-involved young people and their families. Moreover, Operation Shield also laid itself open to accusations of racism.

Of the 3,422 people listed in 2015 on the Metropolitan Police Gangs Matrix 78.2 % were identified as Black, while a further 8.7 % were from other ethnic minority groups. London's population is approximately 60 % White Caucasian. According to Patrick Williams (2014), in Greater Manchester 89 % of individuals on the Gangs Matrix are from ethnic minorities, while the White Caucasian population is higher than 80 %. It is not difficult to see why accusations of racism were levelled at the police and, had they been prepared, they might well have answered that the Matrix also included the names of people deemed to be at risk of gang involvement, who might be diverted via pre-emptive intervention by the welfare and educational agencies with which they worked in partnership, but they did not.

Racism may well play a part in the construction of these matrices but, as Bullock and Tilley (2002) demonstrated in their South Manchester study, it is also the case that ethnic minority young men are significantly over-represented as both victims and perpetrators of lethal, and not infrequently gang-related, violence. In her study of London homicides between 1999 and 2005, Marion Fitzgerald (2008) found that ethnic minority young men aged 10–17 constituted 70 % of victims of homicide, whereas White Caucasians made up only 28 % of the total. In his study of homicides in London between 2000 and 2010, Mark Jackson (2010) found that ethnic minority suspects made up just over 50 % of suspected perpetrators and that, while African-Caribbean males accounted for 32 % of all victims, the most heavily victimised sub-group was African-Caribbean teenagers aged between 15 and 19 who comprised 56 % of this number.

Adoption and Adaptation

A modified version of Operation Ceasefire, with its emphasis on 'Co-ordinated Leverage, Enhancing Community Relations and Engagement with Gang Members' has been adopted in both Glasgow and Manchester. Although these cities have faced different problems from those in Boston, as well as from each other, in terms of the origins, nature, volume and prevalence of gang violence, the programmes they have developed appear to have had a significant impact.

While Glasgow has placed considerable emphasis upon the individual and familial risk factors contributing to youth violence, the Manchester strategy tends to emphasise extrinsic, environmental factors. Whereas Glasgow has embraced a 'public health' model (Ritter 2009) in which gang-related violence is regarded as a kind of inter-generationally trans-mitted 'epidemic', Manchester has adopted what might be described as an 'ecological' model (Suttles 1972), in which gang-related youth violence is seen primarily as a function of neighbourhood alliances, local cultures, the social networks in which individuals are embedded, their relationship with upper echelon criminal business organisations and the effects of social and ethnic change.

These differences of approach are partly conceptual and partly shaped by real differences in the histories of gang conflict and the nature of the violence. Present day Glasgow gangs have their origins in the conflicts which arose in the city in the 1880s. The original Glasgow gangs were divided between those which were solely territorial and those that combined territorial and sectarian allegiances. While originally a largely Protestant city, in the late nineteenth and early twentieth centuries large numbers of poor,

Irish, Roman Catholics migrated to Glasgow, drawn by the job opportunities in the heavy industries around the Clyde and the better quality of life they offered. However, one of the results was that sectarian youth gangs formed in the low-income neighbourhoods in which the migrants settled. With the advent of mass unemployment in the early 1930s these conflicts intensified and it became fairly common for men in their twenties and thirties to remain active members of street gangs (Davies 1998).

Unlike gang-affected neighbourhoods in Manchester and London, which are characterised by relatively high levels of 'housing churn' as successive waves of migrants pass through them, the populations of Glasgow's gang-affected neighbourhoods have remained relatively stable over several generations. Moreover, whereas gang-involved young people in Manchester and London tend to be implicated in drug dealing, in Glasgow the problem of violence is compounded by high levels of alcohol consumption and illicit drug use (Pitts 2008; Harding 2014).

The Glasgow Model

Research undertaken by the Glasgow police in 2007 identified 170 street gangs in the city, with an estimated 3,500 members aged between 11 and 23. Comparing police reports with the accounts of trauma surgeons and A&E staff showed that as many as two-thirds of knife crimes were not being reported to the police. Thus in October 2008 the police Violence Reduction Unit launched its Community Initiative to Reduce Violence (CIRV). The Glasgow initiative has three basic components:

- *A zero-tolerance police warning* that if the violence doesn't stop, relentless targeted enforcement will follow.
- *Call-ins* at which identified gang members were invited to attend the Glasgow Sheriff Court where family members of injured or deceased gang members, police and doctors detailed the human cost of gang activity and gang culture and the participants were invited to sign a pledge to renounce violence and work with the CIRV programme.
- *A commitment from educational, youth serving and social care agencies* that if young people desist from violence they will be helped with education, training and employment.

Alongside this, Glasgow police began stopping buses coming into the city from the outlying housing estates at weekends, when most of the stabbings occurred, and searching young people who they believed could be carrying a weapon.

There have been ten call-ins since 2008, and of the 473 gang members who have attended, 400 have signed up to a pledge of non-violence. CIRV (2011) claim that since its inception there has been a 46 % reduction in violence amongst this group. Moreover, those who have taken part in the most intensive programmes are said to have cut their offending by 73 % and knife-carrying amongst participants has dropped by almost 60 %. However, as CIRV's initial research indicates, these tend to be offences with low levels of reporting.

Moreover, during the same period there has been a 25 % drop in violent offending amongst gang members in areas of the city where the CIRV does not operate, which could suggest that either knowledge of the programme is having some kind of palliative effect or, conversely, that the CIRV programme outcomes are benefitting from a more general decline in youth violence in the city.

These outcomes, while not conclusive, suggest that CIRV is having an impact on violent gang crime in Glasgow.

The Manchester Model

The evidence from Manchester, where the lessons of Operation Ceasefire were implemented differently, is more substantial but less well known, because the architects of the initiative believed that a high media profile given to gang violence was one of the factors sustaining it.

Gang violence in South Manchester in the twenty-first century has its origins in the struggles between the Gooch Close, Doddington and Longsight gangs in Cheetham Hill and Moss Side for control of the city centre drugs market in the early 1990s. In June 1997, five members of the Young Gooch were sentenced to 43 years in prison for firearms related offences (Carter 2012). Nonetheless the violent conflict continued into the twenty-first century until, in late 2007, on the basis of evidence from gang members and an elaborate wire tap, Greater Manchester Police arrested 11 senior members of the Gooch Close Gang who, in April 2009, were convicted at Liverpool Crown Court of 154 shootings, including five murders, five attempted murders and 94 serious woundings.

Although the trial of the Young Gooch marked the end of what was, in effect, a criminal business organisation linked with several street gangs, it did not signal the end of gangs and crime in South Manchester. Instead, it presaged a proliferation of more chaotic gangs of younger people claiming affiliation to the original Gooch and Doddington gangs. However, this generation of 'gangstas' also claimed affiliation to the Cripz and the Bloodz and Blue Team and Red Team, (Manchester City and Manchester United football clubs). Newcomers included the OTC (Old Trafford Cripz), the Fallowfield Mandem/Mad Dogs, HGC (Home Grown Crew) and HCG (Holdgate Close Gang) which claimed affiliation to the Gooch and the Longsight Crew, the Young Doddington Crew and the MSB (Moss Side Bloodz) who operated under the banner of the Doddington. This structure is akin to that of the Los Angeles gangs in which the various gang factions are affiliated to one of two main gangs, the Bloods or the Crips (Carter 2012). Whereas some of the original members of the Gooch and the Doddington made a great deal of money from drug dealing, this new generation of gangstas were primarily involved in violent conflict to gain or maintain respect.

The Manchester Multi-Agency Gang Strategy (MMAGS) was launched in 2002 in the wake of research undertaken by Karen Bullock and Nick Tilley (2001). Based on data compiled by Greater Manchester Police, the research revealed that between April 2001 and March 2002 South Manchester gangs were responsible for 11 fatal shootings, 84 serious woundings and 639 other incidents of violence involving firearms. It also showed that a large number of those responsible for the shootings had themselves been shot. This important, but seldom cited, study is notable for being one of the few that has ventured into the ideologically precarious terrain in which poor, often ethnic minority, young people are committing appalling crimes of violence against one another.

Most of the perpetrators and victims were young men in their teens. These shootings were highly localised. Of those recorded in 1999, for example, 68 % were in the two main gang-affected neighbourhoods in South Manchester. Of the 46 gun-crime victims identified in the study, 30 lived in these two areas, where, in the second half of 1999, there were six gang related murders in five months (Bullock and Tilley 2001).

The ensuing strategy was based in part on the Boston (USA) Operation Ceasefire model, but MMAGS added three additional elements to the model:

- *A gang mediation service* to address long-standing rivalries and emerging tensions that caused shootings.
- *Targeted protection/containment* for victims and repeat victims, because those who survive attacks may retaliate or be victimised again.
- *Sensitisation of agencies* to the conditions that foster gang violence, its effects and their responsibilities under Section 17 (Community Safety) of the Crime and Disorder Act (1998).

Although MMAGS was, in effect, a statutory partnership it had an independent advisory group that included community representatives, and it met regularly with Mothers Against Violence, Victim Support and several other local voluntary sector organisations. In its first 12 months of operation MMAGS made contact with over 200 gang-involved young people and during this time only around 10 % of this target group were known to have re-offended (Corrigan 2007).

MMAGS had a remarkable impact upon the young people it targeted and from 2001 played a major role in the steady reduction of gang-related firearms discharges, deaths and associated injuries. The other key element in the success of the Manchester gang strategy was the creation of the Xcalibre gangs unit, launched by the Greater Manchester Police in August 2004. Charged with creating 'gun free streets' in Greater Manchester Xcalibre has three elements:

- *A small squad that focuses on the criminal business organisations* supplying firearms and Class A drugs to gangs.
- *A critical incident team that investigates gang-related shootings*
- *The Xcalibre Taskforce*: a team of one inspector, two sergeants and 15 constables.

Prior to the deployment of Xcalibre, when a firearms incident occurred, police officers would flood the streets stopping and searching any young person who fitted the profile of a likely perpetrator. This meant that many uninvolved Black young people in the area would be stopped and searched and this had the perverse effect of maximising resentment while minimising information flow.

The Xcalibre team set out to identify the young people and adults who were actually involved in gangs and gang crime and to meet them on the streets. The teams went out on patrol every evening, sometimes with MMAGS outreach workers and peer mentors, covering the areas where gang-involved young people congregated. They adopted a policy of never driving past a suspect but always stopping and talking to them. What they talked about were the risks to the gang members, their families and their friends from continued gang involvement.

At the outset, this talking served primarily as a warning to these young men and women about the potential consequences of their gang involvement but it was accompanied by offers of legitimate routes out of the gang via programmes developed by MMAGS and tailored to the circumstances, interests and capabilities of individual young people. But this was also the beginning of a conversation that began to work away at the sense of omnipotence and invulnerability, which is the greatest thing that gang involvement bestows because it is the mirror image of the experience of powerlessness, fatalism and vulnerability that drew these young people to life in the gang in the first place. This talking, because it is delivered with warmth and respect, and accompanied by offers of legitimate routes out of the gang to a place where they might construct a plausible identity of their own choosing, also chips away at their nihilistic sense of victimhood which legitimates their depredations; what Cornell West (1993) calls their 'numbing detachment from others and the coldhearted, mean-spirited outlook that destroys both the individual and others'. Practically, this strategy of intensive contact had the immediate effect of reducing the numbers of firearms on the street and hence the danger to which the young people could be exposed.

Street gangs are sustained through the recruitment of younger siblings and their associates (BRAP 2012) and so Xcalibre focuses particularly on minors—the younger siblings and associates of known gang members, who they find hanging out with them on the streets and are therefore assumed to be at risk of gang involvement. The police and social workers take them to their homes and issue their parents with a Statement of Concern. This Statement of Concern triggers a multi-agency case conference, which includes representatives from Education, Health, Probation, the Youth Offending Team and the local Safeguarding Board. The conference considers the vulnerability of the child or young person, their siblings and associates, and puts in place a relevant intervention. From 2007, the average age of gang-involved young people began to rise, indicating that the strategy of diverting younger siblings and associates away from gang crime was working.

Another early sign of success for this new strategy came in the summer of 2008 when Greater Manchester Police recorded the largest gap in time between firearms discharges in Manchester since 1990, from mid-February to July. This coincided with the sentencing of 11 high-profile members of the Gooch Close gang, which demonstrated that gang-related offending would attract severe sentences. Taken together, these factors— the long prison sentences imposed on notorious local gangsters, 'intensive' policing and the co-location of a multi-disciplinary team—saw firearms crime, death and injury fall even further from 2009, until in 2012/13 there were no firearms fatalities in Moss Side and Longsight.

The success of the Manchester strategy is rooted in an agreement between the leader of the council and the chief constable to ring-fence expenditure on the gang strategy and to offer incentives for personnel to stay in their respective roles for several years to develop a culture of trust between the statutory agencies and voluntary sector providers and effective formal and informal mechanisms for sharing information. This was also the model developed in the Young Hackney initiative in London. In Manchester this process has been facilitated by the co-location of senior personnel from the YOT, Probation, Safeguarding, Housing and Children and Young People's services and the Greater Manchester Police Xcalibre Gangs Taskforce. A large part of the success of MMAGS/ Xcalibre is attributable to its longevity, the co-location of the police with other agency personnel and locally recruited outreach workers and peer mentors. The programme built trusting relationships with the families of gang-involved children and young people, the youngsters themselves and the schools and statutory and voluntary sector agencies, organisations and community groups in the area. In short, it was an embedded intervention.

Embedded Interventions

Recent research tells us that in gang-affected neighbourhoods in English towns and cities, although the violent and sexual victimisation of children and young people may be commonplace it is seldom reported (Beckett et al. 2013). This is because of a widespread belief amongst young people in these neighbourhoods that 'the authorities' would be powerless to stop it and that official intervention might well make matters worse by setting them up for further victimisation. Most young respondents were pessimistic about the possibility of change and feared that the situation was, if anything, getting worse; not least because of the closure of local youth projects, mentoring schemes and street-based youth work programmes. This withdrawal of public services tended to compound their sense of fatalism.

The problem is that like many of the projects set up under the auspices of the EGYV programme, the agencies and organisations established to protect and safeguard these young people are essentially reactive; intervening after the event in response to an incident or a referral and putting victims or perpetrators through time-limited agency-based programmes (Beckett et al. 2013). This is because, in the UK, most safeguarding and criminal justice agencies are still working to a model in which expertise is located within a bureau staffed by specialists to which the hapless victims or the culpable perpetrators are taken to have their victimisation or their offending worked on by the experts.

But for these young people the risks are out there in the gang-affected neighbourhood, where the experts seldom venture; the perpetrators are their peers and the problem lies, first and foremost in the dynamics of the neighbourhood rather than the behaviours, attitudes and beliefs of particular young people ensnared in the social field of the gang. The young people know this but they also know what kinds of support and intervention, in the neighbourhood, in the school and in the peer group, could ameliorate the situation. They are also aware that, all too often, the victims of gang crime, particularly young women, are regarded as in some way responsible for their own victimisation by some professionals (Firmin 2015).

Abstracted, bureau-based responses to the gang problem may improve the lot of some gang-involved individuals. However, they cannot antici-

pate gang violence and victimisation in order to make pre-emptive interventions. Nor can they respond to the, almost invariably unreported,
victimisation of gang-involved and gang-affected girls and young women
and their parents (Beckett et al. 2013). And, in particular, they cannot
mediate between potential adversaries in inter-gang violence, which is
the forum where most gang fatalities occur. In short, most safeguarding
and criminal justice agencies are destined to be in the wrong place at the
wrong time.

This is, at the very least, unfortunate since the research tells us that a
key feature of effective gang strategies and gang mediation appears to be
that the workers are embedded in the neighbourhoods and the groups
involved in, and most affected by, gang crime (Spergel and Grossman
1998; Braga et al. 2001; Pitts 2008; Centre for Social Justice 2009). These
workers are best placed to undertake an assessment of the gang problem,
to work with local agencies, organisations and community groups to
establish which aspects of the local gang problem they are best equipped
to deal. Moreover, it is only when gang-involved and gang-affected young
people are engaged in such a strategy that their fatalism and nihilism can
be called into question by their experience of making better things happen, and their reflexivity mobilised in the struggle to effect bureaucratic,
neighbourhood and individual change.

Conclusion

Such an approach fits well with the critical realist project which holds
that interventions to stem gang violence should be rooted in a recognition that the destinies of gang-involved and gang-affected young people
are shaped in crucial ways by the interplay of history, social structure,
local cultures and individual biographies (Mills 1957; Young 2011). This
being so, it follows that interventions should focus on: (a) the social,
economic and historical factors that sustain gang involvement within the
neighbourhood; (b) the networks, relationships and locales which demar-
cate the social field of the gang; and (c) the individuals, both victims and
perpetrators, who constitute and reproduce these social fields; the threats
they pose and the risks they run.

References

Adorno, T., & Horkheimer, M. (1944). *The dialectic of enlightenment: Philosophical fragments* (G. S. Noerr (Eds.), trans: Jephcott, E.). London: Verso Classics.

Aldridge, J., Medina, J., & Ralphs, R. (2008). Dangers and problems of doing gang research in the UK. In F. van Gemert, D. Peterson, & I.-l. Lien (Eds.), *Street gangs, migration and ethnicity*. Cullompton: Willan.

Aldridge, J., Medina, J., & Ralphs, R. (2011). Collateral damage: Territory and policing in an english gang city. In B. Goldson (Ed.), *Youth in crisis: Gangs territoriality and violence*. London: Routledge.

Archer, M. (1995). *Realist social theory: The morphogenetic approach*. Cambridge: Cambridge University Press.

Balasunderham, A. (2009, April). Gang-related violence amongst young people of the tamil refugee diaspora in London. *Safer Communities*, 8(2).

Baum, D. (1996). Can integration succeed? Research into urban childhood and youth in a deprived area of Koblenz. *Social Work in Europe, 3*(3).

Becker, H. S. (1966). Whose side are we on? *Social Problems, 14*(3), 239.

Beckett, H., Brodie, I., Factor, F., Melrose, M., Pearce, J., Pitts, J., et al. (2013). *It's wrong … But you get used to it, a qualitative study of gang-associated sexual violence towards, and exploitation of young people in England*. London: The Children's Commissioner for England.

Bhaskar, R. (1989). *Reclaiming reality*. London: Verso.

Bhaskar, R., & Callinicos, A. (2003). Marxism and critical realism: A debate. *Journal of Critical Realism, 1*(2).

Bjerregaard, B., & Smith, C. (1993). Gender differences in gang participation, delinquency, and substance use. *Journal of Quantitative Criminology, 9*, 329–355.

Bourdieu, P. (1990). *The logic of practice*. Cambridge: Polity Press.

Bowling, B., & Phillips, C. (2006, October). *Young black people and the criminal justice system*. Submission to the Home Affairs Committee Inquiry.

Braga, A., Kennedy, D., Waring, E., & Morrison, A. (2001). Problem-oriented policing deterrence and youth violence: An evaluation of Boston's operation Ceasefire. *The Journal of Research in Crime and Delinquency, 38*(3), 195–225.

Brand, A., & Ollerenshaw, R. (2009). *Gangs at the grass roots: Community solutions to street violence*. London: The New Local Government Network.

BRAP. (2012). *Stuck: Current approaches to the design and delivery of interventions to address gang-related violence in Birmingham: A research report*. Birmingham:

BRAP. Accessible at http://www.barrowcadbury.org.uk/wp-content/uploads/2012/09/stuck-brapresearchreport1.pdf

Brotherton, D., & Barrios, L. (2004). *The Almighty Latin King and Queen Nation: Street Politics and the Transformation of a New York City Gang.* New York: Columbia University Press.

Carter, R. (2012). *History, affiliation, tactics and structure of the Gooch Close Gang.* Unpublished, Greater Manchester Police.

Centre for Social Justice. (2008). *Broken Britain.* London: Centre for Social Justice.

Centre for Social Justice. (2009). *Dying to belong: An in-depth review of street gangs in Britain.* London: Centre for Social Justice.

CIRV. (2011). *The violence must stop.* Glasgow: CIRV.

Cummings, D. (2013).David Cummings on Startups. https://davidcummings.org/2013/12/27/overestimate-the-next-two-years-and-underestimate-the-next-ten.

Davies, A. (1998). Street gangs, crime and policing in Glasgow during the 1930s: The case of the beehive boys. *Social History, 23*(3), 251–267.

Davison, T., van Staden, L., Nicholas, S., & Feist, A. (2010). *Process evaluation of data sharing between emergency departments and community safety partnerships in the South East* (Home Office Research Report 46). London: Home Office.

Disley, E., & Liddle, M. (2015). *Urban street gangs in ending gang and youth violence areas: Local perceptions of the nature of gangs and whether they have changed in the last two years.* London: Ministry of Justice.

Elias, N. (2000). *The civilizing process: Sociogenetic and psychogenetic investigations.* Oxford: Blackwell.

Farrington, D. P., Coid, J. W., & Murray, J. (2009). Family factors in the intergenerational transmission of offending. *Criminal Behaviour and Mental Health, 19,* 109–124.

Firmin, C. (2015). *Peer on peer abuse: The safeguarding implications of contextualising peer on peer abuse between young people within their social fields.* Doctoral Thesis, University Of Bedfordshire, Institute of Applied Social Research.

Giddens, A. (1984). *The constitution of society.* Cambridge: Polity Press.

Gingerbread (2013). http://www.gingerbread.org.uk/content.aspx?CategoryID=365.

Hagedorn, J. (2012). *A world of gangs: Armed young men and gangsta culture.* London: University of Minnesota Press.

Hallsworth, S. (2013). *The gang and beyond: Interpreting violent street worlds.* Basingstoke: Palgrave/Macmillan.

Hallsworth, S., & Duffy, K. (2011). Confronting London's violent street world: The gang and beyond. A report for London council's centre for social and evaluation research. London: London Metropolitan University.

Hallsworth, S., & Young, T. (2008). Gang talk and gang talkers: A critique. *Crime, Media and Culture, 4*(2), 175–195.

Harding, S. (2014). *The street Casino.* Bristol: Policy Press.

Harding, S. (Ed.). (forthcoming). *Global perspectives on youth violence gangs and weapons.* Philadelphia: GIB Publishing.

Jackson, M. (2010). *Murder concentration and distribution patterns in London: An exploratory analysis of ten years of data.* Cambridge: University of Cambridge. Accessible at http://www.crim.cam.ac.uk/alumni/theses/Jackson,%20M

Katz, J. (1988). *Seductions of crime: Moral and sensual attractions in doing evil.* New York: Basic Books.

Katz, J., & Jackson-Jacobs, C. (2004). The criminologists' gang. In C. Sumner (Ed.), *The Blackwell companion to criminology* (pp. 91–124). Malden: Blackwell.

Kennedy, D. (2007). *How to stop young men shooting each other.* London, Presentation to the Metropolitan Police Authority.

Levi-Strauss, C. (1966). *The savage mind (La Pensée Sauvage).* Chicago: University of Chicago Press.

Matthews, R. (2014). *Realist criminology.* Basingstoke: Palgrave/Macmillan.

Moynihan, D. (1965). *The Negro family: The case for national action.* Washington, DC: Office of Policy Planning and Research, U.S. Department of Labor.

Murray, C. (1984). *Losing ground: American social policy 1950–1980.* New York: Basic Books.

Muncie, J., & Hughes, G. (2002). Modes of Youth Governance: Political Rationalities, Criminalization and Resistance. In J. Muncie & G. Hughes (Eds.) Youth Justice: Critical Readings. London: Sage Publications.

Palmer, S. (2009). The origins and emergence of youth 'gangs' in a British inner-city neighbourhood. *Safer Communities,*8(2) 17–26.

Patterson, O., & Fosse, E. (2015). *The cultural matrix: Understanding black youth.* Cambridge, MA: Harvard University Press.

Pitts, J. (2008). *Reluctant gangsters: The changing face of youth crime.* Cullompton: Willan Publications.

Pryce, K. (1979). *Endless pressure.* Harmondsworth: Penguin Books.

Ritter, N. (2009, November). 'Ceasefire': A public health approach to reducing shootings and killings. Washington, *National Institute for Justice, 264.*

Rose, N. (1996). The death of the social? Refiguring the territory of government. Economy and Society, 25(3), 327–346.

Rodger, J. (2008). *Criminalising social policy: Antisocial behaviour and welfare in a de- civilised society.* Cullompton: Willan.

Sampson, R., & Lauritsen, J. (1994). Violent victimisation and offending: Individual, situational and community-level risk factors. In A. Reiss & J. Roth (Eds.), *Social influences: Understanding and preventing violence 3.* Washington, DC: National Academy Press.

Short, J. (1997). *Poverty, ethnicity and violent crime.* Boulder: Westview Press.

Simon, J. (2007). Governing through crime. In I. Friedman & G. Fisher (Eds.), *The crime conundrum: Essays on criminal justice.* Boulder: Westview Press.

Smith, D. (2005). *The Edinburgh study of youth transitions.* Edinburgh: University of Edinburgh.

Social Science Research Unit. (2009). *Commissioning public services.* London: Institute for Education.

Spergel, I., & Grossman, S. (1998). The little village project: A community approach to the gang problem. *Social Work, 42,* 456–470.

Spergel, I., Curry, D., Chance, R., Kane, C., Ross, R., Alexander, A., Simmons, E., Oh, S. (1994). *Gang suppression and intervention: Problem and response.* National Youth Gang Suppression and Intervention Research and Development Program, School of Social Service Administration, University of Chicago.

Suttles, G. (1972). *The social construction of communities.* Chicago: University of Chicago Press.

Thomas, W. I., & Thomas, D. S. (1928). *The child in America: Behavior problems and programs.* New York: Knopf.

Unger, R. (1987). *Social theory: Its situation and its task.* Cambridge: Cambridge University Press.

van Gemert, F., Peterson, D., & Lien, I.-L. (Eds.) (2008). Street gangs, migration and ethnicity. London: Willan Publishing.

Wacquant, L. (2008). *Urban outcasts: A comparative sociology of advanced marginality.* Cambridge: Polity Press.

West, C. (1993). The Nihilistic threat to black America the major enemy of black survival in America is neither oppression nor exploitation but rather the loss of hope and absence of meaning. http://articles.philly.com/1993-05-09/news/25966287_1_black-america-black-business-expansion-second-camp

Williams, P. (2014). Police, gangs and racism. http://www.crimeandjustice.org.uk/resources/police-gangs-and-racism

Wilson, W. J. (1989/2012). *The truly disadvantaged: The inner city, the underclass, and public policy* (2nd ed.). Chicago: Chicago University Press.

Young, J. (2011). *The criminological imagination.* Cambridge: Polity Press.

Young, J., & Matthews, R. (1992). *Rethinking criminology: The realist debate.* London: Sage.

Youth Justice Board. (2007). *Groups gangs and weapons.* London: Youth Justice Board.

5

Middle-Range Radical Realism for Crime Prevention

Nick Tilley

Let us not assume that there has been no effective and ethical crime prevention. Let us also not assume that current research, beliefs, policies and practices are not open to improvement. This chapter argues in favour of middle-range radical realism as a framework for developing and delivering progressive crime prevention.

I begin by highlighting some crime prevention successes. I then go on to make some critical comments on: (a) conventional assumptions about crime prevention discourse, which lie behind policy and practice decision-making; (b) much crime prevention research; and (c) the use of the term administrative criminology to disparage some crime prevention theory and practice. Next, I sketch out what I mean by middle-range radical realism. Finally, I discuss the implications of middle-range radical realism for research, policy and practice.

N. Tilley (✉)
Department of Security and Crime Science, University College, London

© The Editor(s) (if applicable) and The Author(s) 2016
R. Matthews (ed.), *What is to Be Done About Crime and Punishment?*,
DOI 10.1057/978-1-137-57228-8_5

Crime Prevention Successes

Many crime rates have been falling in most western countries since the early- to mid-1990s (Van Dijk et al. 2012). They have fallen against assumptions that long-term increases in crime would continue. There are many reasons why crimes may rise and fall (Tonry 2014). The evidence suggests, however, that at least some of the recent and sustained falls were due to deliberate efforts to reduce crime risks (Farrell et al. 2014). There is no consensus as yet on the causes of all the drops in crime that have occurred and many of the early explanations invoked idiosyncratic developments in the United States, when it appeared that the drops were confined to that country. However, as the falls have followed in many other countries more generic causes have been sought (Farrell et al. 2014).

It has become clear that security improvements have played a large part in producing falls in a wide range of crimes (Farrell et al. 2014). The clearest example comprises the dramatic and sustained drop in car theft. Here, central locking, alarm setting and the activation of electronic immobilisers have been shown to play a key role in reducing the number of offences (Farrell et al. 2011a, b; Brown 2004, 2013; Van Ours and Vollaard 2013). The much greater drop in forced entry MOs and in temporary, as against permanent, thefts, as well as the association of the fall with dramatic increases in the amount and quality of security built into cars, suggest that it is indeed increases in security that have reduced the rate of offences. Moreover, it is those who previously stole cars for temporary use, because it was so easy to do so, whose offences have been prevented by security improvements (Farrell et al. 2011a). Although the evidence is not quite so compelling, it also appears that security improvements have played a substantial part in reducing levels of domestic burglary, which have also seen a dramatic fall since the early- to mid-1970s in many countries (Tseloni et al. 2010). There is still weaker evidence that the security-generated falls in, so-called, debut or gateway crimes (such as car theft, burglary and shop theft that mark entry points to periods of prolific offending) inhibit the onset of crime careers that encompass a wide range of crime types (Farrell et al. 2015). Hence, security improvements may indirectly be reducing a wide range of crimes and criminality (Farrell et al. 2014). It may also be that the spread of security which has occurred in many countries in the form of, for example, CCTV cameras, security staff,

RFID tags, Crime Prevention Through Environmental Design (CPTED) and alley-gating, comprises a common denominator reducing many types of crime in many jurisdictions, whilst those crimes where security improvements lag behind the emergence of new opportunities have been increasing. The clearest example of increased crime opportunity relates to information and communications technology and here, although measuring rates of victimisation is very tricky, it would appear that crime is booming. Identity theft, child pornography, internet frauds and romance scams all comprise examples (UNODC 2013; see McGuire in this volume).

So, nationally and internationally, security improvements have led directly to drops in some crimes, with possible further preventive side effects where debut crimes have been inhibited, whilst at the same time other crimes have increased following a growth in opportunity for new forms of crime, notably those associated with the growing use of the internet (see Goodman 2015).

In addition to large-scale national falls in crime that can be attributed to deliberate efforts to reduce crime, there is evidence that local crime prevention efforts have also enjoyed some success. For instance, well-targeted and highly publicised deterrence has yielded substantial falls in specific crimes within specific groups (Kleiman 2009; Kennedy 2008). The best case study showing this concerns gang-related homicides in Boston. Here, Operation Ceasefire was used to tell those involved that firearms offences by any gang member would trigger a general crackdown on all (the many) offences in which members were involved (Braga et al. 1999). No one wanted gang-related killings and no gang wanted to elicit concerted enforcement attention on all their infractions. The effect was to reduce dramatically the number of gang-related shootings (Braga et al. 1999). Part of the process involved an intense communications strategy to make sure all understood the situation including family and community members who also applied informal controls over those belonging to gangs.

Another example of locally effective crime prevention that returns to the security motif relates to alley-gating (Bowers 2004; Sidebottom et al. 2015). Alley-gating is a widely adopted technique, mainly used to reduce domestic burglary in terraced housing that backs on to an alleyway giving rear access to dwellings. Closing off public access to the alley by gating it off makes it more difficult for offenders to enter properties surreptitiously. There is a good deal of evidence that well-targeted alley-gating of this kind can reduce levels of domestic burglary.

More generally, in terms of local strategy, evidence strongly suggests that systematic problem-solving is effective (Weisburd and Eck 2004; Weisburd et al. 2010). This does not describe specific actions but rather an approach that homes in on specific problems, analyses them in detail and then tailors a set of measures (often involving a third party) to change the situation that is enabling or encouraging the specific criminal behaviour. Such problem-solving is often led by the police, but can also be undertaken by partnerships or other individual organisations (see Bullock et al. 2006).

A focus on repeat victimisation, which has led to substantial reductions in crimes where implemented well, comprises one form of problem-solving. It draws on the widespread research finding that crime tends to concentrate on particular targets (Farrell and Pease 1993, 2001; Pease 1998; Grove and Farrell 2014). Targets that have been victimised once are at higher risk than those who have not (yet) been targeted. Those victimised twice are at higher risk of a third incident than those victimised (so far) only once. And so on. Moreover the repeats tend to come quickly and risks of further incidents decay quite rapidly (Grove and Farrell 2014). Concentrating preventive efforts promptly on the recently victimised, and increasing the dosage if further incidents occur, comprises a general strategy that has enjoyed success, for example, in relation to domestic violence (Hanmer et al. 1999).

Many other examples of specific crime prevention successes could be given. My point here is that in advancing alternative policy approaches that are more realistic, viable and progressive than those that have been in place in the past—which is the main focus of this book—needs to take account of what has already been found to be effective in practice.

I turn now to a critique of current positions.

Critiques of Current Orthodoxies

Current Assumptions That Lie Behind Much Policy and Practice Decision-making

Although much has been achieved by way of crime prevention, the prevailing assumptions in much policy, practice and research are open to criticism. Fortunately some crooked thinking has largely disappeared. However, some myths remain.

I begin with myths that were once widely believed, but are heard much less often now:

1. *'Crime, like lightning, doesn't strike twice.'* Victims were once reassured with the comforting advice that they had had their turn as victims, so they should no longer worry. A wide range of research confirms, as already indicated, that victims are at elevated risk, at least in the short term. Victims now tend to be told this and to receive advice and sometimes, where necessary, material support to reduce the risk of revictimisation.
2. *'Crime is randomly distributed.'* This is a more general version of the lightning doesn't strike twice myth. A large body of research shows that crime is highly patterned and that practitioners are often poorly placed to identify the patterns due to their experience of only specific and occasional events and the tendency to remember and assign too much significance to exceptional rather than typical events (Goldstein 1979; Tilley 2009). Crime analysts, improved data collection, cheap computers and user-friendly software now allow patterns to be more readily identified and used in operational decisions. One recent version of this is 'prospective hotspotting', which uses research-based algorithms to estimate where and when future crime is most likely to inform preventive resource allocation, also known as predictive policing (Johnson and Bowers 2007).
3. *'Prevented crime is simply displaced by time, place, MO, victim, offender or crime type.'* This, so called, hydraulic theory of crime, which has it that there is a fixed volume of crime or crime harm, still occasionally surfaces, even within the research community and more often amongst policymakers and the general public. However, it has become difficult for those with responsibility to advise on and execute policies to remain ignorant of the large volume of research that casts doubt on this crime theory, although equally it is not possible to falsify the most loosely formulated version of the displacement hypothesis which suggests that displacement may be by any method, at any time or place (Guerette and Bowers 2009). Absent a specific hypothesis about where and how displacement will surface, testing whether or not it is occurring is simply impossible. It can thereby become an article of faith that is liable to paralyse many preventive endeavours.

4. '*Responsibility for crime prevention can be lodged with the police in particular and the criminal justice system more generally.*' Although it is doubtful if any serious police or criminal justice practitioner, researcher or policymaker would seriously advance this view, it continues to lie behind some crime related rhetoric. For example the police and criminal justice policymakers are sometimes apt to claim credit for drops in crime, and critics of the police and criminal justice system are apt to blame it for rises in crime. Whilst credit and blame may sometimes be warranted in specific cases, any general assumption that crime levels simply reflect what the police do or do not do is not warranted. It is now widely accepted that the practices, policies, products and plans of other agencies and organisations are crucial to much crime prevention (Laycock and Tilley 1994). This is not to say that police conduct is irrelevant to crime or crime prevention. The application of 'procedural justice principles' (achieving perceived legitimacy by being trustworthy, involving citizens in decision-making and treating them fairly and with respect) appears, unsurprisingly, to encourage compliance and avoid provocation (Tyler 2003; Mazerolle et al. 2013).

I turn now to myths that continue to obstruct effective crime prevention.

5. '*To prevent crime we need to address the root causes of criminality.*' This commits the 'fundamental attribution error' (Wortley 1997; Ross and Nisbett 2011; Tilley and Sidebottom 2015), which involves explaining behaviour in terms of disposition. Behaviour, and in this case criminal behaviour, fundamentally reflects the dispositions of those engaging in it. The inference is that only altering the basic dispositions behind behaviour can change it. However, there is by now a very large body of research showing that behaviour is heavily shaped by the immediate situation. The Asch experiments showed that expressed opinions could be manipulated quite easily by the views expressed by others (Asch 1955). Zimbardo's Stanford prison experiments showed how allocating individuals a role could quickly lead them to take on the attributes of the role holder (Zimbardo 2007). Milgram showed how experimental subjects could be put in a situation where they willingly administered what they believed to be substantial and potentially fatal electric shocks

(Milgram 1974). In each case the immediate situation played a crucial role in eliciting the behaviour. This is not to say that disposition will play no part. It is only to say that situations play a large part in shaping what people do and that those situations can be altered in ways that will produce more or less of any particular behaviour. Much discourse on crime prevention, where it invokes a common-sense need to address the root causes of crime (whether these be moral, psychological or sociological) makes the fundamental attribution error. Moreover, those police who refer to prolific offenders as irredeemable 'scrotes', who treat them as unproblematically embodying criminality and who assume that all prevention depends on the suppression of such scrotes, embrace the fundamental attribution error (see Tilley 2014). The same goes for many popular newspapers and populist politicians. The fundamental attribution error crosses political boundaries and is, indeed, fundamental.

6. '*Effective and ethical crime prevention requires wholesale social reform to deal with basic inequalities and inequities.*' This view tends to be rooted in the fundamental attribution error and, in this sense, is social scientifically naïve. It flies in the face of much effective crime prevention that has not addressed basic inequalities and inequities (Clarke 1997, 2005). It is also politically and ideologically objectionable and a danger for those committed to an agenda that aims to reduce or remove social inequalities and inequities. Hanging arguments for social reform on its expected crime prevention benefits jeopardises that reform if the crime prevention benefits do not follow. Moreover, there are reasons to believe that much egalitarian reform may inadvertently generate rather than reduce crime. If this is the case, should radicals be any less committed to egalitarian reform? I think not. The post-war emergence of the welfare state created higher levels of consumer durable consumption by the poor, who thereby came to own more products typically targeted by local acquisitive offenders. Likewise, higher rates of participation by women in a labour market with reduced employment discrimination created more unoccupied properties in the daytime, which thereby became more vulnerable to burglary (Cohen and Felson 1979). Is a radical reformist agenda to be compromised because of criminogenic side effects? Or is it better to try to address the crime fall-out with specific measures aimed at reducing the levels of crime experienced?

The latter view takes crime prevention to be focused properly on the prevention of crime, rather than mixed in with other social policy agendas. That said, there is indeed a radical agenda that would (a) focus crime prevention efforts where they are needed, to reduce unequal vulnerability to crime, and (b) apply pressure on those whose inattention to the ways in which they may inadvertently create crime opportunities allows avoidable crime waves to take place. These themes are the focus of later sections of this chapter.

7. *'Victims are never to blame.'* This view has it that offenders are fully to blame for all crimes. The grounds are sometimes linked to adherence to the fundamental attribution error, which I've already touched on. There are also moral grounds. We should be able to conduct ourselves any way we choose provided that what we do is lawful, and it is up to the state to protect us. We cannot be held responsible in any way for the behaviour of others who offend against us. The case most often invoked in this argument is that of assaults against women, most notably rape. Although I have no argument at all with this position as it relates to women (or for that matter to many other victim groups), there may be cases where victims do bear some responsibility. Take shop theft, for example. In the past, at any rate, the number of shop thefts has exceeded the total number of crimes captured in the British Crime Survey (Tilley 2010). It is a high volume crime. It also seems to be a gateway crime—an offence that helps kick-start many criminal careers (Owen and Cooper 2013). The expectation that the state will bear the costs of control over shop theft, even assuming that the state were competent to do so, seems unreasonable. Assigning some responsibility to the retailer makes sense, where the form of retailing provokes or enables shop theft to occur and where the costs of processing offenders falls to the public purse (see Ekblom 1986).

Crime Prevention Research Orthodoxy

Effective crime prevention, it is held, needs to be evidence-based, and that requires the conduct of large numbers of new trials and meta-analyses of results from previous trials (Sherman 1997, 2013). There is a substantial and well-meaning movement advocating evidence-based policing and evidence-based crime prevention (Sherman 2013). At first sight it seems sensible and benign, a pitch for the policy-development counterpart of motherhood and apple pie.

The idea behind the movement is that most of what is done in the name of crime prevention is untested. The best tests are ones that establish a counterfactual (what would have happened in the absence of the intervention) to ascertain both whether there has been an impact and the size of that impact. And the best way of establishing the counterfactual is to conduct a randomised controlled experiment (RCT). RCTs assign potential intervention targets randomly to treatment and control groups (preferably with blinding of subjects, practitioners and analysis). By using this method what would have happened absent the intervention can be estimated and the net effect calculated by subtracting control group change from treatment group change. With proper costing of both crime and intervention, it then becomes possible to gauge objectively, quantitatively and in a common currency whether the crime prevention benefits are worth the crime prevention investment. Moreover, it becomes possible to compare several interventions to ascertain which is most cost-effective.

Given the uncertainties that are inevitable in any individual study, the results of all (published and unpublished) studies relating to a given intervention need to be combined to produce an unbiased estimate of overall effects, with a point estimate and confidence limits surrounding it. Moreover, given the problems of blinding and random assignment of sufficient units for statistical analysis with large entities as the target of interventions, quasi experiments are often deemed necessary which come as close as practical to mimicking the RCT to establish the counterfactual (Sherman 1997).

Armed with evidence from the best trials available policymakers and practitioners can make informed decisions. Where there is no evidence or where new interventions are planned, advocates of evidence-based policing and crime prevention urge investment in trials that approximate as closely as practicable to RCTs that can plug evidence gaps (Shepherd 2003). Over time, the vision is of policy and practice that is increasingly informed by an ever-growing evidence base.

There are, however, five main problems with evidence-based crime prevention of the sort advocated. These relate to induction, complexity, diversity, change and relevance to infrequent high-cost events.

1. Problems in the logic of induction have been well known ever since Hume (1793) and its lack of necessity in science has been known since Popper (1959). That something has been seen to happen in the past is no guarantee that it will happen in the future. Indeed, even the probability does not increase. That the sun has been seen to rise and fall by innumerable people over human history does not mean that the sun does routinely move round the Earth—it does not do so. Observations can be used to test (falsify) theories, not to prove universal generalisations. Smart experimentalists seem to realise this, which is why they emphasise internal validity (that in any specific instance the intervention in question really did produce the measured outcome). However, less generally recognised is that replications do not do the trick either (what counts as a replication is not obvious—duplication is not possible and, even if a measure could be duplicated, past findings do not entail that the same would be found in the future) (Tilley 1996). RCTs are also poorly equipped to deal with complexity.

2. Complexity refers here to the ways in which the effectiveness of measures depend on conditions that they themselves transform, altering the effects that the measures have (Ekblom 2011). This is not difficult to understand. Self-fulfilling and self-defeating prophesies are cases in point (Merton 1968). The prediction of a traffic jam due to road works and the suggestion of an alternative route can lead to route switches, which means that the predicted event does not occur because its prediction changes the conditions for drivers' decision-making. Likewise, the prediction of a shortage of some good leads to that shortage as buyers stock up, again because of decision-making informed by the prediction. In both cases adaptation creates a system change that affects the outcome. In crime prevention, the naiveté of those liable to offend in the light of claims about the efficacy of some measure are liable to evaporate as they learn either to adapt to it or they realise that it is not as efficacious as once believed. In settings where mutual adaptation and strategic decision-making occurs amongst multiple agents the sources of internal instability proliferate (Ekblom 1997). What

went at time one for a given measure to have its effects cannot be assumed to go at time two. CCTV furnishes an example where the technology, operators, managers, offenders and potential targets of crime adapt to one another in complex ways that mean that the consequences of cameras at one time and in one situation are unlikely to produce robust evidence of the likely outcome at another place or time. Whilst complexity manifests in many systems, it is especially acute where human intentional agents are involved.

3. Diversity refers to the variability in apparently similar presenting problems and the conditions in which an intervention is put in place. CCTV can again provide an example. CCTV placed in car parks to try to reduce crime, with monitoring where there are security guards on hand and where a small number of prolific offenders operate, can work by catching them, but this is not the case where CCTV cameras are not watched live, where there are no security guards and where large numbers of occasional car thieves operate (Tilley 1993).

4. Social change can be quite rapid, in comparison to change in the natural or biological worlds (Popper 1957, 1972). The tools for crime (such as the electronic screwdriver), the targets for crime (for example the lightweight laptop), the opportunities for crime (such as those furnished by the internet), and the routine activities creating conditions for crime (movement patterns of targets, likely offenders and potential guardians and handlers), are all changeable and create emergent properties for criminal behaviour and for specific measures aimed at prevention.

5. Assessing the efficacy of measures aiming to prevent high cost, low frequency events, such as terrorist attacks, are not open to RCTs and kindred methods (Laycock 2012).

A later section in this chapter describes a more realistic agenda for research to inform crime prevention.

The Dismissal of Administrative Criminology

Administrative criminology has been dismissed as right realist and reactionary (Young 1986; Matthews 2014). References to administrative criminology seem to have begun as a (pretty good) joke to try to highlight the distinctiveness of another approach in criminology, when the Home Office was both undertaking and funding much research about crime in the UK. Those researchers targeted within the Home Office could not reply robustly, because either they were within a government department and, as such, could not contradict any formal views held, or they were dependent on Home Office funding. Hence the jibes remained largely unanswered. But those jibes rather missed their targets, at least at the time they were originally levelled (see Hough 2014 for suggestions that matters may have changed). For example, it was a Home Office review of research that raised questions over the capacity of the police to control crime in a report whose publication faced quite serious obstacles at the time it was produced (Clarke and Hough 1984). It was Home Office researchers who conducted the first national victimisation survey, which estimated empirically the volume of unreported and unrecorded crime and hence jeopardised official accounts (Hough and Mayhew 1983). It was Home Office research that challenged conventional accounts of the causes of crime, which had previously attributed it to wickedness, inequality, poor social conditions or a defective background or personality (Mayhew et al. 1976; Clarke 1980). It was Home Office research that challenged assumptions that the, then taken-for-granted, methods of controlling crime through prison and efforts at rehabilitation were effective (Sinclair 1971; Brody 1976). It was Home Office research that fingered big business interests as sources of criminality and hence needed pressure to persuade them to change to reduce the crime fallout from their products, policies and practices (Ekblom 1986; Laycock 2004; Houghton 1992). Any notion that Home Office research seriously acted as the voice of capital or the administrative elite, or that it contained no critique of conventional administrative thinking, or that it lacked any kind of radical agenda is misplaced. Moreover, although it is not relevant to the critique of the criminological position alluded to here, as it happens many of those tarred with the administrative criminology brush hold radical political views that they take to be consistent with the criminological research they have produced.

I turn now to an alternative agenda for crime prevention, which I refer to as middle-range radical realism.

Middle-range Radical Realism for Crime Prevention (MRRR for CP)

Middle-range

Middle-range radical realism suggests an approach to research, policy and practice that aims: (a) to achieve progress in crime prevention and preemption; (b) to provide for adaptation in the face of change; and (c) is orientated to achieving socially just outcomes by reducing inequality and inequity in relation to crime outcomes. It is unapologetically piecemeal in its methods. There will be no magic wands to wave, no rabbits to be pulled out of a hat, no magic bullets to fire, no panaceas to prescribe, and no quick fixes to apply. Instead, as in medicine and engineering, what I aim to lay out is a way of thinking and acting that promises incremental but uneven steps towards improved safety, albeit that that they will inevitably be interspersed with reversals.

So, what exactly do I mean by middle-range radical realism? First, I spell out what the key terms refer to. I then go on to describe an agenda for research, policy and practice that it implies.

Middle-range. Robert Merton, of course, wrote about and advocated middle-range theory (see also Pawson 2000 for an account of middle-range realism). Less well known, T. H. Marshall (1968) wrote about 'stepping stones into the middle distance' as a principle of social research. Karl Popper talked about 'piecemeal social engineering', rooted in theoretically informed social science, to address specific harms (Popper 1945, 1957). All stressed operating at a level of abstraction beyond 'descriptions of particulars' (Merton 1968: 39) but short of 'vast generalisations, universal laws, and a total comprehension of human society' (Marshall 1963: 22) or 'all-embracing, unified theory' (Merton 1968: 45). Instead of either of these, middle-range theory, taking inspiration from practices in the physical sciences (Merton 1968: 40, cites Gilbert on magnetism, Boyle on atmospheric pressure and Darwin on the formation of coral atolls), begins with relatively simple ideas specifying causal mechanisms, and from these generates propositions relating to their out-workings in the real world that are open to empirical test. Examples from criminology include Felson's routine activities approach (Cohen and Felson 1979; Felson 1998), Clarke's situational crime prevention techniques (Clarke 1980) and Wilkins' account of deviancy amplification spirals (Wilkins 1964), all of which have been found fertile. They are general theories relating to specific phenomena that are open to empirical test as their applications are worked through.

Popper, at least, acknowledged the importance of 'emergent properties', which describe new and intrinsically unpredictable developments that could comprise game changers in specific situations (Popper 1957). Although he didn't talk of complexity theory, his ideas closely align with it. His 'three world interactionism', whereby creative minds, ideas and things interact, and his consequent indeterminism, including his account of knowing humans who construct knowledge in the light of which they act (and produce physical objects with causal properties of their own), echo some key themes of complexity theory (Popper and Eccles 1977). One example is the human invention of the internet (as a product of the mind using ideas and physical matter), which created new conditions for human action, including new crime opportunities. The novel crime problems could not have been anticipated in advance of the invention of the internet, albeit that they appear to reflect the out-workings of opportunity theory and routine activities in a new setting. That is not to say that, once the internet had been invented, it would not have been possible to foresee and pre-empt some of the unwanted side effects that have emerged.

Middle-range crime prevention does not attempt to find a universal solution to the crime problem across all space or time. Instead it focuses on specific crimes and the conditions producing or enabling them. It eschews all-encompassing theories and all-encompassing solutions that target the root cause of crime. Instead it is more interested in the near causes of crimes and, where possible, foreclosing emergent ones before they are widely exploited.

Radical

Radicalism here has five dimensions. The first is to doubt conventional wisdoms or intuitions, of which there are many. Much discussion of crime turns on assumptions about crime patterns, causes of crime, and about methods of prevention, which turn out to be mistaken (see the earlier discussion in this chapter). The radicalism of middle-range radical crime prevention takes an empirical and skeptical approach to the nostrums that wash through much policy, much practice and much commentary on crime. The notions that crime is irregular and unpredictable, that it is committed only by a handful of wicked people, or that it is the preserve of the poor, all turn out to be mistaken. Likewise, the notions that severe punishment, mass imprisonment, running holiday play schemes, Neighbourhood Watch, more police officers, motor projects, better welfare, capital punishment and so on will *automatically* lead to the prevention of crime require sceptical responses.

The second dimension is to be rather uninterested in crime per se. Many crime categories come and go. What is of interest to middle-range radicalism are the harms caused by crimes, rather than adherence to a set of rules. Many rules do attempt to rule out harmful behaviour, but not all. Much harmful behaviour is criminal, but not all. Passing laws to exclude harmful behaviour and having a system to promulgate and enforce, where possible, rules against harmful behaviour may be important in reducing those behaviours (see Homel 1995). But it is not the only method. Part of the radicalism of middle-range radical crime prevention is to change the focus from crime and rule-following per se to harmful interpersonal behaviour, which may or may not be unlawful. Hence, for example, domestic violence/rape is within scope, even in jurisdictions that do not make it unlawful.

The third dimension of radicalism relates to leverage and responsibility attribution (Eck and Eck 2012; Tilley 2012; Scott 2005; Laycock 2004). The winners and losers from crime prevention will often differ from one another. Those creating the conditions for crime are often not those who experience it. Crime frequently falls on third parties. Property developers, publicans, football clubs, car park proprietors, motor vehicle manufacturers, producers of lightweight electrical goods, internet service providers, manufacturers of pistols, landlords, hoteliers and supermarkets, for example, all make profits but in doing so create many crime opportunities that cause harms to third parties. This is not to say that the producers of harmful crime opportunities do so intentionally, nor is it to say that they do not also produce beneficial goods and services. Indeed, in some cases those involved may be unaware of the nature and extent of the harms they are generating. Middle-range radical crime prevention, however, is committed to identifying inadvertently produced crime harms and applying pressure on those producing them to minimise or remove the unwanted side effects that are created. In this sense crime can be considered a form of pollution (Farrell and Roman 2006).

The fourth dimension of radicalism relates to ethics and social justice. There are many ways to prevent crime and there are many types of crime that may be focused on in crime prevention. Moreover, there can be trade-offs between crime prevention measures and other policy and practice principles (Ekblom 2011). Crime prevention, thus, involves more than mere technical efficacy. There is a range of considerations relating, for example, to aesthetics (unacceptably ugly devices), convenience (hard to use devices), social exclusion (keeping those who look threatening out of certain locations), threats to privacy (some CCTV systems), threats to civil liberties (some versions of stop and search) and social justice (the changed distribution of crime harms consequent on crime prevention measures). Radicalism here refers to concerns to develop and deliver crime prevention that is socially inclusive and is orientated to reducing harms to those who are most vulnerable by virtue of previous crime experience, lifestyle, place of residence, age, ethnicity or gender. Crime is treated as a distributive 'bad' rather than 'good' (Tilley et al. 2011; Ignatans and Pease 2015). As with standard discussions of distributive justice there is no assumption that there is a fixed volume of the good (or bad) (Rawls 1971). Totals can change as can their distribution. An increase in utility to the more advantaged is deemed socially just, provided that it is not at the expense of the worse off. Hence a reduction of crime to all, even if there is still inequality in crime, is preferable to an increase in crime to all, even if the increase is to those less vulnerable to crime. What we observe in the crime drop is a fall for all but a greater fall amongst better off members of the community (Tilley 2011). Given that we are now pretty confident that improvements in physical security can lead to falls in crime risk and that the less well off tend to have less security, MRRR for CP would favour subsidies for security upgrades for those most vulnerable to crime who are least well off.

The final dimension of radicalism here relates to social policy. MRRR for CP refuses to criminalise social policy and discourse on social policy on two grounds. First, it risks distorting agendas that are properly concerned primarily with other objectives, such as education, health, housing and social welfare, all of which comprise goods in their own right. Using them as vehicles for crime prevention risks distorting them. This is not to say, of course, that their side effects on crime do not warrant attention. The design of schools may permit less or more bullying and youth sexual violence and abuse. Hospitals are routinely hot spots of crime and they may be managed and designed in ways that reduce risks to staff and to patients (Smith 1986). Housing designs can build in crime (for example Radburn layouts, poor locks, windows and doors) or build out crime (for example Secured by Design) (Armitage 2013). Welfare payments systems can be operated in ways that make fraudulent claims easier or more difficult to make. In each of these examples the inclusion of crime prevention is subservient to and orientated towards better service of the aims of the service rather than mobilising the service towards efforts at broader crime prevention aims. Second, for MRRR for CP crime is the problem, *sui generis*. It is not treated as some kind of malaise, symptomatic of other shortcomings in society. Much can be done to reduce crime harms without dealing with other social ills and injustices. Failing to deal with crime as a preventable harm-in-itself, is taken by MRRR for CP to be morally reprehensible in neglecting to attend to what can be achieved to improve welfare, especially of the disadvantaged.

Realist

The term realist, as used here, is to be understood in two different ways. The first relates to causal mechanisms—regularities and changes in regularities in both the social and natural worlds are the result of causal mechanisms, many of which cannot be observed directly. In the natural world magnetism, gravity, germs and natural selection comprise examples. Examples in the social world are anomie (Durkheim 1951), opportunity (Mayhew et al. 1976), reinforcement (Skinner 1965) and the contradictions of capitalism (Marx 1867). We invoke such causal mechanisms to explain observed patterns. In engineering, medicine and social life we intervene to alter the patterns of causal mechanism (either inhibiting old mechanisms or exciting new ones) to try to change behaviours or states that we find problematic or unsatisfactory, or to create new objects or institutions to further our ends.

Causal mechanisms are deemed real, rather than fictions invented to tell stories (Pawson and Tilley 1997; Sayer 1984, 2000). However, the activation of specific mechanisms is rarely unconditional. They exist as causal forces or powers that may or may not prevail, depending on the context. The tendency of gravity to pull objects towards the earth, for example, is counteracted when a tennis ball is released under water.

Our accounts of causal mechanisms are fallible. That is, although causal mechanisms are real they are known through their manifestations in what we can observe, and our observations sometimes suggest that accounts of causal mechanisms have been mistaken. In astronomy, for example, there have been a series of conjectured causal mechanisms to explain observations of the movements of heavenly bodies. Over time, old accounts of mechanisms have been found inadequate to explain new observations and new accounts have been developed. In laboratory sciences, artificial contexts are created in controlled experiments, which are designed to release conjectured mechanisms (and exclude others) to test whether or not they produce the expected observed results (Bhaskar 1975; Harre 1972). In the social world laboratories holding external influences at bay—where standardised manipulations of standardised experiments are conducted, holding all else deemed potentially relevant constant—are not available.

In the social (including crime) world, history, biography, culture, social embeddedness, meaning and intentionality make for chronic messiness whose exclusion does violence to the realities of testing explanatory theories or theories embedded in measures aiming at amelioration.

In everyday life, we casually and routinely refer to causal mechanisms. For example, when we ask why George killed his girlfriend Maisie, we may say that he did so out of jealousy because he believed she had betrayed him. Our account conjectures that the key causal mechanism lying behind the crime was jealousy, which we cannot directly observe but which we understand as a causal potential within human beings that can be activated if the context is right, and (perceived) betrayal by a girlfriend comprises a contextual condition, we speculate, for the activation of jealousy that has the causal potential to produce murder. Of course, jealousy is not sufficient to produce murder. Plenty of jealous men do not murder girlfriends who betray them; a complex of other contextual conditions are necessary to provide for jealousy to become sufficient to produce the murder itself (see Cartwright and Hardie 2012 on causality, drawing on Mackie 1965).

In relation to crime prevention, realism in this first sense of the term requires that efforts be made to deactivate causal mechanisms causing crime and to activate causal mechanisms that reduce risk to prospective victims. As with all social programmes interventions aimed at crime prevention embody tacit theories about what they will do to reduce or prevent crime. Realism requires that those theories be explicated in advance to check (a) their *a priori* plausibility, and (b) their consistency with relevant research findings.

The second meaning of realist here relates to practicality, in other words to being realistic. What can be achieved in practice, in the relatively short term, to reduce crimes against those who are most at risk of serious crime harms? It is one thing to daydream about a world with little or no crime harm. It is another to take steps to reduce current vulnerability in the real conditions in which people are suffering it. Focusing on this requires that attention be paid to the conditions of those who are competent to take preventive measures and what can be done to persuade them to implement those measures. So, in this sense of realism, MRRR for CP is concerned with the 'art of the possible' (cf Medawar 1967), with plausible and practicable piecemeal efforts that are liable to reduce real crime harms to the most vulnerable.

Crime and Crime Prevention

MRRR for CP assumes that harm-engendering crime is normal, just as parallel behaviours are normal in other parts of the animal world. Angry bees sting, aroused males impose themselves on females, carnivores kill weaker animals to eat them, cuckoos oust other birds' offspring in the interests of securing the welfare of their own, and so on. Taking what one wants, attacking those one dislikes, and attempting to eliminate competitors need no special explanation. It is the socially organised prevention of such behaviours that is interesting. The passage of laws, the creation of enforcement institutions and everyday patterns of socialisation provide a backcloth, de-normalising much predation in human society (and social breakdown sees the eruption of predatory criminality). Crime prevention, as a distinctive set of practices, is undertaken against this background.

Crime is unevenly distributed so it makes sense to focus publicly supported preventive efforts where it is most harmful, most concentrated and most open to preventive intervention amongst those least able to provide for their own protection from predation. The best evidence we have suggests that fears of displacement from crime prevention have been overstated and that a happy by-product of crime prevention is a diffusion of benefits. Where a penumbra of preventive effects are experienced beyond the operational range of specific measures, there is little need to worry much about privately funded prevention leading to increased crimes on those not able to fund their own protection (see Guerette and Bowers 2009; Clarke and Weisburd 1994). Insofar, however, as these private efforts may have led to crime displacement towards those who are most vulnerable and least able to fund preventive measures to protect themselves, this comprises an additional reason to concentrate publicly funded measures on the relatively poor or weak who are most at risk.

As already indicated, many high volume crimes have been falling in number since the early- to mid-1990s and the best (although fallible) evidence suggests that improvements in security have been directly responsible for most of the drops, and may also have contributed indirectly to some other falls by inhibiting youngsters' entry into careers of prolific offending, although more research is needed to corroborate this. More speculatively, it would be reasonable to conjecture that those whose criminality has been most inhibited through security improvements are likely to be least embedded in criminal lifestyles, where high levels of commitment to crime and competence in sidestepping security might be expected. The changing age-crime curves and patterns of prolific, detected offending are consistent with this view, with falling numbers of young, occasional offenders and increasing numbers of older and prolific offenders (Owen and Cooper 2013; Farrell et al. 2015). If these developments are, indeed, occurring they would indicate that further progress in crime prevention will need to look to ways in which those who do become heavily involved in prolific offending lifestyles can be effectively encouraged to desist before their criminality wanes anyway as they eventually age out of crime (see, for example, Laub and Sampson 2003). There is a range of types of intervention operating through a variety of preventive mechanisms, which warrant attention. These include, for example, targeted deterrence of gang-related crime, cognitive-behavioural therapy to change the thinking of those who offend and targeted incarceration of committed, prolific drug-dependent offenders (see Tilley 2009; see Pitts and Chatwin in this volume).

Meanwhile, as some crimes fall with improvements in security, new crime opportunities emerge and are likely to continue to emerge, producing new crime waves. These occur as and when political, social and technological developments inadvertently create fresh criminogenic conditions (Pease 1997; Farrell and Tilley forthcoming). To preempt the crime harvests that frequently attend new developments, MRRR for CP emphasises the importance of: (a) assigning, wherever possible, responsibility on those developers to consider the possible crime consequences of what they are doing and to try to contain the crime opportunities they may be producing; and (b) of trying to anticipate and pre-empt new crime developments that spring from the exploitation of emergent crime opportunities. Given that social and technological developments are continuous and that they are likely to create new crime opportunities, this readying for their closure is unlikely to come to an end. Moreover, just as new developments are liable to create new opportunities for crime commission, they can also promise new opportunities for reduction whose potentiality needs to be tracked.

MRRR for CP acknowledges the openness and plasticity of the social, as well as its openness to intervention to prevent crime harm fallouts from developments that may otherwise be welcomed. In this sense, it is Popperian in inspiration (Popper 1957; Tilley 2004). Popper counselled against historicism—the notion that there are inexorable social laws that allow the future to be predicted with confidence. Human inventiveness and the new causal powers introduced by human invention puts paid to that, as the example of the internet mentioned earlier illustrates. However, Popper also advocated cautious attention to what might result from new developments. He wrote of 'hypotheses dying in our stead' to refer to our efforts to prevent the creation of inadvertent harms. He wrote of harm-reducing piecemeal social engineering as a means of addressing specific harms through targeted, theoretically informed interventions. MRRR for CP understands predatory crime to be open to this approach (Popper 1957).

I have tried to sketch in broad terms what I mean by middle-range radical realism for crime prevention. In the next section, I go on to outline a research, policy and practice agenda.

An Agenda for MRRR for CP Research, Policy and Practice

The following agenda follows from the previous discussion and attempts to set out briefly what would be involved in delivering MRRR for CP.

Research

MRRR for CP would need substantial research support. The research would be directly orientated to informing policy and practice, by attending to its needs rather than the expressed preferences of policymakers and practitioners. This might sound like enormous hubris on the part of the researcher, which I would like to avoid. The reason for stipulating matters in this way follows from what are often rather poorly formulated questions whose underlying assumptions are false. For example, a policymaker might ask what effect a given measure has, as if there is and can be a simple answer to that question. Take Neighbourhood Watch. Gloria Laycock was asked by a government minister's private secretary if Neighbourhood Watch works. The no-nonsense minister was demanding a yes/no answer. Laycock said, 'Yes', on the basis of a report she and I had written (Laycock and Tilley 1995). I would have said, 'No'. The correct answer based on our work is, 'sometimes, it depends on the context and how Neighbourhood

Watch is implemented'. Laycock and I would have agreed on that. The assumption behind the minister's question was wonky. There can be no simple answer to that question. But it is a conventional and understandable question. Moreover, it is a question policy wonks are apt to ask. Indeed, treasury folk charged with getting value for money from public spending want just such superficially simple works/doesn't work answers and if the answer is 'Works', in addition they require effect size estimates to build into their models to inform decisions on public spending. The real complexity, variability and change across the social world may be a nuisance, but to treat it as other than it is is to pretend we are in fairyland and the answers we give, if we succumb to those asking questions based on erroneous assumptions, will be fairytales.

If research is to inform policy and practice properly it needs to refuse to provide answers to questions rooted in false premises. As Ekblom (2011) has emphasised, although we may value simplicity in science, that should not be at the expense of doing fundamental violence to the phenomena being examined.

What MRRR for CP does have to recognise, however, are the realities facing policymakers and practitioners and that those realities lie behind some of the wonky questions asked. Policymakers and practitioners cannot do everything that may be asked of them. Resources are always limited. There are always opportunity costs from decisions; doing A rules out doing B or C or D at the same time. Moreover, there is often an imperative on policymakers and practitioners to do something. Even doing nothing comprises a policy/practice decision. If the issue is presented a decision has to be made about how to respond or not to respond at all. Crime comprises just the kind of issue that demands a decision from policymakers and practitioners, even if that decision is to do nothing. In the face of this, what can MRRR for CP offer?

We have devised EMMIE as an acronym to capture what we think research may most realistically be able to provide to crime prevention policymakers and practitioners to inform their decisions in the face of crime harms they have to address (Johnson et al. 2015).

The two E's of EMMIE provide the best answers that can be given on *E*ffects and *E*conomy, which comprise inexorable imperatives that policymakers and practitioners have to take account of. Although there can be no fixed and final answers, as emphasised repeatedly in this chapter, the policymaker and practitioner need to gauge, however roughly, what effects will be brought about at what cost. Both individual studies and reviews of previous studies thus need to include best estimates on the effects that were produced and costs that were incurred in the initiatives covered as considerations that policymakers and practitioners can draw on in their decision-making, however hedged and qualified those estimates have to be and however weakly related past findings in different conditions may be to current circumstances.

The two M's of EMMIE capture what produce the intended and unintended effects created from interventions put in place to try to reduce crime harms. The first M refers to the underlying causal *M*echanisms that are activated or inhibited in the effort to produce the reduced crime harms that the policymaker or practitioner is concerned with; the second refers to *M*oderators that condition the causal mechanisms activated. In effect, it is used as a synonym for what realists more usually refer to as context, but is preferred here in part to steer conventional statistical analysis towards causally relevant moderators rather than the research design variables often included, and in part because the M contributes helpfully to the EMMIE acronym! In deciding what to do in their own, idiosyncratic conditions, policymakers and practitioners need to take account of what is known of how measures work out, in what conditions to produce the range of winners and losers from interventions they might put in place. Primary studies and reviews of research thus need to be organised around articulating, testing and refining hypotheses concerning the mechanisms at work in producing crime harm (and other) outcomes and the contextual conditions that are relevant to the activation or deactivation of those mechanisms.

The 'I' refers to *I*mplementation. The implementation of crime prevention measures can be difficult. Particular schemes may face real organisational, community, legal, ethical or cultural obstacles. Hence, even if a strategy has the causal potential to prevent crime if fully implemented, it may not do so in practice given the nature of the communities, agencies and organisations involved. Alley-gating, for example, may reduce rear-access burglary in terraces of houses. Those contemplating introducing such a scheme, however, need to know what is involved in putting it in place and maintaining it in ways that will continue to keep crime down, assuming that it has the intended initial impact (Sidebottom et al. 2015): permissions required (given ownership, rights of way, and community preferences); provision for maintenance; replacement of lost keys; access by emergency services and refuse collectors; obtaining the necessary capital and revenue funding; and so on. These are all issues that need to be understood and addressed. To be useful to policymakers and practitioners primary studies and reviews need to include reports on what is involved in delivering a specific intervention or overall strategy.

The research agenda of MRRR for CP requires both primary studies and reviews to adopt an EMMIE framework to inform the development and delivery of strategies and tactics aimed at reducing crime-related harms.

The research agenda for MRRR for CP also needs to identify where and amongst whom the most extensive and serious crime-related harms of various sorts are experienced. Crime related harms include not only direct loss and injury, but also adverse emotional and health consequences. Research relating to fear of crime, signal crimes, repeat victimisation and high crime neighbourhoods are all relevant here and help 'get the grease to the squeak', in the sense of targeting efforts where harms are greatest in the interests of furthering distributive justice.

Finally, the research agenda for MRRR for CP includes provisions for attempting to identify sources of emergent crime problems (Pease 1997). New developments produce new crime opportunities and provocations, as well as new tools to try to prevent crime. These relate in part to science and technology, for example the internet referred to earlier and the crime prevention devices now fitted to most cars. These also relate to changing economic, social and political conditions. For example mass migration, new tax regimes, changes in retail methods, alterations in leisure pursuits, the development of new payment methods, changes in work patterns and so on may all produce new opportunities for crime and crime prevention. The research agenda relating to MRRR for CP includes sustained attention to the emergent as it relates to crime harms, as well as experienced in the past. It does not assume that either crime or crime prevention is or can be fixed.

The framework for MRRR for CP research requires a teacher–learner relationship with policymakers and practitioners (Tilley 2014). Both parties benefit, although here the primary interest lies in informing improvements to policy and practice. Practitioners and seasoned policymakers have many ideas informed by their experience. Some of these ideas may be mistaken, the result of selective perception or perhaps particular experiences. Nevertheless, they have often seen a lot and their ideas are therefore informed. The researcher can be helped to draw on practitioners, in particular, in formulating and developing middle-range theories that can be tested (see Pawson and Tilley 1997). The empirical corroboration of some of that theory can help inform later work and work by others. The falsification of some of that theory can help remove erroneous suppositions that lie behind what is done. In addition to learning from and testing policymaker and practitioner theory, MRRR for CP can 'teach' tested realist theory back to policymakers and practitioners for its application in light of the specific conditions they encounter.

Policy and Practice

The public policy and practice agenda follows from what has already been said in this chapter. It includes ten elements.

1. *Being piecemeal:* Do not expect or aim to implement panaceas. Real crime prevention achievements have been made through piecemeal efforts. Be sceptical of those offering such panaceas.
2. *Using situational crime prevention:* Invest in developing and encouraging situational crime prevention, whose theory is well-supported by evidence and which has been found to deliver crime drops, although not to the exclusion of other methods of crime prevention to address specific crime harms.
3. *Focusing on specific problems:* Adopt a problem-oriented approach that targets efforts on those places, people, processes and products where the production or experience of crime harms is most concentrated. This will require strong data and strong analytic capacity.
4. *Involving third parties:* Persuade those inadvertently creating criminality and crime temptations, provocations and opportunities, especially where the victims are third parties, to accept responsibility for preventing the crime fallout from what they do. Examples of those to be targeted include manufacturers of CRAVED goods, planners of

new developments, landlords, hoteliers, shopkeepers, nightclub owners and publicans

5. *Ensuring procedural justice:* Avoid unintentionally provoking criminality. Police services that do not adopt the principles of procedural justice, for example, may inadvertently provoke harm-inducing criminality amongst young people.

6. *Allocating resources to produce harm-reducing distributive justice:* Concentrate crime prevention efforts on improving distributive justice as it relates to crime harms, not other harms. This provides a routine mechanism for the socially equitable allocation of public resources for crime prevention.

7. *Specifying causal mechanisms:* Draw on evidence to construct crime prevention efforts rooted in theories that have been corroborated by empirical research. The theory needs to specify plausible causal mechanisms that will be activated by the proposed measures in the context in which the targeted problem surfaces, whilst at the same time avoiding unintended harmful side effects.

8. *Using informed discretion:* Develop the skills and knowledge base to use informed discretion in deciding what to do in local conditions. Informed discretion comprises the framework through which skilled physicians work, drawing on extensive research and experience in their practice.[1]

9. *Investing via EMMIE:* Commission EMMIE-focused research when investing heavily in a programme or trying new policy to ensure that robust findings are produced that speak to improvements in future policy and practice needs.

10. *Anticipating new crimes:* Try to anticipate emergent crime problems with a view to pre-empting avoidable crime and criminality harvests.

---

[1] Informed discretion is preferable to uninformed routine responses, uninformed discretionary responses, or informed rule-bound responses insensitive to idiosyncratic conditions. An alternative may be normal defaults, rooted in evidence of what has been found in typical conditions with scope for discretionary departures where there is evidence that the conditions are atypical. The development of those skills and the improvement in the knowledge base will require a long-term programme. It will also involve the teacher–learner relationship with the research community mentioned in the agenda for research.

The key motifs of MRRR for CP policy and practice are a concern with reducing crime harms (rather than crimes per se), continuous improvement (in theory and practice), adaptation (in light of changing conditions and emerging new generators of crime), equity (in the distribution of crime harms and crime prevention efforts), realism (in the sense of practicability, and a focus on deactivating causal mechanisms to achieve prevention in harms without generating unintended negative side effects), responsibilisation (by mobilising those inadvertently creating crime harms to modify their practices to avoid doing so), informed discretion (in building capacity amongst decision-makers to come to informed judgements relating to planned practices and policies and their implementation), and commitment to funding and working with researchers using EMMIE (to extend the policy and practice related evidence base to inform decisions).

Conclusion

This chapter has argued in favour of middle-range radical realism for crime prevention. Although critical of some widespread crime prevention thinking and research it does not entail a wholesale repudiation of what has already been delivered and achieved in research, policy and practice. Middle-range radical realism for crime prevention aims, instead, to provide a coherent agenda, building on the past and providing a foundation for improvements in the quality of life of those most susceptible to crime-related harms. *Mutatis mutandis* middle-range radical realism might also offer a more general agenda for socially progressive social improvement.

References

Armitage, R. (2013). *Crime prevention through housing design*. Basingstoke: Palgrave Macmillan.
Asch, S. E. (1955). Opinions and social pressure. *Scientific American, 193*(5), 31–35.
Bhaskar, R. (1975). *A realist theory of science*. Brighton: Harvester.

Bowers, K. J., Johnson, S. D., & Hirschfield, A. F. (2004). Closing off opportunities for crime: An evaluation of Alley-Gating. *European Journal on Criminal Policy and Research, 10*(4), 285–308.

Braga, A., Kennedy, D., & Piehl, A. (1999). *Problem-oriented policing and youth violence: An evaluation of the Boston Gun project,* Unpublished report to the National Institute of Justice, Washington, DC.

Brody, S. (1976). *The effectiveness of sentencing* (Home office research study no. 35). London: HMSO.

Brown, R. (2004). The effectiveness of electronic immobilisation: Changing patterns of temporary and permanent vehicle theft. In M. G. Maxfield & R. V. Clarke (Eds.), *Understanding and preventing car theft* (pp. 101–119). Monsey: Criminal Justice Press.

Brown, R. (2013). Reviewing the evidence of electronic vehicle immobilisation: Evidence from four countries. *Security Journal.* doi:10.1057/sj2012.55.

Bullock, K., Erol, R., & Tilley, N. (2006). *Problem-oriented policing and partnerships: Implementing an evidence-based approach to crime reduction.* London: Routledge.

Cartwright, N., & Hardie, J. (2012). *Evidence-based policy.* Oxford: Oxford University Press.

Clarke, R. (1980). Situational crime prevention: Theory and practice. *British Journal of Criminology, 20,* 136–147.

Clarke, R. (1997). *Situational crime prevention: Successful case studies* (2nd ed.). New York: Harrow and Heston.

Clarke, R. (2005). Seven misconceptions of situational crime prevention. In N. Tilley (Ed.), *Handbook of crime prevention and community safety.* London: Routledge.

Clarke, R., & Hough, M. (1984). *Crime and police effectiveness* (Home Office Research Study 79). London: HMSO.

Clarke, R., & Weisburd, D. (1994). Diffusion of crime control benefits: Observations on the reverse of displacement. In R. Clarke (Ed.), *Crime prevention studies* (Vol. 2). Monsey: Criminal Justice Press.

Cohen, L. E., & Felson, M. (1979). Social change and crime rate trends: A routine activities approach. *American Sociological Review, 44,* 588–608.

Durkheim, E. (1951). *Suicide.* New York: Free Press.

Eck, J., & Eck, E. (2012). Crime place and pollution. *Criminology and Public Policy, 11*(2), 281–316.

Ekblom, P. (1986). *The prevention of shoptheft* (Crime Prevention Unit Paper 5). London: Home Office.

Ekblom, P. (1997). Gearing up against crime: A dynamic framework to help designers keep up with the adaptive criminal in a changing world. *International Journal of Risk, Security and Crime Prevention, 2*(4), 249–265.

Ekblom, P. (2011). *Crime prevention, security and community safety using the 5Is framework*. Basingstoke: Palgrave Macmillan.

Farrell, G., & Pease, K. (1993). *Once bitten, twice bitten: Repeat victimisation and its implications for crime prevention* (Crime Prevention Unit Paper 46). London: Home Office.

Farrell, G., & Pease, K. (Eds.). (2001). *Repeat victimization* (Crime prevention studies series 12). Monsey: Criminal Justice Press.

Farrell, G., & Roman, J. (2006). Crime as pollution. In K. Moss & M. Stephens (Eds.), *Crime reduction and the law*. London: Routledge.

Farrell, G., & Tilley, N. (Forthcoming). Technology for crime prevention: A supply side analysis. In B. Leclerc, and E. Savona (Eds.) *Crime Prevention*. Springer.

Farrell, G., Tseloni, A., & Tilley, N. (2011a). The effectiveness of vehicle security devices and their role in the crime drop. *Criminology and Criminal Justice, 11*(1), 21–35.

Farrell, G., Tseloni, A., & Tilley, N. (2015) Why the crime drop? In M. Tonry (Ed.) Why Crime Rates Fall and Why They Don't. Crime and Justice Vol. 43 (pp 421–490). Chicago: Chicago University Press.

Farrell, G., Tseloni, A., Mailley, J., & Tilley, N. (2011b). The crime drop and the security hypothesis. *Journal of Research in Crime and Delinquency, 48*, 147–175.

Farrell, G., Laycock, G., & Tilley, N. (2015). Debuts and legacies: The crime drop an the role of adolescence-limited and persistent offending. *Crime Science*.

Felson, M. (1998). *Crime and everyday life*. Thousand Oaks: Pine Forge Press.

Goldstein, H. (1979). *Problem-oriented policing*. New York: Wiley.

Goodman, M. (2015). *Future crimes*. London: Bantam Press.

Grove, L., & Farrell, G. (2014). Once bitten, twice shy: Repeat victimisation and its prevention. In B. Welsh, and D. Farrington (Eds.), *The Oxford Handbook of crime prevention*. Oxford: Oxford University Press.

Guerette, R. T., & Bowers, K. (2009). Assessing the extent of crime displacement and diffusion of benefit: A systematic review of situational crime prevention evaluations. *Criminology, 47*(4), 1331–1368.

Hanmer, J., Griffiths, S., & Jerwood, D. (1999). *Arresting evidence: Domestic violence and repeat victimisation policing research series paper 104*. London: Home Office.

Harré, R. (1972). *The philosophies of science*. Oxford: Oxford University Press.

Homel, R. (1994). Drink-driving law enforcement and the legal blood alcohol limit in New South Wales. *Accident Analysis and Prevention, 26*(2), 147–155.

Homel, R. (1995). Can police prevent crime? In K. Bryett & C. Lewis (Eds.), *Contemporary policing: Unpeeling tradition*. Sydney: Macmillan.

Hough, M. (2014). Confessions of a recovering 'administrative criminologist': Jock Young, quantitative research and policy research. *Crime Media Culture, 10*(3), 215–226.

Hough, M., & Mayhew, P. (1983). *The British crime survey: First report* (Home Office Research Study 76). London: HMSO.

Hough, M., Jackson, J., Bradford, B., Myhill, A., & Quinton, P. (2010). Procedural justice, trust and institutional legitimacy. *Policing, 4*(3), 203–210.

Houghton, G. (1992). *Car theft in England and Wales: The Home Office car theft index* (Crime Prevention Unit Paper 33). London: Home Office.

Hume, D. (1793). *A treatise on human nature*. London: John Noon.

Ignatans, D., & Pease, K. (2015). Distributive justice and the crime drop. In M. Andresen & G. Farrell (Eds.), *Routine activities and the criminal act*. Basingstoke: Palgrave Macmillan.

Johnson, S., & Bowers, K. (2004). The Burglary as clue to the future: The beginnings of prospective hot-spotting. *European Journal of Criminology, 1*, 237–255.

Johnson, S., & Loxley, C. (2001). Installing alley-gates: Practical lessons from burglary prevention projects. *Home office crime reduction research series, 2*(1). London: Home Office.

Johnson, S., Birks, D., McLaughlin, L., Bowers, K., & Pease, K. (2007). *Prospective mapping in operational context*. London: Home Office.

Johnson, S., Tilley, N., & Bowers, K. (2015). Introducing EMMIE: An evidence rating scale to encourage mixed-method crime prevention synthesis reviews. Journal of Experimental Criminology, 11(3), 459–473

Kennedy, D. M. (2008). *Deterrence and crime prevention: Reconsidering the prospect of sanction*. New York: Routledge.

Kleiman, M. (2009). *When Brute force fails: How to have Less crime and less punishment*. Princeton: Princeton University Press.

Laub, J., & Sampson, R. (2003). *Shared beginnings, divergent lives*. Cambridge Mass: Harvard University Press.

Laycock, G. (2004). The U.K. car theft index: An example of government leverage. In M. Maxfield & R. V. Clarke (Eds.), *Understanding and preventing car theft, crime prevention studies* (Vol. 17). Monsey: Criminal Justice Press.

Laycock, G. (2012). Happy birthday. *Policing, 6*(2), 101–107.

Laycock, G., & Tilley, N. (1994). Implementing crime prevention. In M. Tonry & D. P. Farrington (Eds.), *Building a safer society: Strategic approaches to crime prevention* (Crime and Justice: A review of research). Chicago: University of Chicago Press.

Laycock, G., & Tilley, N. (1995). *Policing and neighbourhood watch: Strategic issues* (Crime detection and prevention series paper 60). Home Office: London.

Mackie, J. (1965). Causes and conditions. *American Philosophical Quarterly, 2,* 245–264.

Marshall, T. (1963). *Sociology at the crossroads.* London: Heinemann.

Marx, K. (1867). *Capital, many editions.*

Matthews, R. (2014). *Realist criminology.* Basingstoke: Palgrave/Macmillan.

Mayhew, P., Clarke, R., Sturman, A., & Hough, M. (1976). *Crime as opportunity* (Home Office Research Study 34). London: HMSO.

Mazerolle, L., Bennett, S., Davis, J., Sargeant, E., & Manning, M. (2013). Legitimacy in policing: A systematic review. *Campbell Systematic Reviews.* doi:10.4073/csr.2013.1.

Medawar, P. (1967). *The art of the soluble.* London: Methuen.

Merton, R. (1968). *Social theory and social structure* (3rd ed.). New York: Free Press.

Milgram, S. (1974). *Obedience to authority: An experimental view.* New York: Harper and Row.

Owen, N., & Cooper, C. (2013). *The start of a criminal career: Does the type of debut offence predict future offending?* London: Home Office.

Pawson, R. (2000). Middle range realism. *European Journal of Sociology, 41*(2), 283–325.

Pawson, R., & Tilley, N. (1997). *Realistic evaluation.* London: Sage.

Pease, K. (1997). Predicting the future: The roles of routine activity and rational choice theory. In G. Newman, R. Clarke, & S. Shoham (Eds.), *Rational choice and situational crime prevention.* Aldershot: Dartmouth.

Pease, K. (1998). *Repeat victimisation: Taking stock* (Crime detection and prevention series paper 90). London: Home Office.

Popper, K. (1945). *The open society and its enemies* (Vols. 1 and 2). London: Routledge.

Popper, K. (1957). *The poverty of historicism.* London: Routledge.

Popper, K. (1959). *The logic of scientific discovery.* London: Hutchinson.

Popper, K. (1972). *Objective knowledge: An evolutionary approach.* Oxford: Clarendon Press.

Popper, K., & Eccles, J. (1977). *The self and its brain: An argument for interactionism*. Berlin: Springer-Verlag.

Rawls, J. (1971). *A theory of justice*. Cambridge, MA: Harvard University Press.

Ross, L., & Nisbett, R. (2011). *The person and the situation*. London: Pinter and Martin.

Sayer, A. (1984). *Method in social science: A realist approach*. London: Hutchinson.

Sayer, A. (2000). *Realism and social science*. London: Sage.

Scott, M. (2005). Shifting and sharing police responsibility for crime prevention. In N. Tilley (Ed.), *Handbook of crime prevention and community safety*. London: Routledge.

Shepherd, J. (2003). Explaining feast or famine in randomised field trials: Medical science and criminology compared. *Evaluation Review, 27*(3), 290–315.

Sherman, L. (1997). Thinking about crime prevention. In L. Sherman, D. Gottfredson, D. MacKenzie, J. Eck, P. Reuter, & S. Bushway (Eds.), *Preventing crime: What works, what doesn't, what's promising. A report to the United States Congress*. Washington, DC: US Department of Justice..

Sherman, L. (2013). The rise of evidence-based policing. *Crime and Justice, 42*, 377–451.

Sidebottom, A., Tompson, L., Thornton, A., Bullock, K., Tilley, N., Bowers, K., & Johnson, S. (2015). *Gating alleys to reduce crime: A meta-analysis and realist synthesis*, Unpublished report.

Sinclair, I. (1971). *Hostels for probationers*. London: HMSO.

Skinner, B. (1965). *Science and human behavior*. New York: Free Press.

Smith, L. (1986). *Crime in hospitals: Diagnosis and prevention* (Crime prevention unit paper 7). London: Home Office.

Tilley, N. (1993). *Understanding car parks, crime and CCTV* (Crime prevention unit paper 42). London: Home Office.

Tilley, N. (1996). Demonstration, exemplification, duplication and replication in evaluation research. *Evaluation, 2*, 35–50.

Tilley, N. (2004). Karl Popper: A philosopher for Ronald Clarke's situational crime prevention. In S. Shoham & P. Knepper (Eds.), *Tradition and innovation in crime and justice*. de Sitter: Willowdale.

Tilley, N. (2009). *Crime prevention*. Cullompton: Willan.

Tilley, N. (2010). Shoplifting. In F. Brookman, M. Maguire, H. Pierpoint, & T. Bennett (Eds.), *Handbook on crime*. Willan: Cullompton.

Tilley, N. (2012). Crime reduction: Responsibility, regulation and research. *Criminology and Public Policy, 11*(2), 361–378.

Tilley, N. (2014). There is nothing so practical as a good theory: Teacher-learner relationships in applied research for policing. In E. Cockbain & J. Knutsson (Eds.), *Applied police research: Challenges and opportunities* (pp. 141–152). London: Routledge.

Tilley, N., & Sidebottom, A. (2015). Routine activities and opportunity theory. In M. Krohn & J. Lane (Eds.), *Handbook on juvenile delinquency and juvenile justice*. Wiley.

Tilley, N., Tseloni, A., & Farrell, G. (2011). Income disparities of burglary risk: Security availability and the crime drop. *British Journal of Criminology, 51*, 296–313.

Tonry, M. (Ed.). (2014). *Why crime rates fall and why they don't* (Volume 43 of Crime and justice). Chicago: University of Chicago Press.

Tseloni, A., Mailley, J., Farrell, G., & Tilley, N. (2010). Exploring the international decline in crime rates. *European Journal of Criminology, 7*(5), 375–394.

Tyler, T. (2003). Procedural justice, legitimacy, and the effective rule of law. *Crime and Justice, 30*, 283–357.

UNODC. (2013). *Comprehensive study on cybercrime*. New York: United Nations.

Van Dijk, J. J. M., Tseloni, A., & Farrell, G. (Eds.) (2012). *The international crime drop: New directions in research*. Basingstoke: Palgrave Macmillan.

Van Ours, J. C., & Vollaard, B. (2013). The engine immobilizer: A non-starter for car thieves. CESifo working paper: Public choice, no. 4092 (Centre for Economic Studies and Ifo Institute). Munich: University of Munich.

Weisburd, D., & Eck, J. (2004, May). What can police do to reduce crime, disorder, and fear? *The Annals of the American Academy of Political and Social Science, 593*, 42–65.

Weisburd, D., Telep, C., Hinkle, J., & Eck, J. (2010). Is problem-oriented policing effective. *Criminology and Public Policy, 9*(1), 139–172.

Wilkins, L. (1964). *Social deviance: Social policy, action and research*. London: Tavistock.

Wortley, R. (1997). Reconsidering the role of opportunity in situational crime prevention. In G. Newman, R. Clarke, & S. Shohan (Eds.), *Rational choice and situational crime prevention*. Aldershot: Ashgate Publishing.

Young, J. (1986). The failure of criminology: The need for a radical realism. In R. Matthews & J. Young (Eds.), *Confronting crime*. London: Sage.

Zimbardo, P. (2007). *The Lucifer effect*. New York: Random House.

6

Policing: Past, Present and Future

Ben Bowling, Shruti Iyer, Robert Reiner, and James Sheptycki

Introduction

The question of what is to be done about law and order set in motion an important transformation in criminology in an earlier era (Lea and Young 1984). Questions about how policing should be conducted and how the police service can be improved confront the discipline again as the second decade of the twenty-first century draws to a close. But what a difference an era makes! When critical criminologists asked what was to be done in the 1980s, some lamented that the problems of crime and victimisation in poor communities were not taken seriously enough and that the police were 'losing the fight against crime' (Kinsey et al. 1986). Others were critical of

B. Bowling (✉) • S. Iyer
King's College, London, UK

R. Reiner
London School of Economics, London, UK

J. Sheptycki
McLaughlin College, York University, Toronto, ON, Canada

© The Editor(s) (if applicable) and The Author(s) 2016
R. Matthews (ed.), *What is to Be Done About Crime and Punishment?*,
DOI 10.1057/978-1-137-57228-8_6

the drift towards law, order and the authoritarian state and rejected the contention that the police were the solution to the crime problem (Scraton 1987). We do not intend to rehearse these older debates here, but it would do to acknowledge them, to forestall the problem of chronocentrism in our understanding of criminology (Rock 2005) and to tackle head-on new theories of policing which suggest that 'the police' have been superseded as objects of enquiry by a more diffuse notion of 'policing' (Reiner 2010 a,b).

David Bayley (1985) evocatively expressed the relationship between the state and the body of men and women charged with exercising authority on its behalf: 'the police are to government as the edge is to the knife'. Although 'all that is policing does not lie with police' (Reiner 2010a: xi), and that under transnational conditions the state has become a different kind of institution than was contemplated by the architects of the modern police, there is good reason to take 'the police' seriously as an idea. In one form or another they exist in every country and are an important aspect of a much broader apparatus of social control. What makes them particularly important is their capacity to use force in social ordering. This chapter seeks to ask how we can improve the quality of policing and make the police accountable to the people that they serve.

The challenge set for us by the editors of this volume was to answer the question: what is to be done about the police? This deceptively succinct question begs a series of theoretical and normative questions concerned with what policing is, who should do it, how it should be done, how its fairness and effectiveness should be evaluated and how it should be made accountable. To address these normative enquiries and to focus our arguments about what is to be done, we draw on theoretical and empirical police research and set out to answer six sets of questions.

Our first concern is the function of the police. We ask: *what is policing and what do the police do?* Before we can offer a prescription for what we think the police should do, we must consider the claims made about the role of the police and the research evidence on what day-to-day police work actually consists of. This leads to our second question: *who carries out the policing function?* The public police are most prominent in discussions about order maintenance, crime investigation and control, but there is competition from private policing and various other providers of security. The, so-called, pluralisation of policing raises questions about the place of 'the police' in social ordering. We turn next to the ways and means of policing. Controversy has raged for decades about police powers and, in particular, the use of force and intelligence-led methods including, but not limited to, electronic surveillance and undercover police work. This generates our third question: *what powers do the police have?*

Our fourth set of questions are concerned with how the police achieve their overall social function, how well they do it and at what cost? Do the police successfully maintain order and control crime? And at what social and economic cost is this achieved? In short, we ask: *what is 'good policing' and how can it be achieved?* Our fifth concern relates to the evidence that police powers have differential effects for different groups in society. The young, the poor, women and ethnic minorities are more likely to suffer the ill effects of policing, such as being stopped, searched and arrested. These same groups are less likely to feel properly protected by the police. We ask: *how does policing impact on different social groups?* With police accountability under close scrutiny, current debates focus on the relations between police and public; this leads to our sixth question: *how are the police policed?* Finally, in our conclusion, we bring the strands or our analysis together to ask: *what is to be done about the police?*

What Do the Police Do?

Our first question—*what is the police role?*—has been at the centre of debate in the sociology of policing ever since empirical research on police began in the early 1960s in both the USA and the UK.[1] The backdrop to the interpretation of early empirical research on the police role was evident in media representations and in popular discourse that framed them as crime fighters in the dominant cultural imaginary of cops 'n' robbers. The alternative to this rather constricted conception of the police was a radical Marxist analysis of the police as repressive agents of a capitalist State. According to this view, the police exercised overt class repression and capitalist injustice was disguised by reductive visions of the police mission as

---

[1] There had been a single precursor, the seminal empirical research conducted by William Westley in the late 1940s, only published in a couple of journal articles until a belated book in 1970. It was a crucial influence on researchers in the early 1960s (Reiner 2015).

suppression of routine street crime. Leaving aside the definitional issues concerning the core concept of crime it seems reasonably clear that law 'n' order and cops 'n' robbers mythologies have been common to both fans and critics of the police. Empirical research findings about policework in practice revealed the shortcomings of these popular understandings.

Observation of police patrol work, still the mainstay of urban policing around the world, showed that the police routinely *under-enforce* the law. Michael Banton showed this in his pioneering ethnographic research in the UK and the USA (Banton 1964). According to him the predominant role of the patrol officer was peacekeeping not law enforcement. This was subsequently confirmed by numerous studies. In itself this could be interpreted as officers neglecting their duties, taking the easier way out and avoiding the rigours of paperwork involved in invoking the criminal justice process. Numerous studies concerning public demand for policing services confirmed that crime calls were only a small part of the policing picture. Most police patrol work is concerned with diverse matters, including looking for missing people, dealing with mentally ill people in distress, with accidents and other social emergencies. As Cumming, Cumming and Edell (1965) memorably put it, when people called the cops what they wanted was a 'philosopher, guide and friend'. The police were, basically, the 'secret social service' (Punch 1979). During the 1980s some research showed that a significant proportion of police calls for service involved 'potential crime' (Shapland and Vagg 1988), nonetheless the evidence suggested that the bulk of calls were not clearly about crime (Waddington 1993).

This was theorised in an influential analysis of the police function by Egon Bittner (1970, 1974). This analysis suggested that, beneath the diversity of problems the police are called upon to tackle there lies, not a distinctive social function, but the core capacity to use force. More recently Jean-Paul Brodeur (2010) expanded this view by observing a wider set of police coercive powers that are not legally available to ordinary citizens. This does not mean that the police typically (or even often) use coercion or force to accomplish a resolution of the troubles they respond to. In putatively democratic societies, the craft of effective policing is to use the background possibility of legitimate coercion so skilfully that it does not need to be foregrounded.

Policework remains contradictory. It is Janus-faced, encompassing both 'parking tickets and class repression' (Marenin 1982). Another way of thinking about this is through the distinction between the reproduction of general and specific order. Policing in the interests of general social order is a general social good. For example, enforcing the rules of the road makes the roads safer for all road users, so this is policing in the interests of some sense of the general order. Policing in the interests of specific social order is rather opposite. An example would be policing the social order of the shopping mall, which is largely in the interests of the consumptive enterprise. Such fine distinctions and nuanced analyses have been largely absent in public politics since New Labour adopted its own brand of crime control rhetoric in the 1990s. The class issue remains pertinent, nonetheless, as many recent *causes célèbres* indicate. These range from the fabrication of official accounts of the 1989 Hillsborough tragedy (and by the same force five years earlier at Orgreave), to the abuse of police force during the G20 and other political protests (Greer and McLaughlin 2010, 2012a, b; Hillsborough Independent Panel 2012; Conn 2015). It has been submerged, however, by a focus on the economics of crime control in which all the conceptual and ethical problems of defining crime are simply bracketed out and the main task becomes efficient repression. This marks a profound shift in official pronouncements about the police role.

From the foundation of the English police by Robert Peel, with the 1829 establishment of the London Metropolitan Police, down to the early 1990s, official statements about the purpose of policing played down the straightforward crime control element (implicitly and sometimes explicitly challenging popular conceptions). In its original formulation by Peel and the Commissioners he appointed, Rowan and Mayne, the purpose of policing was the prevention of crime, peacekeeping and the preservation of 'public tranquillity'. This last phrase was revived by Lord Scarman in his *Report on the Brixton Disorders* in 1981, which explicitly prioritised peacekeeping over law enforcement. In this conception, public support is crucial for policing, and a broad service role is encouraged to facilitate this. Law enforcement and catching criminals were explicitly downplayed by Peel and Scarman, both of whom saw these as evidence of failure in the primary police task of peacekeeping, and as potentially undermining order by inflaming tensions.

The historical context in which the British police developed is crucial for understanding the Peelian statement of purpose. The police had an acutely controversial foundation in the teeth of widespread opposition, in and out of Parliament. Although a key motive for their creation was safeguarding threats to public order, this was downplayed by Peel, in favour of preventing routine property crime, in order to get the 1829 Act passed. The prophets of the 'police science' of the eighteenth century that underpinned Peel's conception—Patrick Colquhoun, Adam Smith and others—saw the police as only a small part of preventing crime, with political economy and culture as basic to peacekeeping and the police, in the institutional sense, only plugging the gaps. This perspective remained fundamental in official enquiries into policing right up to the early 1990s, receiving a major fillip from its centrality to the reform agenda stemming from Scarman, and underpinning the unique 1990 collaboration of the three police professional associations, which produced the Operational Policing Review (Joint Consultative Committee 1990).

Contemporary government pronouncements about the purposes of policing embody a substantial shift, following the politicisation of law and order in the 1970s and, more particularly, the embedding of a new consensus on toughness since the early 1990s, as neo-liberalism became firmly entrenched (Reiner 2007). Thatcher's Home Secretaries had largely mounted a 'phoney war' on crime (apart from in the public order arena), despite the Leader's blazing speeches. But real policing policies and rhetoric toughened up after 1993. The new orthodoxy was made bluntly explicit in the Conservative government's 1993 *Police Reform* White Paper: 'The main job of the police is to catch criminals' (Home Office 1993: s.2.2). This thief-taking priority was undercut by the very next sentence: 'In a typical day, however, only about 18% of calls to the police are about crime.' But, from the law and order perspective, this is a problem rather than an indication of public demand that is to be respected. The hunt was on for identifying 'extraneous' tasks from which the police should be liberated, although this initially proved abortive. The 2010 Coalition's *Policing in the 21st century* pays lip service to Peel's preventive priority, but focuses primarily on 'putting the public in the driver's seat' in order to cut crime through 'common sense' policing (Home Office 2010: 3). In a 2011 speech in the aftermath of the summer riots that year, Home Secretary Theresa May emphasised that the test of police effectiveness, 'the sole objective against which they will be judged, the way in which communities should be able to hold them to account, is their success in cutting crime'. If the point were not made emphatically enough, at three separate points her speech, the Home Secretary exhorted the police to be 'single-minded crime fighters' (May 2011).

There is no doubt that a variety of innovative methods have boosted the crime control capacity of the police in recent years. It is, of course, vitally important that the police can respond effectively to violent and property crimes, conduct thorough investigations of those that are reported and bring offenders to justice. Nonetheless, this remains only a small part of serious emergency work that the police are called upon for by the public. The police are rightly compelled to maintain a significant proportion of resources to respond to these, and the popular representation of policing as being all about crime (and crime control as being all about the police) is misleading and dangerous. It both threatens the effectiveness of emergency service delivery and places unrealistic expectations of CSI-level crime fighting upon a police force that could never deliver.

At present, most public discussion focuses on the role of the police in crime reduction. But, this is a very narrow and distorted view of the police function in terms of what policing is and should be about, and what the police actually do. We concur with Jesse Rubin that the 'police are occupied with peacekeeping—but preoccupied with crime fighting' (Rubin 1972: 25; cited by Kleinig 1996: 11). In our view, the first thing that should be done about the police is to ensure that people understand that policing is not all about crime control. The police are, in fact, an all-purpose emergency service charged with responding to a wide range of different urgent social problems. In our opinion, emergency order maintenance—so-called fire-brigade policing—is the true purpose of police work and should be protected from budget cuts (Reiner 2012c).

Who Does Policing?

Many agents and agencies can and do perform policing tasks, and always have. Policing may be done by professionals employed by the state in an organisation with an omnibus policing mandate—the archetypal modern idea of the police—or by state agencies with other primary purposes (like the Atomic Energy Authority Police, parks constabularies, the British Transport Police, and other 'hybrid' policing bodies;

see Johnston 1992: Chap. 6). Police may be professionals employed by specialist private policing firms (contract security), or security personnel hired by an organisation whose main business is something else (in-house security). Patrols may be carried out by bodies without the full status, powers, equipment or training of the core state police, such as Police Community Support Officers (PCSOs). Policing functions may also be performed by citizens in a voluntary capacity within state police organisations (like the Special Constabulary), in association with the state police (like Neighbourhood Watch schemes), or in completely independent bodies (such as the many vigilante bodies which have flourished at many times and places). Policing functions may be carried out by state bodies with other primary functions, like the army in Northern Ireland, or by employees (state or private) as an adjunct of their main job (like concierges, bus conductors or shop assistants, *inter alios* guarding against theft). Policing is also carried out by technology, such as CCTV cameras or listening devices. Policing can be designed into the architecture and furniture of streets and buildings, as epitomised by Mike Davis's celebrated example of the bum-proof bench (Davis 1990). It is increasingly carried out by transnational agencies (Bowling and Sheptycki 2012, 2015).

All these policing strategies proliferate today, even though only the state agency has the omnibus mandate of order maintenance that is still popularly understood by the label 'the police'. A much debated question is whether the apparent shift away from state policing towards private, citizen and transnational forms amounts to a fundamental and qualitative transformation (Bayley and Shearing 1996). This claim has been subject to cogent critique. Although the personnel employed by private security have indeed grown to be more numerous than public constabularies in many countries, they were already coming close in the supposed heyday of state policing in the post-war decades (Jones and Newburn 2002).

Moreover, part of the increase in private security numbers occurred because corporations have increasingly substituted contracted in-house security, thus boosting the private security employment statistics. More broadly, Jones and Newburn show that the growth of private security represents an increasing formalisation of social control as the number of employees with *secondary* but still substantial security functions (bus and rail conductors and inspectors, park-keepers, roundsmen, etc.) has declined sharply. Some forms of citizen auxiliary police, like the Special Constabulary, have declined (Jones and Newburn 2002), but the introduction and rapid proliferation of PCSOs since 2002 indicates the diversity of the 'extended policing family'. The mushrooming of private security performing an increasing array of functions, and the internal diversification of state policing, certainly are significant developments, but what is debatable is whether they amount to a qualitatively new model of policing, requiring an entirely new analytic paradigm (cf. the arguments in Shearing 2007 and Shearing and Stenning 2012 versus Newburn 2007 and Jones 2007).

The state has never had a monopoly of security arrangements (Zedner 2006), even though in stable liberal democracies it has claimed control over *legitimate* force—but there is no evidence that this domination of *legitimacy* is under challenge. The new policing theorists claim that the status and image of private security has been transformative and not just because of their quantitative presence. Whilst they are certainly more in demand, it is far from clear whether they have become viewed more positively by the mass of the public. Although, primarily for economic reasons, it has been government policy to develop civilianisation and auxiliaries like the PCSOs, these do not threaten the hold over the mainstream 'sworn' constables in the public imagination. Indeed, the popular media have regularly reviled PCSOs ('Blunkett's Bobbies') and similar initiatives. Whilst there has undoubtedly been a pluralisation of policing in recent decades, in neither substance nor symbolism does it amount to a qualitative transformation. In our opinion, the public police are, and should remain, the lynchpin of state governance.

What Powers Do the Police Have?

Police officers usually require only the power of persuasion to do a good job. Coaxing a suicidal person away from a ledge, escorting a drunk from a bar and asking children calmly but firmly to stop disturbing their elderly neighbours can all be achieved with good communication skills and the personal and institutional authority vested in the police uniform.

However, as we have argued above, to do the job the police require the power to use *non-negotiable force* and the power to intrude into privacy. The reason that people call the cops (rather than anyone else) is because they have the 'capacity and authority to overpower resistance to an attempted solution in the natural habitat of the problem' (Bittner 1970: 40–41). This raises the question of what powers the police should have and how powerful they should be.

The police share a number of features in common with the military (Townsend 1993). They are both specialists in the use of force and are disciplined organisations arranged hierarchically in a rank-structured bureaucracy. Both have access to armaments of various degrees of lethality and share similar uniforms, helmets and badges of rank. Both are drilled to march in step and have command and control systems that guide and manage deployment. A fundamental difference exists because democratic policing emphasises minimal force in the maintenance of social order, whereas military use of force aims to conquer an enemy by 'killing people and breaking things' (Dunlap 2001).

The architects of the modern British police emphasised the distinction between soldiers and constables. Indeed, the historical origins of the police lie in the public opposition to the use of military force in domestic situations—the deployment of the Yeoman at Arms at Saint Peters Fields Manchester in 1819 (the, so-called, Peterloo Massacre)—which is often cited as a significant feature in the development of non-military means of responding to riot (Townsend 1993). Key ideas have underscored the distinction between police and military forces: the idea of the constable as a citizen in uniform; the doctrine of the minimum use force; the rule of law; and the subordination of police powers to judicial processes required to collect evidence and arrest suspects. These ideas provide legitimacy to the monopoly on the use of force granted to the police in maintaining public order and investigating crime. In Britain this distinction is underscored by the fact that most police officers are armed only with batons (and increasingly Tasers) and do not routinely carry firearms. Elsewhere, of course, the routine arming of the police is usually defended on the grounds of officer protection.

The police–military boundary is becoming increasingly narrow (McCulloch 2004) and this trend is not limited to the United States, although it is particularly pronounced there (Kraska 2001, 2007). Military personnel in many 'new wars'—ranging from involvement in civil war and intervening in weak, failing and failed states—are frequently called upon to undertake constabulary duties in riot control and crime investigation. At the same time, the threat of serious public disorder and an actual or perceived growth in armed criminality and terrorism have led governments to equip police forces with heavier armaments and to develop military training and deployment programmes. Police officers in special paramilitary units are often virtually indistinguishable from soldiers (Goldsmith and Sheptycki 2007).

Police in Britain rarely shoot people, but when they do the consequences are far-reaching for the victims and families of those involved, as well as for wider society. The shooting of Jean Charles de Menezes illustrated the capacity of the police to act in a quasi-military fashion. Following a botched surveillance operation in the wake of the 2005 mass casualty attacks on London, no attempt was made to arrest de Menezes who was mistaken for a suicide bomber and shot seven times in the head to prevent any possibility that a device could be detonated. In 2011, the shooting of Mark Duggan—who was unarmed at the time he was killed—provoked demonstrations and triggered widespread rioting. In many parts of the world, police shootings are much more common than in Britain. In Jamaica, with a population of around 2.5 million, around 140 people are killed by the police every year. The Brazilian police shoot 2,000 people every year. Police violence in the USA shot to prominence in 2014 following the shooting of Michael Brown, an unarmed teenager, in Ferguson, Missouri, which sparked days of rioting. The issue has remained prominent with the regular publishing of video film of police shooting unarmed civilians. The US government does not collect data on police shootings, but the Guardian newspaper launched a project called The Counted, which has a tally of 709 people shot dead by the police in the USA in the first nine months of 2015. By contrast, in Britain 23 people were shot dead by the police between 2004 and 2014 (IPCC 2015, Table 2.2).[2] In Ontario,

---

[2] There are, of course, many other deaths following contact with the police; this includes those caused by 'less lethal' weapons such as Tasers, the use of restraints, collisions with vehicles and deaths arising when police neglect their duty of care to people in their custody.

Canada, the Special Investigations Unit, which is responsible for inquiring into cases of police use of force throughout the province, released a report indicating that between 2010 and 2014 police were responsible for 39 fatal shootings, of which 16 took place in Toronto (a city of over two million people) (Gillis 2015).

In much the same way that the police–military distinction rests on restrictions in the use of force, the division between police and spies rests on constraints in the use of intrusive surveillance. In a similar fashion, the police have also sought to distinguish themselves from spies and police services from secret intelligence services. In recent years, however, the lines demarcating police from secret intelligence agencies have blurred. This can be seen in the rise of intelligence-led policing and with it: the growth of intelligence collection, analysis and dissemination capacities in police services; the convergence between policing and secret intelligence values in the provision of national security (especially in counter terrorism, but in organised crime); the growing role of the secret intelligence and security services in ordinary law policing; and increased use of criminal informers and undercover policing tactics (Sheptycki 2003; Innes and Sheptycki 2004; Sheptycki 2004; Fyfe and Sheptycki 2006).

A number of recent scandals in the UK illustrate the problems arising from these forms of policing (Lewis and Evans 2013). For example, the National Public Order Intelligence Unit (NPOIU), a 70-strong undercover unit, was set up by the Association of Chief Police Officers (ACPO) to monitor 'domestic extremists', that is, environmental activists. In 2010, information about the unit led to the collapse of a trial of six people accused of planning political protest activity. NPOIU officer Mark Kennedy was revealed to have spent seven years working undercover as part of the environmental protest movement. During this period, he had participated in police operations involving 22 countries, which involved initiating long-term meaningful friendships and engaging in sexual relationships under false pretences. An even more remarkable case involves Bob Lambert, a former Special Branch officer with the Metropolitan Police Special Demonstrations Squad (SDS), who embarked on a series of long-term relationships with women activists (one of whom bore his child) as a way to establish a cover story. After these revelations concerning long-term relationships with undercover police officers, eight women initiated legal action against the police for deception. An equally troubling set of cases concern the infiltration of social justice campaigns relating to deaths in custody or failures of policing, such as the Stephen Lawrence Family campaign. A series of judge-led public inquiries into the management of undercover policing are now underway.

Public debate about police powers has taken a radical shift in recent times as a consequence of the, so-called, IT revolution, which has been a mixed blessing for police agencies (Marx 2007). Techno-policing has turned out to be a double-edged sword: on the one hand it enhances police power, promises effectiveness, efficiency, expeditiousness and the reduction of administrative burdens (Bowling et al. 2008). On the other, the infusion of technology is giving rise to an increasing sense of insecurity (Ericson 2007). The shift towards techno-policing should be cautiously received. Luddism is not an option since the history of policing reveals these institutions to be at the forefront of many technological shifts (Brodeur 2010). The coming age of techno-policing, predictive analytics, geo-spatial analysis and computer-aided police management (Prox and Griffiths 2014) should be anchored with democratic and community-led police intelligence analysis (Bullock 2013, 2014; and Ronn 2012).

Policing moves with the times, of course. The 'innovations in policing' that occurred in the 1960s and 1970s (Weatheritt 1986) arising from the introduction of new technologies–such as motor vehicles, two-way radios, computer aided despatch systems, centralised criminal records databases–are now taken for granted by both police and public. Similarly, today's new scientific techniques, data collection devices and mathematical analytical procedures are shaping numerous aspects of policing, including crime investigation, intelligence analysis and the management of public order (Bowling et al. 2008). Such technologies as body-worn cameras, personal digital assistants, mobile fingerprint and DNA testing analysis devices blur the boundary between evidence collection, evidence testing and punishment. These technologies also blur the boundary between the innocent person and the suspect, since they enable the surveillance of entire populations. Numerous policing processes are being automated and temporally and procedurally compressed. This, for Marks, Bowling and Keenan (2016) indicates a move towards an automated policing and criminal justice process that is mediated by technology in ways that minimise human agency and undercut due process safeguards. Few countries have been able to ensure the social democratic basis of techno-policing (Reiner 2012a, b). In the United States and Europe there is an observable move towards a highly militarised and invasive form of techno-policing (Kraska 2001, 2007; Flyghed 2005; Fassin 2013). The façade of community policing has been destroyed (Parenti 2004) and its techniques integrated into a militarised model of policing (DeMichele and Kraska 2001).

What Is Good Policing and How Can It Be Achieved?

The 'blue uniformed' police force is a modern invention (Rawlings 2002). Originally, policing in England was equated with parish constables, night watchmen, thief takers, the Charlies (the King's Men, so named after King Charles) and so forth. The police as an established body of state employees, lightly armed men and women paid to patrol towns, cities and villages with the goal of maintaining order, preventing and investigating crime emerged in the Victorian era. In Britain, traces of the police idea can be found in the late eighteenth century, but police forces really only came into being across the country during the mid-nineteenth century with the Metropolitan Police Act (1829), the Municipal Corporations Act (1835), The Rural Constabulary Act (1839) and the County and Borough Police Act (1856). The extent of geographical penetration of the police is not that great. For example, work carried out by the UK Audit Commission in the 1980s showed that in a British shire force with 2,500 police officers, once headquarters staff, management, specialists and abstractions were accounted for, and the force divided into the four shifts required for twenty-four-hour cover, there would only be 125 police on the streets at any one time. Amounting to one police officer on patrol for every 18,000 residents. In some places a police presence is hardly necessary for more or less quiescent social order. But elsewhere people do not see the police as an organisation that can be trusted to be called upon to prevent or detect crime, or to help with other emergency situations—this is especially true in contexts where there is deep-rooted social conflict—and call upon other forms of self-help policing. The role of the Irish Republican Army (IRA) in policing nationalist communities during the Troubles in Northern Ireland are but one example among many of how non-state paramilitary organisations fill a vacuum in state provision (Mulcahey 2005).

Policing is 'carried out by a diverse array of people and techniques' and can be found in all known societies. The 'modern idea of police' is only one of the ways in which policing can be conducted (Reiner 2010a: 5). As has been noted by generations of sociologists and criminologists, everyday social order is maintained, for the most part, by ordinary people without police involvement. However, there is a wide range of circumstances, especially in advanced modern societies, that authoritative intervention from specialists in order maintenance is not only valuable but essential. Responding to major accidents and civil emergencies bring this to the fore: whether the incident is a train crash, flood or exploding bomb, police are required to manage the closure of streets and transport networks; in the investigation of serious and volume crime requiring people skilled in evidence collection, analysis and case preparation; for the protection of infrastructure such as power generation and supply, ports and airports or telecommunications. All of these tasks call for well-organised state policing that can coordinate with other 'blue light' organisations, such as ambulance and fire services. And, as argued above, the police in contemporary society operate as the only all-purpose emergency service that is available twenty-four hours a day, seven days a week to respond to a wide range of social problems.

What, then, constitutes good policing? Here we reiterate Reiner's 'neo-Rethian' perspective (1985, 2010a: 65). It might seem strange for critical policing scholars to draw on the views of Charles Reith, the conservative 'cop sided' police historian. We reject Reith's (1956) romanticised view of the emergence of 'new police' as an unequivocally beneficent institution. However, we do think there is value in Rethian principles of policing, derived from those originally formulated by Peel and set out in the first General Instructions issued to the police by Rowan and Mayne, the first joint Commissioners of the Metropolitan Police (Reith 1956: 286–7; Metropolitan Police 1829). These may not have been realised in practice, but they can be taken as 'an aspiration for *what a police force should be like*' (Reiner 2010: 47, emphasis added).

For Peel, peaceful cities rather than the visible activity of the police was the criterion on which the police should be judged. This emphasises the point made above that policing is not only about crime control, and it is that crucial the police—as an institution and as a body of individuals—should be aware of their broader social function. In exercising their functions and duties, Peel's principles insisted that the police should recognise that their 'existence, actions and behaviour' are 'dependent on public approval... and on their ability to secure and maintain public respect'. To the extent that policing is concerned with crime and disorder, good police work is not founded on the use of military force, the threat of severe punishment or the infiltration of criminal groups. Rather, it is based on securing public cooperation, bearing in mind that the police are only one agency among many public and private bodies contributing to social order.

This also relates to principles minimising governmental use of coercion, surveillance and other intrusive measures. Physical force should be used 'only when the exercise of persuasion, advice and warning is found to be insufficient to obtain public cooperation to an extent necessary to secure observance of law or to restore order, and to use only the minimum degree of physical force which is necessary on any particular occasion for achieving a police objective' Metropolitan Police (1829). As Peel's principles warn, 'the extent to which the cooperation of the public can be secured diminishes proportionately the necessity of the use of physical force and compulsion'. Police powers should be used fairly, kept in check and be democratically accountable. The police should adhere strictly to executive functions and refrain from 'even seeming' to usurp the powers of the judiciary in avenging individuals or the state or judging guilt or punishing the guilty. Preserving public confidence requires 'not pandering to public opinion' but by demonstrating impartiality, service, independence and by offering 'individual service and friendship to all members of the public without regard to their wealth or standing, by ready exercise of courtesy and friendly good humour; and by ready offering of individual sacrifice in protecting and preserving life' (Ibid).

The rise of global neo-liberal ideology has had consequences for the way people talk about the economics of policing. In several countries a general pattern has been observed whereby the official crime rates have been dropping for some years and yet the cost of policing has continued to rise (Boyd et al. 2011; Gascón and Foglesong 2010; Leuprecht 2014; Ruddell and Jones 2013; Walker and Archbold 2014: 248–260). There are strong political cross-currents dictating that the costs of public policing need to be curtailed, whilst at the same time democratic social forces seek to assert more overt control over public policing (Walker and Archbold 2014). These forces for change within professional policing are occurring at the same time as an increasing drift towards enhanced forms of High Policing (Brodeur 2007; O'Reilly 2015) and other forms of political policing, not least in the context of counter-terrorism (Weisburd et al. 2009). These raise complex questions about how to assess the quality of policing at odds with Peelian policing values.

In the final decades of the twentieth century, policing in most Western democracies moved towards predominantly community and problem-oriented approaches (Bayley 1996). Current changes in the police operating environment are reshaping the internal structure and governance of policing and these adaptations are weakening the connections between police and public (International Association of Chiefs of Police 2005; McCulloch 2002). Bayley and Nixon (2010) argue that early in the twenty-first century, the institutions of policing entered a period of historical discontinuity equivalent to that which presaged the rise of modern policing in London in 1829. It is too early to tell if efforts by coalitions of progressive academics (e.g. Hough et al. 2010) and police practitioners (e.g. Neyroud 2008) can transcend the historical conditions by melding internal methods of police performance management with external markers of procedural fairness.

The odds are stacked against this for a number of reasons. One is declining budgets for municipal policing and the rise in the costs of sworn police officers. Another is resistance by rank-and-file police, especially in North America where police unionism in urban policing institutions is strong (Police Practice and Research 2008). This has inhibited innovation and organisational change in many police organisations. Increasingly since the 1960s there has been growing resistance to racially biased policing that, in the early years of the twenty-first century, has been exacerbated by demographic changes brought about by large-scale transnational migration (Bowling et al. 2012).

One possible response to the growing individuation of police officer accountability would be the development of a corresponding 'constabulary ethic' (Sheptycki 2007). The constabulary ethic stresses the existential position of the individual police agent who is, first and foremost, a human being who freely accepts a professional role that imparts the responsibility of interfering in people's conflicts with one another for the good of the community as a whole (Sheptycki and O'Rourke-Dicarlo 2011). What makes this ethic particularly fraught is that, *in extremis*, police agents may use force, up to and including deadly force, to accomplish the goal of social ordering. The constabulary ethic demands that society owes all individuals, including but not limited to police officers, a duty of care, just as individuals, including police officers, freely accept the responsibilities that go with living in a caring society. Ultimately, what is needed is policing that is 'good enough' since it is 'unhelpful and unrealistic to demand perfect police' (Bowling 2007).

How Does Policing Impact on Different Social Groups?

For most people, the police are the first point of contact with the criminal justice system and with the coercive arm of government more generally. Therefore, their impact on different social groups—particularly those most marginalised—feeds into inequity in other spheres and can often exacerbate existing inequalities. The impact of policing begins from selective police deployment and targeting, for example with the *over-policing* of neighbourhoods where minority ethnic communities are concentrated. This propensity to treat such areas as intrinsically criminal contributes to the rate at which people of African, Caribbean and Asian origin are brought into contact with the criminal justice system. Such practices contribute to the ongoing *criminalisation* of minority communities—the process by which the law is used against minorities to demonstrate their criminality through systemic and selective targeting and deployment of coercive power (Gordon 1983: 33). This leads to the disproportionate rate at which marginalised people come into contact with the criminal justice system, through discretionary practices such as stop and search targeting young men of minority ethnic communities and the consequent disproportionate rates of arrest, conviction and imprisonment.

Concurrent to this process of criminalisation, people from minority communities often experience a failure of *service provision* from the police. They are more likely to be treated by the police in a racially abusive manner, and speak of police apathy towards them as victims of crime (Bowling and Phillips 2002). Numerous reports indicate that the police response to minority ethnic communities as victims has been: an unwillingness to provide protection; inactivity; and abuse by the police to complainants. The way in which policing provision is perceived by ethnic minority people is available from survey evidence (Bowling and Phillips 2002: 135). This indicates that ethnic minority satisfaction with the police tends to be much lower than that of white respondents. Unsurprisingly, this also affects the propensity of minority ethnic communities to cooperate with the police (Bowling and Phillips 2002: 136).

The failure of the police to provide a fair and equal service to ethnic minorities is particularly visible in cases of racist violence (Bowling 1999). Despite a documented rise in racially motivated attacks through the 1970s and 1980s, the general consensus was that the police were either indifferent to the concerns of minority ethnic people or actively prejudiced. Additionally, the police harassment of minority ethnic people often occurs because of their insecurity about their immigration status, and those arrested after going to the police for help in cases of domestic violence or robbery may be asked to produce their passport, deterring people from seeking police protection. Moreover, immigration checks motivated by racial bias will only confirm such bias; if minority ethnic people are predominantly questioned about their immigration status, more minority ethnic people will be found to be 'illegal', thus confirming the initial suspicions. The effects of such discriminatory policing have been detrimental; not only have the police failed to provide a fair and equal service and protection to minority citizens, but it has also criminalised them through selective targeting and enforcement of laws against them.

The experiences of women at the hands of the police have also been shaped by stereotypes of 'acceptable' or 'conventional' femininity. The criminal justice system tends to mirror everyday stereotypes and assumptions, and the concept of the 'guilty victim' (Tchaikovsky 1989: 185) (or the woman who has, in some way, invited harm) is applied to women, and police attitudes to women are based on conditions of *appropriateness* where women may be subject to harsher treatment if they are deemed to be behaving *inappropriately*. Police culture, alongside being in many ways institutionally racist, is also entrenched in an occupational culture of sexism. Domestic violence has traditionally been low on the police list of priorities, possibly because convictions in such cases are rare and the attrition rate is high. The police tend to collude with male perpetrators of domestic violence, feeling that they should not intervene forcefully and disrupt the privacy of families. Worse, repeated incidents of domestic violence have been traditionally treated *less* seriously and as disputes or nuisances. Women of colour are particularly vulnerable to disbelief, blaming and dismissal directed at them not only as women, but as ethnic minority people who are stereotyped as criminals, and as women of colour who are sexually stereotyped in different ways (Solanke 2009: 733). Women who arrive in the country as dependants and then suffer domestic violence are put at risk of deportation if they approach social services (Sarwar 1989: 48). A lack of response and a refusal to prosecute are a common police response to racist attacks and their historical response to domestic violence (Sheptycki 1991). Where the police have taken concerted steps to tackle domestic violence, through multi-agency policing initiatives for example, this has come at the cost of stigmatising households as problem families, whilst continuing to hold that cultural differences are the reason for a lack of swift and effective police intervention when women call. This is compounded by stereotypes of minority ethnic women as having a 'higher tolerance' to male violence and pain (Southall Black Sisters 1989: 43), or being stereotyped as submissive.

The experiences of women of colour are crucial nodal points from which we can understand the impact of criminal justice policing on those who face *intersecting* oppressions, or are multiply marginalised (Bowling and Phillips 2002: 50). The experience of women of colour then indicates a higher degree of victimisation along the lines of race, gender and class, and qualitatively *different* concerns when it comes to improving police response. Such intersectional discrimination goes beyond mere addition, where discrimination is an aggregation of racism and sexism, and requires an approach that considers how such characteristics *interact* to produce distinct outcomes. For example, the police response to women of colour who are victims of domestic violence by seeing them as naturally submissive, tolerant to pain or bound to their cultures is an *interaction* of misogyny and racism to produce an outcome that fails to assist victims, rather than the mere addition of the racism and sexism that minority ethnic women face.

Minimising the differential impact of policing on marginalised people requires a broader understanding of what it is that gives rise to structural inequality and discrimination in the first place. It is no surprise that those who suffer the most as a result of discriminatory policing practices are those who also suffer the most in other social spheres. We should turn our attention instead to the *sources* of economic, social, political and structural inequality and cultural marginalisation. Safe and peaceful communities require investment in public services—housing, health, education and employment—that operate in the interests of marginalised and vulnerable people. The current economic programme of cuts to services and austerity can only exacerbate the conditions of criminalised populations. We should turn away from focusing on the enforcement of laws that penalise people for being the products of a system deeply rooted in inequality and hurtling towards ever greater inequality.

Good policing, ideally, would primarily provide reliable emergency services and assistance. This is not utopian if the infrastructure to alleviate inequality exists elsewhere. Cultural change is necessary, where prejudice is tackled and treated as a *cause* rather than a consequence of the conditions of marginalised people, alongside a broader agenda of economic and political reform. Exclusionism sustains discriminatory practices and reform requires a reorientation and rebalancing of decision-making power. This exclusionism is reinforced by cuts to public services that help disproportionately marginalised communities. Exclusion will have the greatest impact on the poor and create widespread xenophobia when combined with the call for tougher immigration measures. If we are serious about challenging discriminatory practices in policing, we must be serious about tackling their root causes.

Prospects for change come from the possibility that those at the receiving end of the sting of 'total policing' and law and order campaigns may be able to instrumentalise their victimisation as a power base from which to claim short-term concessions and long-term reform in the arena of economic and political equality. Alliances between marginalised groups, activists, academics, lawyers and others may provide the basis for effective collective action to demand accountability and the fair use of police powers, in the light of the failure of law to effect the fundamental changes required. Whilst the scope for reform from within representative democracy is limited by the exclusion of minorities from politics and a lack of institutional interest, pressure groups and extra-parliamentary collectives may succeed by uniting people in their shared, if varying, experiences of marginalisation. Achieving both justice and peace depend on short-term interventions with a vision of a long-term future for fair and accountable policing.

Who Polices the Police?

Thinking about police accountability takes us to the first question of political philosophy: 'who will guard the guards?' Some people, including police officers, think that the public should trust the police to get on with the job of protecting society from dangerous criminals, investigating crime and maintaining public order. To such people mechanisms of accountability might seem a bit like 'handcuffing the police'. Observing Lord Acton's famous dictum—that 'power tends to corrupt and absolute power corrupts absolutely'—we persist in thinking that democratic police accountability matters (Beare and Murray 2007).

Arguments for the necessity for police accountability derive essentially from the difficulty in holding power in check. The conundrum stems from the empirically observable fact that achieving the goals of policing—the maintenance of peace, order and safety in society—routinely involves the use of physical violence, deception and intrusion into the private lives of people suspected of committing crime, which can be threatening to the social order. As Kleinig (1996) argues, the exercise of state powers, simply because they interfere with the fundamental rights of citizens, are morally suspect. Police powers, therefore cannot be taken for granted but must be justified in general and in each individual instance in which they are used. Although policing is justified by reference to 'goods' it is intended to achieve, it also inevitably places 'bads' or burdens on particular individuals

(Bowling 2007). Policework routinely involves the use of force ranging from the persuasion and threat to carry out a search, the physical force required to conduct an arrest to the use of deadly force in extreme circumstances. There should always be some mechanism to ensure that that the 'evil means' used by the police are used for the 'good ends' that they seek to achieve (Kleinig 1996).

Debates about the regulation of law enforcement powers focus on the means by which the police can be held to account in two senses (Marshall 1978). The first dimension, which could be called answerability, requires that the police are explanatory and cooperative—that they can explain what action they have taken, against whom, why and with what effect. The second dimension, which could be called control, requires that the police are subordinate and obedient to some form of legitimate authority. This means that there must be some means by which the use of police powers can be constrained to the minimum required and that there is liability and sanction where lawful powers are exceeded and, indeed, where there is corruption and incompetence. The precise mechanisms through which both senses of police accountability can be achieved are a matter of debate and internationally there is considerable variety of practice (Goldsmith and Lewis 2000; Reiner and Spencer 1993).

Police are held to account through diverse institutional processes. Police organisations have internal systems of officer accountability. Due to the powerful advances in computing and communications technology in recent years, frontline police officers are constantly measured in terms of a variety of key performance indicators. This accountability is primarily facilitated through technologies such as the mobile data terminals in police patrol vehicles, but with the miniaturisation of computer technology, officers are increasingly being evaluated according to performance metrics communicated to them in the palm of their hands. This internal managerial accountability has been enhanced in recent times through mobile camera surveillance. Firstly in police patrol cars and increasingly in the form of body-worn cameras; individual patrol officers are highly scrutinised in terms of their occupational performance. The observations of earlier generations of police sociologists—that officer discretion increased as one moved down the hierarchy and that frontline officer's decisions were made under conditions of 'low visibility'—are no longer true (Wilson 1968; Goldstein 1960). Routine technological surveillance of police officers has fundamentally changed the conditions of the occupational culture.

Police are also held to account through the institutions of law, that is to say, police are compelled to give an account of their activities during court processes and to legislative and judicial bodies. Traditionally this has been done through one branch of law—criminal law—but increasingly police are drawing on other branches of law—for example administrative law when undertaking civil proceedings to confiscate proceeds of crime. Law is becoming increasingly complex and so police capacity to give an account in legal terms has increased. One Canadian study (Malm et al. 2005), determined that the amount of police time spent on paperwork had increased by a factor of ten in the preceding twenty years. Whereas in the mid-1980s it might have taken a police officer an hour and a half to fully process a person for driving a vehicle under the influence of alcohol, by the mid-2000s, that work time had increased to around five hours. Or, to cite another example, at the time of this study the empirical evidence suggested the average domestic violence call would take several police officers about eight hours to complete, whereas historical cases typically took up about one hour of one officer's time. These increases are due to changing legal requirements that oblige police officers to account for their actions (Malm et al. 2005).

In some jurisdictions civilian institutions have some political policy purview over policing and this requires both individual police officers and the organisation as a whole to give an account. For example, in Toronto there is a civilian review board which oversees police policy and in Ontario there is the Special Investigations Unit, a civilian agency charged with the power to investigate police wrongdoing. Although relatively rare, some scholars would argue that, at least in the English-speaking world, there is an increasing tendency towards institutional arrangements for external accountability and review (Goldsmith and Lewis 2000). In the United Kingdom, numerous bodies are responsible for various aspects of police accountability—the Independent Police Complaints Commission, locally elected police authorities or commissioners, HM Inspectorate of Constabulary, Parliamentary Committees and so forth.

Studies confirm that in the United Kingdom and North America the avenues by which police, both as individuals and as institutions, are required to give accounts have increased over recent years (Ericson 2007; Haggerty and Ericson 1997; Stenning 1995). In addition to the growing power of technical surveillance of police officers at work and the increasingly complex legal requirements for police accountability, there is the possibility of criminal prosecutions, disciplinary proceedings and civil actions against police officers. Increasingly, the power of commercial media to expose police to scandal are being amplified by new social media, thereby creating yet more lines of police accountability (Doyle 2003).

British police forces have traditionally been highly decentralised and the vestiges of that tradition are clearly evident today. With the exception of specialist squads and agencies created to carry out particular policing functions—such as serious organised crime—there is still no national police force. Policing in England and Wales is geographically dispersed to 43 local police forces, organised along county or metropolitan boundaries headed by a Chief Constable who answers to an elected Policing and Crime Commissioner (PCC). This latter role was created by the coalition government's Police and Social Responsibility Act (2011), which abolished local police authorities. The idea behind the PCCs was to introduce a public voice to policing, to bring local democracy into the way in which policing was governed. The PCCs replaced the police authorities that had been part of local democracy, although they are directly elected they are not really accountable to the Police and Crime Panels that are linked to the local democratic institutions. The 2010 Conservative election manifesto promised to make the police 'more accountable through oversight by a directly elected individual', but the increase in accountability is highly questionable at best. The average turn out in the 2012 election was 15 % and there were large numbers of spoiled ballot papers. A review by the former Metropolitan Police Commissioner Lord Stevens (2011) concluded that the model had 'fatal systematic flaws' and should be discontinued once the existing PCCS had served their term.

It can be argued that, whether the police are accountable to an elected politician (such as the PCC) or a combination of elected and appointed persons, police decision-making will retain a high degree of autonomy. This is because the common law doctrine of constabulary independence, which states that police constables should be answerable to the law and the law alone, has been interpreted as meaning that police decision-making cannot be directed or controlled by any national or local politician or institution. Despite decades of changes in accountability mechanisms, the Chief Constable remains sovereign in deciding operational matters. As the former president of ACPO puts it, this deliberate insulation from political control makes the police 'autonomous professional agents of the law' meaning that the public must rely on police 'expertise, judgement and experience in taking professional decisions on operational policing' (Orde 2011). This perspective raises fundamental questions about how the police can be policed and by whom.

Conclusion: What Is to Be Done About the Police?

Having worked through a description of police powers, their role, control, impact on different social groups and mechanisms for accountability, we turn in our conclusion to the question: *what is to be done about the police?* Whatever else, we have to come to terms with the fact that every social order has some kind of formal policing mechanism. Policing is both inevitable and inevitably dirty work (Kleinig 1996; Reiner 2010a). Civilising the powers of surveillance, coercion and punishment means coming to terms with the police. By way of conclusion we draw from the preceding analysis of policing to articulate what we think should be done to improve the quality of policing and the police.

Our first recommendation is that discussions about policing should shift above and beyond the goal of crime reduction; the idea that crime control should be the sole (or even main) job of the police has become a political fetish. This is wrong in theory and is flatly contradicted by the evidence of what policing consists of in practice. Marshalling resources in pursuit of maximal crime control is, in our view, not only unproductive but also skews the reality of the policing task. It is worth noting that the crimes recorded by criminal justice systems tend to be ones committed by the disadvantaged against the disadvantaged. In our view, we should recognise that the police exist primarily as a first line response to people in distress and that the 'emergency social service' role of policing should be paramount.

In our understanding of the role of the police we underline the importance of other institutions in helping to maintain social order and community safety, including the family, schools, tenants and residents' associations, faith groups, private security guards, wardens, stewards and a plethora of neighbourhood organisations. The police are only one among many public, private and voluntary sector providers of services concerned with order maintenance, crime prevention, crime investigation and the provision of security. This is a highly plural operating environment that needs police, public and government to maximise the potential of these agencies to provide an effective, as well as fair and democratically accountable, social order for all. This also requires that we ensure the police service is comprised of the right people in terms of police staffing, leadership and integrity. This is concerned with recruitment, retention, promotion of the people who have the right values and are committed to the highest quality of service and with the highest integrity. These qualities are not only important in relation to public policing, but also because there is a need for leadership across the policing sector.

Police powers should operate on the principled basis of harm minimisation and proportionality. That is, the police should use the least possible coercive force and intrusion into privacy to achieve their aims. In all instances, the least intrusive or coercive option should be used. The drift towards militarised policing techniques, equipment, methods and organisation should be reversed. The use of covert investigative methods is highly problematic; the police should be visible symbols of democratic social order, which they cannot be if policy and practice are shrouded in secrecy and routinely performed at the boundaries of legality and ethical conduct. We need more robust accountability mechanisms to regulate 'high policing' and intelligence-led forms of policing such as surveillance, undercover policing and the use of informers. Models of assessment and accountability need to be examined thoroughly to reflect the reality of plural policing. Evaluations of policing have to take into consideration the diverse roles and functions of the police. Existing mechanisms for the governance of policing are not fit for purpose since they are politicised, yet seemingly unable to hold police action properly to account, and they may, in fact, inflame police–community relations. We need a properly democratically accountable, human and humane response to the problems of crime and disorder within communities.

The idea of the police as a public service is vitally important in a democratic society and should be defended. In a world in which everything is up for sale, the police should not be. This is important for a number of reasons, above all the requirement of public accountability for the common good. Legal regulation of policing is necessary, but not sufficient to bring about real change in how the fundamental goals of policing are shaped and moved towards a greater concern with legitimate peacekeeping. Political and cultural change is required to create a more diverse and ethical police force, one in which the use of intrusive and coercive force is kept to a minimum and which can be held accountable to the people it serves. Apart from strengthening procedures to hold the police accountable, and improving appropriate training and supervision, it is worth noting that that those who bear the brunt of the criminal justice system's coercive power are generally those who are at the margins of society.

Official responses to police wrongdoing or occurrences involving the police abuse of force and other problematic policing events should be dealt with by an external agency. It is unacceptable for allegations of police misconduct to be investigated by the police themselves. Robust external review is a fundamental requirement of police accountability. Official policies should be enforced through training, supervision and monitoring that is sensitive to the possible intersecting oppressions that members of the public may face, and the unique obstacles that these pose to current policing practice. The police should be accountable to the citizenry they serve and policing policies need to be monitored so that the emergency social service function can be most effective at the operational level.

Women, people from ethnic minorities, the poor, the mentally ill and the young (and the various intersections of experience between these distinct categories) are among the most vulnerable members of society, who face political, social and economic marginalisation in every sphere of public and private life. Those that are the most marginalised come into contact with the police as a consequence of their marginalised status, and have laws selectively enforced against them, which only serves to entrench their marginalisation. Policing evidently has the greatest negative impacts on the most marginalised; therefore, the drift towards paramilitary policing and the use of wide surveillance, which undercut safeguards on civil liberties, should be reversed.

Understanding why marginalised individuals and communities are disproportionately targeted by the police returns us to understanding what the police role is in the first place and, more broadly, what activities are deemed objects for crime control. The police are the coercive arm of the state and embody the state's values and interests. If the state embraces neoliberal capitalist values, it will inevitably work in the interests of dominant groups of people. Under such conditions, minorities fall outside the values of the dominant class and hence become targets of inappropriate policing practice. Policing is ambivalent; its repressive functions reproduce the dominant social order and yet the activity of peacekeeping—if it is done well enough—can also contribute more generally to a beneficent social order. Improving policing is, therefore, intrinsically related to refreshing and renewing fundamental democratic values.

References

Banton, M. (1964). *The policeman in the community*. London: Tavistock.

Bayley, D. (1985). *Patterns of policing: A comparative international analysis*. New Brunswick: Rutgers University Press.

Bayley, D. (1996). *Police for the future*. Oxford: Oxford University Press.

Bayley, D., & Nixon, C. (2010). *The changing environment for policing, 1958–2008* (New perspectives in policing). Harvard, Kennedy School of Government and the US National Institute of Justice.

Bayley, D., & Shearing, C. (1996). The future of policing. *Law and Society Review, 30*(3), 586–606.

Beare, M., & Murray, T. (2007). *Police and government relations—Whose calling the shots?* Toronto: University of Toronto Press.

Bittner, E. (1970). *The functions of the police in modern society*. Chevy Chase: National Institute of Mental Health.

Bittner, E. (1974). Florence Nightingale in pursuit of Willie Sutton: A theory of the police. In H. Jacob (Ed.), *The potential for reform of criminal justice*. Beverley Hills: Sage.

Bowling, B. (1999). *Violent racism: Victimisation, policing and social context*. Oxford: Oxford University Press.

Bowling, B. (2007). Fair and effective police methods: Towards 'good enough' policing. *Scandinavian Studies in Criminology and Crime Prevention, 8*(S1), 17–23.

Bowling, B., & Phillips, C. (2002). *Racism, crime and justice*. London: Longman.

Bowling, B., & Sheptycki, J. (2012). *Global policing*. London: Sage.

Bowling, B., & Sheptycki, J. (Eds.) (2015). *Global policing and transnational law enforcement* (Vol. 1–4). London: Sage.

Bowling, B., Marks, A., & Murphy, C. (2008). Crime control technologies. In R. Brownsword & K. Yeung (Eds.), *Regulating technologies* (pp. 51–78). Oxford: Hart.

Bowling, B., Phillips, C., & Sheptycki, J. (2012). Race, political economy and the coercive state. In J. Peay & T. Newburn (Eds.), *Policing: Politics, culture and control: essays in honour of Robert Reiner* (pp. 43–69). Oxford: Hart Publishing.

Boyd, E., Geoghegan, R., & Gibbs, B. (2011). *Cost of the cops: Manpower and deployment in policing*. London: Policy Exchange.

Brodeur, J.-P. (2007). High and low policing in post-9/11 times. *Policing, 1*(1), 25–37.

Brodeur, J.-P. (2010). *The policing web*. Oxford: Oxford University Press.

Bullock, K. (2013). Community, intelligence-led policing and crime control. *Policing and Society, 23*(2), 125–144.

Bullock, K. (2014). *Citizens, community and crime control*. Basingstoke: Palgrave Macmillan.

Conn, D. (2015, July 22). We were fed lies about the violence at Orgreave. Now we need the truth. *The Guardian*.

Cumming, E., Cumming, I., & Edell, L. (1965). The policeman as philosopher, guide, and friend. *Social Problems, 12*(3), 276–286.

Davis, M. (1990). *City of quartz*. London: Vintage.

DeMichele, M. T., & Kraska, P. (2001). Community policing in battle garb: A paradox or coherent strategy? In P. Kraska (Ed.), *Militarising the American criminal justice system: The changing roles of the Armed Forces and the police*. Boston: Northeastern University Press.

Doyle, A. (2003). *Arresting images: Crime and policing in front of the television camera*. Toronto: University of Toronto Press.

Dunlap, C. (2001). The thick green line: The growing involvement of military forces in domestic law enforcement. In P. Kraska (Ed.), *Militarising the American criminal justice system: The changing roles of the Armed Forces and the police*. Boston: Northeastern University Press.

Ericson, R. V. (2007). *Crime in an insecure world*. Cambridge: Polity.

Fassin, D. (2013). *Enforcing order: An ethnography of urban policing*. Cambridge: Polity Press.

Flyghed, J. (2005). Crime-control in the post-wall era: The menace of security. *Journal of Scandinavian Studies in Criminology, 6*(2), 165–182.

Fyfe, N., & Sheptycki, J. (2006). International trends in the facilitation of witness co-operation in organized crime cases (with N. Fyfe). *The European Journal of Criminology, 3*(3), 319–355.

Gascón, G., & Foglesong, T. (2010). *Making policing more affordable: Managing costs and measuring value in policing* (Executive sessions on policing and public safety). Harvard: Kennedy School of Government and the US National Institute of Justice.

Gillis, W. (2015, August 16). How many black men have been killed by Toronto police? We can't know. *Toronto Star*.

Goldsmith, A., & Lewis, C. (2000). *Civilian oversight of policing: Governance, democracy and human rights*. Oxford: Hart.

Goldsmith, A., & Sheptycki, J. (Eds.) (2007). *Crafting transnational policing*. Oxford: Hart.

Goldstein, J. (1960). Police discretion not to invoke the criminal process: Low visibility decisions in the administration of justice. *Yale Law Journal, 69*, 543–594.

Gordon, P. (1983). *White law: Racism in the police, courts, and prisons*. London: Pluto Press.

Greer, C., & McLaughlin, E. (2010). We predict a riot?: Public order policing, new media environments and the rise of the citizen journalism. *British Journal of Criminology, 50*(6), 1041–1059.

Greer, C., & McLaughlin, E. (2012a). This is not justice: Ian Tomlinson, institutional failure and the press politics of outrage. *British Journal of Criminology, 52*(2), 274–293.

Greer, C., & McLaughlin, E. (2012b). 'Trial by media': Riots, looting, gangs and mediatised police chiefs. In J. Peay & T. Newburn (Eds.), *Policing, politics, culture and control* (pp. 135–153). Oxford: Hart.

Haggerty, K. D., & Ericson, R. V. (1997). *Policing risk society*. Oxford: Clarendon.

Hillsborough Independent Panel. (2012). *Report* available at http://hillsborough.independent.gov.uk/

Home Office. (1993). *Police reform: A police service for the twenty-first century*. London: HMSO. White Paper Cm. 2281.

Home Office. (2010). Policing in the 21st century: Reconnecting police and the people. Cm. 7925.

Hough, M., Jackson, J., Bradford, B., Myhill, A., & Quinton, P. (2010). Procedural justice trust and institutional legitimacy. *Policing, 4*(3), 203–210.

Independent Police Complaints Commission. (2015). Deaths during or following police contact: IPCC Research and Statistics Series Paper 27. London: IPCC.

Innes, M., & Sheptycki, J. (2004). From detection to disruption: Intelligence and the changing logics of police crime control in the United Kingdom (with Martin Innes, University of Surrey). *International Criminal Justice Review, 14*, 1–24.

International Association of Chiefs of Police. (2005). *Post 9–11 policing: The crime control-homeland security paradigm—Taking command of new realities*. Alexandria: IACP.

Johnston, L. (1992). *The rebirth of private policing*. London: Routledge.

Joint Consultative Committee. (1990). *Operational policing review*. Surbiton: Police Staff Associations.

Jones, R. (2007). The architecture of policing: Towards a new theoretical model of the role of constraint-based compliance in policing. In A. Henry & D. J. Smith (Eds.), *Transformations of policing*. Aldershot: Ashgate.

Jones, T., & Newburn, T. (2002). The transformation of policing? Understanding current trends in policing systems. *British Journal of Criminology, 42*(1), 129–146.

Kinsey, R., Lea, J., & Young, J. (1986). *Losing the fight against crime*. London: Blackwell.

Kleinig, J. (1996). *The ethics of policing*. Cambridge: Cambridge University Press.

Kraska, P. (Ed.) (2001). *Militarising the American criminal justice system: The changing roles of the Armed Forces and the police*. Boston: Northeastern University Press.

Kraska, P. (2007). Militarization and policing—Its relevance to 21st century police. *Policing, 1*(4), 501–513.

Lea, J., & Young, J. (1984). *What is to be done about law and order?* London: Penguin.

Leuprecht, C. (2014). *The blue line or the bottom line of police services in Canada? Arresting the runaway growth in costs.* Ottawa: MacDonald-Laurier Institute.

Lewis, P., & Evans, R. (2013). *Undercover: The true story of Britain's secret police.* London: Guardian Faber Publishing.

Malm, A., Pollard, N., Brantingham, P., Tinsely, P., Darryl, P., Brantingham, P., Cohen, I., & Kinney, B. (2005). A 30 year analysis of police service delivery and costing. *International Centre for Urban Research Studies (ICURS)*, Simon Fraser University.

Marenin, O. (1982). Parking tickets and class repression: The concept of policing in critical theories of criminal justice. *Contemporary Crises, 6*(2), 241–266.

Marks, A., Bowling, B., Keenan, C., et al. (2016). Automatic justice: Technological innovation, crime and social control. In K. Yeung, R. Brownsword, & E. Scotford (Eds.), *The Oxford handbook on the law and regulation of technology.* Oxford: Oxford University Press.

Marshall, G. (1978). Police accountability revisited. In D. Butler & A. H. Halsey (Eds.), *Policy and politics: Essays in honour of Norman Chester.* London: Macmillan.

Marx, G. T. (2007). Rocky Bottoms and some information age techno-fallacies. *Journal of International Political Sociology, 1*(1), 83–110.

May, T. (2011). *Police reform; Home Secretary's speech of 16 August 2011.* London: Home Office. https://www.gov.uk/government/speeches/police-reform-home-secretarys-speech-of-16-august-2011

McCulloch, J. (2002–3). Counter terrorism, human security and globalization; from welfare state to warfare state? *Current Issues in Criminal Justice, 14*(3), 283–298.

McCulloch, J. (2004). Blue armies, khaki police and the cavalry on the new American frontier: Critical criminology for the 21st century. *Critical Criminology, 12*(3), 309–326.

Mulcahey, A. (2005). *Policing northern Ireland: Legitimacy, reform and social conflict.* Collumpton: Willan.

Newburn, T. (2007). The future of policing in Britain. In A. Henry & D. J. Smith (Eds.), *Transformations of policing.* Aldershot: Avebury.

Neyroud, P. (2008). Past, present and future performance: Lessons and prospects for the measurement of police performance. *Policing, 2*(3), 340–348.

Independent Police Complaints Commission. (2015). Deaths during or following police contact: IPCC Research and Statistics Series Paper 27. London: IPCC.

O'Reilly, C. (2015). The pluralization of high policing: Convergence and divergence at the public-private interface. *British Journal of Criminology, 55*(4), 688–710.

Parenti, C. (2004). *The soft cage: Surveillance in America: From slave passes to the war on terror*. New York: Basic Books.

Police Practice and Research. (2008). Police reform from the bottom up: Police unions and their influence. *Police Practice and Research (Special Issue), 9*(2).

Prox, R., & Griffiths, C. T. (2014). Core policing. *Police Practice and Research and International Journal* (Special Issue), 1–9.

Punch, M. (1979). The secret social service. In S. Holdaway (Ed.), *The British police*. London: Edward Arnold.

Rawlings, P. (2002). *Policing: A short history*. Cullompton: Willan.

Reiner, R. (1985). *The politics of the police* (1st ed.). London: Harvester Weatsheaf.

Reiner, R. (2007). *Law and order*. Cambridge: Polity.

Reiner, R. (2010a). *The politics of the police* (4 ed.). Oxford: Oxford University Press.

Reiner, R. (2010b). New theories of policing: A social democratic critique. In D. Downes, R. Hobbs, & T. Newburn (Eds.), *The eternal recurrence of crime and control: Essays for Paul Rock* (pp. 141–182). Oxford: Oxford University Press.

Reiner, R. (2012a). Policing and social democracy: Resuscitating a lost perspective. *Journal of Police Studies, 25*, 91–114.

Reiner, R. (2012b). What's left? The prospects for social democratic criminology. *Crime Media and Culture, 8*(2), 135–150.

Reiner, R. (2012c). *In praise of fire brigade policing: Contra common sense conceptions of the police role*. London: Howard League.

Reiner, R. (2015). Revisiting the classics: Three seminal founders of the study of policing: Michael Banton, Jerome Skolnick and Egon Bittner. *Policing and Society, 25*(3), 308–327.

Reiner, R., & Spencer, S. (Eds.) (1993). *Accountable policing: Effectiveness, empowerment and equity*. London: Institute for Public Policy Research.

Reith, C. (1956). *A new study of police history*. London: Oliver and Boyd.

Rock, P. (2005). Chronocentrism and British criminology. *The British Journal of Sociology, 56*(3), 473–491.

Ronn, K. V. (2012). Democratizing strategic intelligence?—On the feasibility of an objective, decision-making framework when assessing threats and harms or organized crime. *Policing, 7*(1), 53–62.

Rubin, J. (1972). Police identity and the police role. In R. F. Steadman (Ed.), *The police and the community*. Baltimore: John Hopkins Press.

Ruddell, R., & Jones, N. A. (2013). *Austerity policing: Responding to crime during economic downturns*. Regina: Collaborative Centre for Justice and Safety.

Sarwar, K. (1989). Working with Asian women and the police. In C. Dunhill (Ed.), *Boys in blue: Women's challenge to the police*. London: Virago Press.

Scraton, P. (1987). *Law, order and the authoritarian state*. Milton Keynes: Open University Press.

Shapland, J., & Vagg, J. (1988). *Policing by the public*. London: Routledge.

Shearing, C. (2007). Policing our future. In A. Henry & D. J. Smith (Eds.), *Transformations of policing*. Aldershot: Ashgate.

Shearing, C., & Stenning, P. (2012). The shifting boundaries of policing: Globalisation and its possibilities. In T. Newburn & J. Peay (Eds.), *Policing: Politics, culture and control*. Oxford: Hart.

Sheptycki, J. (1991). Using the state to change society, the example of domestic violence. *The Journal of Human Justice, 3*(1), 47–66.

Sheptycki, J. (2003). The governance of organised crime in Canada. *The Canadian Journal of Sociology, 28*(3), 489–517.

Sheptycki, J. (2004). Organizational pathologies in police intelligence systems: Some contributions to the lexicon of intelligence-led policing. *The European Journal of Criminology, 1*(3), 307–332.

Sheptycki, J. (2007). The constabulary ethic and the transnational condition. In *Crafting transnational policing* (pp. 32–71). Oxford: Hart.

Sheptycki, J., & O'Rourke-Dicarlo, D. (2011). Existential predicaments and constabulary ethics. In R. Lippens & J. Hardie-Bic (Eds.), *Crime, governance and existential predicaments* (pp. 108–128, Chap. 5). London: Palgrave Macmillan.

Solanke, I. (2009). Putting race and gender together: A new approach to intersectionality. *The Modern Law Review, 72*(5), 723–749.

Southall Black Sisters. (1989). Two struggles: Challenging male violence and the police. In C. Dunhill (Ed.), *Boys in blue: Women's challenge to the police*. London: Virago Press.

Stenning, P. C. (1995). *Accountability for criminal justice: Selected essays*. Toronto: University of Toronto Press.

Lord Stevens (2011). Policing for a better Britain. http://www.lse.ac.uk/social-Policy/Researchcentresandgroups/mannheim/pdf/policingforabetterbritain.pdf.

Tchaikovsky, C. (1989). The inappropriate women. In C. Dunhill (Ed.), *Boys in blue: Women's challenge to the police*. London: Virago Press.

Townsend, C. (1993). *Making the peace: Public order and public security in modern Britain*. Oxford: Oxford University Press.

Waddington, P. A. J. (1993). *Calling the police*. Aldershot: Avebury.

Walker, S., & Archbold, C. (2014). *The new world of police accountability*. Thousand Oaks: Sage.

Weatheritt, M. (1986). *Innovations in policing*. London: Croom Helm.

Weisburd, D., Feucht, T., Hakimi, I., Mock, L. F., & Perry, S. (2009). *To protect and serve: Policing in an age of terrorism*. Dordrecht/London: Springer.

Wilson, J. Q. (1968). *Varieties of police behavior*. Cambridge: Harvard University Press.

Zedner, L. (2006). Policing before the police. *British Journal of Criminology, 46*(1), 78–96.

7

Seven Ways to Make Prisons Work

Francis T. Cullen, Daniel P. Mears, Cheryl Lero Jonson,
and Angela J. Thielo

Introduction

Prisons are often portrayed as inherently inhumane and criminogenic and
the explanation proceeds along these lines: prisons' inhumanity stems
from the very nature of total institutions (Goffman 1961); it is not natural for humans to be caged, and enforcing conformity will inevitably
lead to coercion (Zimbardo 2007) and use of the "hole," if not physical
brutality (Rothman 1980) and psychic manipulation (Foucault 1977).

F.T. Cullen (✉)
School of Criminal Justice, University of Cincinnati, Cincinnati, OH, USA

D.P. Mears
College of Criminology and Criminal Justice, Florida State University,
Tallahassee, FL, USA

C.L. Jonson
Department of Criminal Justice, Xavier University, Cincinnati, OH, USA

A.J. Thielo
Department of Criminal Justice, University of Louisville, Louisville, KY, USA

© The Editor(s) (if applicable) and The Author(s) 2016
R. Matthews (ed.), *What is to Be Done About Crime and Punishment?*,
DOI 10.1057/978-1-137-57228-8_7

The omnipresent pains of imprisonment will result in adaptations in which inmates bind closer together to resist their subjugation, creating an oppositional culture that only deepens offenders' commitment to crime (Sykes 1958). In this context, the noble goal of rehabilitation—of correcting prisoners—will be unreachable, as discretionary enforced therapy will become yet another futile tool in the effort to achieve inmate compliance (Martinson 1974; Rothman 1980). Except for the small number of truly predatory criminals for which incapacitation is the only option, imposing a prison sentence has no moral or practical justification. The fact that prisons drain the public treasury, especially when employed on a massive scale, is yet another compelling reason to avoid their use.

This view, which is fundamental to criminologists' professional ideology (Cullen and Gendreau 2001), creates a difficult conundrum. If prisons are inherently damaging, then it makes little sense to try to improve them. Such efforts will achieve, at best, incremental and temporary reform. At worst, they will lend legitimacy to an evil institution, suggesting that incarceration can, in some sense, work. Ignoring prisons, however, only relinquishes their control to more conservative elements that wish to immiserate inmates in the belief that harsh conditions are morally deserved and teach the valuable lesson that crime does not pay. The results, such as those seen in California, have been disquieting (Kruttschnitt and Gartner 2005; Page 2011; Petersilia 2008; Simon 2014).

Although notable exceptions exist (for examples, see Cullen et al. 2014), criminologists have resolved this conundrum by opting to forgo the task of being a major force in improving prisons. Instead, they have mainly retreated to detailing the harms of institutional life (e.g., sexual victimization) and, more often, to writing elegant treatises about the intractable rise of mass imprisonment (see, e.g., Clear and Frost 2014; Currie 2013; Garland 2001; Gottschalk 2006; Pratt 2009; Tonry 2004; Whitman 2003). Although this choice to neglect incarcerated inmates was made independently by individual scholars, the collective consequence has been that criminologists have abandoned millions of prisoners to negotiate incarceration on their own. Progressive critics may have gained moral capital through their outsider status, but only at the expense of remaining powerless to halt the rise of mass imprisonment and conditions of confinement that too often have undermined inmates' human dignity (Simon 2014). Do we not have an obligation to make prison life work better for them?

In *Governing Prisons*, DiIulio (1987) offered a dramatically different perspective, arguing that prisons were manageable and that institutional life could be made safer, healthier, and more reformative. He called for scholars to become engaged in prison research and "to ponder more seriously the strengths and weakness of different ways of thinking about prisons" (1987, p. 275). Ironically, although he wished to improve inmates' living conditions, his perspective was seen as conservative and in violation of criminologists' professional ideology. Part of DiIulio's identification as a right-winger and his subsequent rejection was self-induced. He prominently chose to trumpet the "morality of imprisonment" (1987, p. 259), to demonstrate empirically the cost effectiveness of prisons (DiIulio and Piehl 1991), and to argue stridently that incarceration was crime reducing and the only feasible option for "super predators" (Bennett et al. 1996; more broadly, see DiIulio and Logan 1992). Alas, his controversial policy stances earned him much opprobrium from criminologists and masked an important correctional reality that *Governing Prisons* was meant to reveal.

In this regard, through his comparative analysis of correctional facilities, DiIulio (1987) showed convincingly that the quality of prison life varied across institutions (see also Wright 1994). He also was accurate in rejecting sociologists' nothing works doctrine, taking them to task for assuming that the informal inmate order rendered prison staff impotent to manage institutions more effectively (for a similar critique of crime policy, see Wilson 1975). Regardless of whether his particular theory of efficacious institutional administration has merit, DiIulio made the key insight that prison managers mattered, either enhancing or worsening life in captive society. This argument was no different than saying that good basketball coaches, high school principals, or corporate CEOs produce better organizations than their less talented counterparts. Thus, embracing the "governmentability of prisons," he called for research on "the conditions under which prisons can be improved" (1987, p. 275). Unfortunately, his request was substantially ignored.

Although no advocates of the indiscriminate use of incarceration, we believe that DiIulio was correct in calling for, in essence, a science of institutional life. We favor criminologists using their expertise to inform the conversation about how to improve the quality of and outcomes produced by prisons. Discussions are underway on whether it will be possible to substantially downsize prisons in the United States—and perhaps elsewhere

(Gottschalk 2015; Petersilia and Cullen 2015; Simon 2014). Regardless of where this conversation leads, the stubborn reality is that for the foreseeable future, more than two million offenders will remain locked up each day in the United States. In this context, the imperative seems clear, criminologists should provide realistic ideas on how to make existing prisons more humane and effective. Undoubtedly, a lengthy list of worthy suggestions might be made (see Cullen et al. 2014). For our part, we are able to detail seven ways or recommendations, grouped in three sections to improve the prudent usage, operation, and effectiveness of prisons. Ultimately, appropriate scrutiny will separate the wheat from the chaff. Still, even if some recommendations prove utopian and most are deemed to be chaff, we will have no regrets for having joined with others in encouraging a criminological enterprise aimed at making prison work.

Before proceeding, we must add two caveats. Our recommendations are derived from, and are thus likely to pertain mainly to, prisons located in the United States. We do not have sufficient first-hand experiences or academic knowledge to assess how exceptional the US correctional system is in comparison to institutions and practices in other nations. We trust that American exceptionalism in imprisonment is not so extreme as to make our recommendations irrelevant to other contexts. Still, the potential limits of our commentary should be appreciated prior to embarking on an excursion through our list of recommendations.

Second, our recommendations are writ large for inmates, mainly because we believe that these reforms will have general positive effects across the prison population. This orientation, however, is not intended to downplay the special challenges facing specific groups of inmates, especially African-American and female prisoners. For example, in the United States and elsewhere, minorities are disproportionately incarcerated (Tonry 2011). Prisons are thus a setting potentially marked by racial injustice, segregation, and conflict. Especially in institutions located in rural areas, Black inmates are guarded by White prison officers who may harbor stereotypes that can lead to misunderstanding, if not to inequitable disciplinary action. They are also often unprepared to return to their home neighborhoods—typically, impoverished inner-city communities from which reentering offenders frequently cycle back to prison (Clear 2007; Hemmens and Stohr 2014). Women inmates similarly experience unique difficulties. These may include sexual harassment and abuse, limited contact with their children for whom they are the primary caregivers, vocational programs based on gender stereotypes (e.g., training in domestic skills), inadequate mental health and medical care for problems experienced by women (e.g., trauma from prior physical or sexual abuse, pregnancy), and treatment interventions that do not take gender-specific risk factors into account (Commission on Sex in Prison 2014; Holsinger 2014; Kruttschnitt and Gartner 2005; Stohr et al. 2015). In short, any comprehensive blueprint to "make prisons work" will need to address conditions of confinement that are both general to all inmates and specific to any given group of inmates.

Improve Prison Life

Recommendation 1. Make Prisons Less Crowded

Prisons cannot be seen as an inexhaustible resource and a dumping ground for every sort of offender. Such institutions will not work, or work as well as they could, if policymakers and judges do not care if they are filled to overcapacity. To be sure, most prison sentences are not gratuitous. They can be justified by the seriousness of the current offense, the chronicity of the defendant's criminality, and/or by discretion or mandates tied to existing criminal statutes. Even so, just because a prison sentence can be handed out does not mean that it should be. Fortunately, there is a growing recognition in the United States that high absolute levels of incarceration are not sustainable (Aviram 2015; Petersilia and Cullen 2015). The capacity to actually downsize prisons is likely lacking (Gottschalk 2015), so bolder steps will be necessary to take advantage of this climate of reform and reduce the inmate population.

Discussing concrete downsizing policies is outside the parameters of this essay. Elsewhere, however, we have advocated a cap-and-trade approach in which local communities are given an allotment of prison beds and would have to pay extra for exceeding this usage (Jonson et al. 2014, 2015). The key insight is that most counties will not curtail their use of state imprisonment so long as it is a free service (i.e., the state pays for offenders sent to state prisons). Prosecutors are oriented toward seeking harsh sanctions, and judges incur political liability if they sentence an offender to the community who later commits a heinous crime. Better to incarcerate than be sorry. Thus downsizing is unlikely unless this perverse system of incentives is reversed—whether through a cap-and-trade system, subsidies and justice reinvestment, or other inducements.

Three compelling reasons exist for curtailing the overconsumption of prisons. First, a custodial placement is not effective in changing inmate behavior. On a common-sense level, high recidivism rates for released prisoners undermine any claim that incarceration scares offenders straight. For reentering prisoners, about two-thirds are arrested within three years and three-fourths within five years (Langan and Levin 2002; Durose et al. 2014; see also Mears and Cochran 2015; Jonson and Cullen 2015). More salient, although the effects are complex and the data limited (Mears et al. forthcoming), the available evaluation literature provides no evidence that prisons specifically deter reoffending. Compared to a noncustodial sanction, a stay in prison either has a null effect on recidivism or is slightly criminogenic—results, by the way, that are found crossculturally (Cullen et al. 2011; Jonson 2010; Nagin et al. 2009; Villettaz et al. 2015). Prisons incapacitate to a degree and exact just desserts, but establishing their value beyond these outcomes is difficult.

Given the ineffectiveness and high cost of confinement, every effort should be made to divert offenders from prison. Risk-assessment should be used to identify low-risk offenders who pose little threat to public safety and whose criminality might well be deepened by incarceration (Smith 2006). Low-risk offenders generally require minimal supervision on standard probation. If some sanction is required, these offenders might best be required to provide restitution to victims or be persuaded to engage in a restorative justice conference. For higher risk offenders, the case for imprisonment is perhaps stronger. Still, a preferable alternative for many of these potential inmates would be community supervision and placement in an evidence-based treatment program (Latessa and Smith 2011). Further, specialty courts—such as drug, mental health, and veterans' courts—are a useful mechanism for identifying at-risk offenders with special troubles and then diverting them from incarceration into interventions designed to address their specific social and criminogenic needs (Baldwin 2013; Mitchell 2011).

Second, prisons filled to, or in excess of, designed capacity make the delivery of treatment services and the provision of prosocial structured daily activities difficult, if not impossible (Steiner and Meade 2014). Due to crowding, for example, inmate idleness in California became rampant. In 2006, half of the state's inmates received no work or treatment program assignment during their sentence (Petersilia 2008). In fact, crowded prisons lead to an emphasis on sheer incapacitation and to the embrace of custody as the preeminent consideration in institutional construction and operation (Kruttschnitt and Gartner 2005; Page 2011; Petersilia 2008; Simon 2014).

Third, severe crowding has the potential to create unsafe and unhealthy prisons (Simon 2014; Steiner and Meade 2014). In *Mass Incarceration on Trial*, Simon (2014) provides a compelling account of the evolution of *Brown v. Plata* (131 S.Ct. 1910 [2011]), the US Supreme Court case that mandated the reduction of California's prison population, which had climbed to over 170,000, by 46,000 inmates (33,000 by the time the decision was issued). In its institutional building spree, California designed "infrastructure for water and sewerage to operate at 190 percent of capacity while providing for medical and mental health care not even at a normal occupancy level" (2014, p. 121). Faced with crowded and often chaotic prisons, correctional officials and staff were either unwilling or unable to give inmates timely and needed access to medical services. Mentally ill offenders also often suffered without treatment. Thus, while awaiting transfer to a secure treatment facility, inmates manifesting "psychotic delusions and powerful impulses of self-destruction" were "left to stand naked" for prolonged periods in tiny "dry cells" that gave them "no place to lie down or to relieve themselves" (2014, pp. 146–147). The resulting preventable discomfort, disease, and death led the Supreme Court to find that these conditions were unconstitutional, permitting practices that were "incompatible with the concept of human dignity" and that had "no place in civilized society" (quoted in Simon 2014, p. 133).

Taken together, these considerations suggest that prisons should be used judiciously and should be transformed into more effective social institutions. Much of the remainder of this essay speaks to the issue of how life inside prisons can be made more productive.

Recommendation 2: Make It Possible for Inmates to Earn Rewards

In 1851 Alexander Maconochie published a book on the moral and effective ways to manage prisoners. He had been charged in 1840 by the United Kingdom's Secretary of State for the Colonies with implementing a new system of management at the convict colony on Norfolk Island. His charge included taking responsibility for the convicts' moral welfare. Maconochie developed what came to be known as the Mark's System, which entailed a carrot and stick approach to incentivizing inmates to follow rules. Marks could be earned or lost based on behavior. At the same time Maconochie sought to eliminate cruel or degrading treatment of convicts. His experiment at Norfolk Island, detailed in a fictionalized account by Norval Morris (2002), highlighted tensions in prison management that resonate in contemporary times. These tensions center on a basic question: How exactly should inmates be treated? Or, put somewhat differently: What exactly are the goals of incarceration and how best should inmates be managed or treated to achieve these goals—including retribution and reduced offending?

The questions implicate tensions that persist into the present. The tensions that inhere to them have impeded progress. Consider Maconochie's (1851, p. 26) words:

> It may be said that I thus overlooked, or even sacrificed, the great object— that of punishment—for which the prisoners were sent on the Island; but, as I still conceive, not so. I carried into effect the full letter and spirit of the law, and merely did not indulge in excesses beyond it. Every man's sentence was to imprisonment and hard labour; the Island was his prison. … What I really did spare was, the unnecessary humiliation which is the fashion to impose on prisoners besides; and which, I believe, does more moral injury than all other incidents put together of ordinary Prison life. It crushes the weak, unnecessarily irritates the strong, indisposes all to submission and reform, and is, in truth, neither intended by the law, nor consistent with the professions made by lawgivers when framing it.

Over 150 years later, this tension was explicitly and prominently documented in news coverage about Guantánamo Bay, home of a United

States' detention camp. The *New York Times*, for example, published an in-depth account of the change in leadership at Guantánamo and the opposing approaches the different wardens employed (Golden 2006). The tensions mirrored almost exactly those in which Maconochie had found himself enmeshed. Maconochie arrived at an Island that relied on torture, abuse, and degrading treatment of inmates. Education, treatment, or moral reform were deemed largely irrelevant.

Similarly, when Col. Mike Bumgarner assumed command of the Guantánamo Bay camp, he inherited a camp that emphasized zero tolerance for infractions and employed punishment frequently and, to some observers, excessively. Bumgarner brought a different sensibility. He wanted a peaceful camp. His approach? Work with the inmates and improve living conditions—such as reducing noise, improving food quality, and allowing inmates to have access to religious books—while enforcing rules consistently and fairly. As with Maconochie's experiment, conditions appeared to improve, but in both cases high-profile incidents cast a shadow on the improvements and led to a return to rigid adherence to rule enforcement.

Little evidence exists, however, that a control-oriented approach based largely on punishment reduces prison misconduct. This limited effect occurs in part because it does little to address factors known to contribute to prison violations and infractions (Bottoms 1999; Gendreau et al. 1997), and in part because it does not resemble approaches that research has found to promote rule compliance. For example, the meta-analysis conducted by French and Gendreau (2006) indicated that behavioral programs that target criminogenic factors (e.g., antisocial attitudes and beliefs, association with others engaged in offending) can be effective in reducing prison misconduct (see, generally, Latessa et al. 2014). In short, emphasizing control and punishment over humane, consistent, and fair enforcement of rules, and provision of services that target known causes of offending is likely to be ineffective. It is likely, too, to be counterproductive. Studies suggest that how prisons are governed can greatly affect inmate behavior. Bottoms's (1999) review, for example, emphasized that when the authority of the prison system is viewed as legitimate, inmates comply more with the rules. Thus, how prisons are run may matter far more than developing specific protocols or interventions for particular inmates. Put differently, rather than emphasize control or punishment, or focus on high-risk inmates, prison systems may be safer and more orderly if they emphasize a mode of governance that is fair, reasonable, humane, and aimed at helping inmates.

This observation brings us back to Maconochie and the idea of using carrots and sticks to incentivize inmate behavior. It is almost an axiom of human behavior that individuals pursue goals. Prisons, however, typically operate in ways that act as if this axiom does not exist. What is the motivation for a given inmate on a typical day in prison? To survive? To retaliate against perceived or actual injustice? To complete a work task? To manage the boredom that numerous inmate accounts document? Such goals are unlikely to do much to motivate inmates.

The problem, then, lies in the fact that, on the whole, prisons offer little to motivate inmates in productive ways. This situation stems in part from rapid prison expansion that, in turn, has led to the need to emphasize prison construction and staffing over extras such as programming. What can prison systems do to motivate inmates in ways that may support rehabilitation, improved inmate behavior, and reduced post-release offending?

First, they should emphasize an approach to managing prisons that inmates will view as legitimate. If inmates do not perceive prison authority as being wielded in a legitimate manner, they will have little incentive to comply with rules and will feel justified in subverting prison polices and demands. This change in managerial style is likely the most difficult for prison systems to undertake and is also the least amenable to a formulaic response (see, generally, Bottoms 1999). It also is the one most likely to result in a larger improvement of inmate behavior in the aggregate.

Second, prisons should enable inmates to earn rewards of various types. The rewards should be graduated and attainable, and they should consistently flow from compliance with required behaviors. What rewards can be implemented? In truth, the possibilities are endless and limited primarily by the creativity of prison officials, as Maconochie's (1851) example illustrates (see also Bottoms 1999; Morris 2002). Special privileges, for example, can include extra time in prison yards, more freedoms around "campus," more time in the library, extra visitation, and preferred work assignments. In this latter regard, it might be possible to use as a reward employment in a job that pays the minimum or prevailing local wage and that even involves work release to an outside private business.

At present, if prisoners are employed, they are paid a low amount (often as little as 25 cents an hour) (Cullen and Jonson 2011; Kovensky 2014). Under the Prison Industry Enhancement Certification Program, a number of US states have received permission to establish work opportunities with pay similar to that in the private sector (Bureau of Justice Assistance 2004). Some evidence exists that employment in these positions reduces recidivism (Smith, Bechtel, Patrick, Smith, and Wilson-Gentry 2006). A larger debate exists over whether prison labor, even at prevailing wages, might depress the compensation earned by, or take jobs away from, low-skilled workers (Kovensky 2014; Malik 2012). The issue is complex but, overall, the effects on the economy are likely to be marginal and potential benefits for inmates may accrue (Kling and Krueger 1999; Petersik 2000; see also Cullen and Travis 1984). Settling this policy controversy, however, is not necessary, since no call is being made to fully renovate the work status of all prisoners. Rather, we are suggesting only that, on a limited basis, work assignments involving fair wages and some freedom of movement be used as yet another valued carrot in a broader incentive system that rewards inmates for appropriate conduct and manifesting change in a prosocial direction.

Third, reduced time in prison is another option. It carries with it, however, the risk of political divisiveness because it can lead to the concern that inmates only end up serving a fraction of their prison sentence. Still, the issue here ultimately is not the percentage of time served; it is the total amount of time served. Assuming an inmate serves the minimal amount of time that society deems appropriate and needed for a given crime, it would seem appropriate for correctional systems to allow for "early" release above this minimal threshold.

Recommendation 3: Use Science to Improve the Conditions of Confinement

Prisons are often austere and uncomfortable environments, made worse by crowding and poor management (DiIulio 1987; Simon 2014). Inmate suffering is not an explicit component of a prison sentence, but it is seen, in a general way, as part of the price that offenders pay for breaking the law. More so, harsh conditions of confinement are attributed a special utilitarian effect; experiencing pain increases the cost of imprisonment and can help to scare offenders straight. The debate over whether inmates, beyond loss of freedom, should be made to actively suffer while incarcerated to increase just desserts is a value question that we will not confront. We will note in passing, however, that the principle of just desserts is substantially violated when inmates are unequally exposed to or able to cope with painful conditions. More important, the issue of utility is an empirical matter that can be settled more definitively. Notably, the evidence suggests that harsh or painful experiences in prison have no specific deterrence effect on recidivism. If anything, the effect is criminogenic (Cullen et al. 2011; Listwan et al. 2013; see also Sykes 1958).

In this light, conditions of confinement should not be taken as an inevitable part of imprisonment. Rather, far more should be known about how specific conditions of life in prison affect inmates during and after incarceration. When possible, we should rely on the best science available to approach this issue in an evidenced-based way. Research conducted outside prisons can be relied on to highlight areas worthy of investigation. Three can be suggested here: research on sleep, on atmospherics, and on situational crime prevention.

We have all experienced the unpleasant ramifications of not getting a good night's sleep, that foggy, sluggish, irritable state that seems to hover over us the entire day. However, there are more ominous consequences besides being a bit slower and a tad grumpier that accompany not obtaining a solid eight hours of shuteye each night. Sleep deprivation, as well as enduring sleep restriction (six hours or less sleep a night), has been found to adversely affect a person's mood, short- and long-term physical and mental health, learning capabilities, memory retention, cognitive abilities, judgment, ability to concentrate, or to do physical tasks (Alvarez and Ayas 2004; Banks et al. 2010; Beebe et al. 2010; Billiard and Bentley 2004; Deweerdt 2013; Harrison and Horne 2000; Killgore 2010; Knutson et al. 2007; Von Dongen et al. 2003). These effects can be so detrimental that denying individuals sleep in excess of twenty-four hours has been commonly used as a technique of torture both in the United States and abroad, and it has been deemed to be a violation of the Eighth and Fourteenth Amendments of the US Constitution (Physicians for Human Rights 2007; *Ashcraft* v. *Tennessee* 1944; *Keenan v. Hall* 1996; *Merritt v. Hawk* 2001).

Although more than two million individuals daily say goodnight in America's prisons, remarkably little research exists that examines the relationship between sleep deprivation and prisoner outcomes during and after incarceration. By contrast, sleep-related studies have focused on schoolchildren, athletes, healthcare workers, adolescents, and even rats (Deurveiher et al. 2013; Eastridge et al. 2003; Gildner et al. 2014; Milewski et al. 2014; Spruyt et al. 2011; Telzer et al. 2013). This void in the research is surprising given that science has consistently revealed that sleep problems are associated with an array of disquieting consequences. In addition to those listed above, the lack of sound sleep has been found to increase aggressiveness, hostility, and risk-taking behavior in children, adolescents, and adults (Ireland and Culpin 2006; Kamphuis et al. 2012; Telzer et al. 2013). Even with this information readily available, correctional systems within the United States continue to neglect how conditions of confinement may affect the sleep patterns of its wards.

It is not difficult to imagine why prisoners may be at risk of sleep deprivation (Ireland and Culpin 2006). In a rare study of juvenile and adolescent offenders, Ireland and Culpin (2006) discovered that individuals are likely to report fewer hours of sleep, more night awakenings, and a longer time to fall asleep during their incarceration than they experienced prior to their detainment. Why does the quality of sleep decrease during incarceration? One answer could be that prisons, by their nature, are not built to be quiet, peaceful sanctuaries with plush mattresses and pillows conducive to uninterrupted and sound sleep. Rather, prisons are warehouses of punishment that are often noisy, anxiety-producing, overcrowded places with minimal accommodation. Thus, the thickness of an average-sized mattress purchased by the general public ranges from eight to 18 inches. By contrast, mattresses in prison often range between two to four inches thick with an attached pillow (www.anchortex.com; www.derbyindustries.com). The general public enjoys high-thread count cotton sheets, while the blankets in prison are commonly made of wool (www.northwestwoolen.com). Most of the general public have their own sleeping quarters that they may share with a loved one, while in California over 95 percent of the incarcerated population shares a cell with at least one other person, typically not of their choosing (California Department of Corrections and Rehabilitation 2013). In combination with the stress and anxiety often associated with confinement, these uncomfortable accommodations undoubtedly contribute to sleep deprivation among prisoners. More generally, given that the lack of sleep hinders learning and cognitive functioning, increases aggressiveness and hostility, and reduces overall physical and mental well-being, it is counterproductive to create physical and social environments that may needlessly hinder inmates' quality of sleep.

Second, beyond how the quality of sleep affects our mood, thinking, behavior, and well-being, we are also influenced by the atmosphere around us. Aspects of our environment—or atmospherics as it is called—such as color, lighting, sound, and temperature can impact our actions and emotions, often without our conscious realization (Alter 2013; Jalil et al. 2011). Simply manipulating lighting and music in a restaurant has been found to impact caloric intake, the length of time to finish a meal, and satisfaction (Wansink and van Ittersum 2012), whereas changing the color of an office from red to blue-green has been associated with fewer negative moods among workers (Kwallek 2005). Retailers strategically select the tempo and genre of music played, the type and color of lighting, and even the aromas in their facilities to alter the amount of time consumers spend in their store and increase their sales (Alter 2013; Babin et al. 2003; Jalil et al. 2011; Singh 2006; Turley and Milliman 2000; Yalch and Spangenberg 2000). Hospitals have begun to paint traditionally stark white rooms colors such as blue or soft green to lower apprehension and fear among patients (Bosch et al. 2012). In each of these examples, behaviors, feelings, moods, and thinking are being shaped by stimuli in the environment. However, prisons are often initially built with no consideration given to the vast knowledge surrounding effects of atmospherics on an individual's well-being or behavior.

The atmospherics of most prisons are bleak. Prisons are stark, drab, and plain, punctuated by loud noises and marked by a distinct odor due to poor hygiene and lack of air circulation. When prisons are constructed, meticulous attention is paid to security concerns. By contrast, scant consideration is given to the science showing how color, lighting, temperature, and other environmental stimuli influence certain types of behavior. Some notable strides in the use of atmospherics in prison have been made. In the late 1970s and early 1980s, some correctional facilities painted their cells in what would become known as Baker-Miller, or Drunk-Tank, Pink because it was believed that this soft hue would result in lower aggressive behavior among offenders (Alter 2013; Schauss 1979). Although this practice initially showed success, it was eventually abandoned due to inconsistent results (Alter 2013). These findings do not mean, however, that changing the prison environment is not a worthwhile endeavor. A promising line of research suggests that simply swapping halogen lights for LEDs could result in less vandalism and aggression within prison settings (Custodial Review 2013). Additionally, there are examples, in both the United States and other nations, where the playing of classical music in high-crime areas has been associated with a reduction in robberies, assaults, vandalism, loitering, and other nuisance behaviors (Benzel and Stanley 1990; Hirsch 2007; Timberg 2005). Might such music have similar effects within the confines of prison? Furthermore, taking a cue from the literature on the impact of color in psychiatric hospitals, prisons may want to replace their stark, depressing gray or white wall colors with more calming and soothing colors (such as blue) that reduce the institutional feel of the prison (Gutheil and Daly 1980; Karlin and Zeiss 2006). Using the science of atmospherics, prisons could become a safer and more effective environment for rehabilitation.

Third, one area often ignored when examining the conditions of prisons is the vast literature on the effectiveness of situational crime prevention. Unlike other theories of crime focusing on the motivations of offenders, situational crime prevention argues that altering the opportunity structure of specific crimes is the key to reducing criminal behavior (Clarke 1992; Clarke and Cornish 1985). Cornish and Clarke (2003) provided 25 specific techniques that seek to manipulate the environment in a way to make crime less attractive to potential offenders. The goal is to either increase offenders' perceptions of risks and effort and/or to decrease offenders' perceptions of rewards, provocations, and excuses associated with specific crime events. These techniques, which often involve target hardening, heightening formal and natural surveillance, and avoiding disputes, have been found to reduce crime (Eck 2006; Welsh and Farrington 2008).

Prison administrators, and most scholars who study them, have largely neglected the insights from the situational crime prevention research. An exception, however, is Wortley (2001, 2002), who has sought to apply situational crime prevention specifically to correctional settings. He argues that traditional situational crime prevention's exclusive focus on how the environment impacts opportunities is too narrow. He proposes that the environment can also influence one's motivation for crime. These situational precipitators, which ready individuals to commit crime, include prompts, pressures, permissibility, and provocations. Wortley (2001, 2002) presents a two-stage situation crime prevention model in which both situational precipitators and situational opportunities must be present to engage in crime. Therefore, crime is most successfully reduced when both precipitators and opportunities for crime are reduced.

Most prisons are constructed in ways that focus on the criminal opportunity component of Wortley's theory. Prisons seek to control the opportunities for misconduct, escape, and violence through the use of CCTV, fences, steel doors, formal surveillance, and other custodial measures. However, prisons rarely take into account precipitating factors that may prompt inmates to break rules when an opportunity presents itself—such as the dull cell that triggers depression, the corrupt correctional officer who is serving as a role model for antisocial behavior, the unnecessary regulations that stifle autonomy and create anger, or the noise pollution that fosters noxious stress (Wortley 2002). Thus, according to Wortley (2001, 2002), prisons are ignoring half of the causes of crime. Using some of the techniques mentioned above concerning sleep and atmospherics could be a start in reducing situational precipitators to crime.

It is very possible the goal of having a safe prison while effectively rehabilitating offenders is being undermined by failing to examine the impact that the prison environment itself has on offender sleep, well-being, mood, decision-making, and behavior. This oversight could be contributing to the frequency of violence within prisons, as well as to the high recidivism rates of released offenders, by not developing an environment conducive to rehabilitation. Therefore, states must determine what is more important; making prisons harsh, cold places meant to inflict more suffering beyond the loss of freedom, or using the existing insights of science on what conditions are most conducive to a safer and more rehabilitative prison environment.

Value the Goal of Offender Change

Recommendation 4: Give the Public What It Wants

Coercive prison conditions can exist regardless of the prevailing correctional ideology. As Rothman (1980), among others, has demonstrated, the use of enforced therapy under the guise of saving offenders permitted a range of abuses. Even so, it also is clear that the rehabilitative ideal is a restraint against the purposeful infliction of pain and the enthusiastic embrace of custody. The decline of the Progressives' model of individual treatment ushered in not a system committed to due process and justice but a mean season in corrections marked by austere living conditions and little concern about offender well-being (Cullen 2013; Cullen and Gilbert 2013; Kruttschnitt and Gartner 2005).

Simon (2014, p. 17) details this movement from a correctional system based on a clinical or therapeutic model to a system embracing the "extreme penology" of "total incapacitation." The rehabilitative ideal had recognized not only that some offenders were dangerous but also that others were not. Its logic thus compelled the view that inmates were individuals who had distinct risks and strengths. By contrast, the emergent common sense of the get-tough era portrayed all offenders—regardless of their convicted offense—as potentially violent, prisons as incapable of reforming anyone, and all reentering criminals as a threat to community safety. In this context, expanding institutional capacity—either by prison construction or cramming offenders into already crowded facilities—became a common practice. An emphasis on custody and security thus trumped a concern about offender treatment or general well-being.

According to Simon (2014, p. 157, emphasis in original), the inability to sustain mass imprisonment is now generating a "new common sense" that rejects the old common sense that inmates comprise a "permanent criminal *class* whose threat of future felonies [is] not precisely knowable but presumptively high and unchanging." Instead, there is a recognition that offenders vary in risk levels and that not all offenders need to be incarcerated or, if so, not locked up forever. In short, political and correctional elites are rejecting the logic of total incarceration (when in doubt, lock everyone up), and instead are favoring a more differentiated or individualized view of inmates. By conceptualizing offenders as having individual differences who vary in their potential for change, the new common sense thus contributes to the legitimacy of the rehabilitative ideal in contemporary corrections.

These considerations suggest that, in the end, the social purpose of corrections matters (Allen 1981). Institutions shorn of a firm commitment to offender reform have a dismal record, often becoming austere, custodial, and little more than part of what Simon (1993) calls a "waste management system" (see, e.g., Kruttschnitt and Gartner 2005; Page 2011). Ensuring that rehabilitation serves as a core correctional goal does not guarantee a better institutional environment since, as Rothman (1980) brilliantly demonstrated, "conscience" can be corrupted by "convenience." But even if the aspiration of the rehabilitative ideal is not realized, the aspiration is still present. The warehousing of offenders is immediately seen as illegitimate and counterproductive. Not delivering effective treatment is no longer a sad fact of a custodial regime but an administrative failure to be rectified. And when reentering prisoners recidivate soon thereafter in high numbers, the potential exists to cast some blame on correctional officials.

Phrased bluntly, prisons are unlikely to be improved unless rehabilitation—the correction of offenders—is a preeminent organizational goal. But will the public endorse treatment as a central purpose of imprisonment? Notably, survey research is clear in showing that respondents embrace rehabilitation as a main goal of imprisonment and support virtually all treatment programs aimed at improving offenders' skills, substance abuse problems, and mental health (for overviews, see Cullen 2013; Cullen et al. 2000; Jonson et al. 2013). For example, a 2001 national poll in the United States found that among the sample, 92 percent agreed that "it is a good idea to provide treatment for offenders who are in prison." When asked about specific programs, 71 percent supported giving offenders a "good education," 88 percent supported teaching "them a skill that they can use to get a job when they are released from prison," and 89 percent supported trying to help inmates "change their values and to help them with the emotional problems that caused them to break the law" (Cullen et al. 2002, p. 137). More recently, a 2010 poll in Oregon found that 53.4 percent of the public believed that "rehabilitation" should be the main emphasis of prison; only 37.5 percent chose "protect society" and 9.2 percent "punishment." Further, more than nine out of ten Oregonians favored providing inmates who returned to society with mental health services (94. 2 percent), drug treatment (91.7 percent), education (91.3 percent), and job training (92.8 percent) (Sundt et al. 2015). This finding is not idiosyncratic to a left-leaning state such as Oregon. A 2013 survey of likely voters in the "red state" of Texas found broad support for the policy of not incarcerating non-violent offenders. When asked about "dealing with non-violent criminals in Texas," 58.2 percent said that rehabilitation was either the "most important" or "second most important" correctional goal (Thielo et al. 2015).

Also relevant is a 1999 study conducted by Applegate (2001) in Orange County (Orlando), Florida. In the midst of the mass imprisonment movement, residents were asked if they preferred to make prisons more austere. Presented with a list of 26 "programs, services, or privileges," they were instructed to state whether they wanted to "eliminate" or "keep" each amenity (2001, p. 257). Two findings are instructive. First, few in the sample favored eliminating educational, vocational, and psychological programs. Amenities that were opposed involved sex (e.g., condoms, pornography), entertainment (e.g., R-rated movies, tennis), exercise that made offenders more dangerous (e.g., weightlifting, martial arts), or physically harmful practices (e.g., smoking cigarettes). Second, the sample members were asked what considerations would make them more likely to keep a given prison amenity. Notably, the prospect of rehabilitation mattered most. Thus, 92.9 percent responded that they would oppose austerity and retain amenities if they could be "convinced that these services and activities lower the chances that inmates will commit new crimes after they are released from prison" (2001, p. 262).

In short, the public supports using imprisonment for a valid social purpose—in this case, employing rehabilitation programs to save inmates from a life in crime. Under the auspices of the authentic pursuit of offender treatment, citizens are willing to endorse the wide use of programs and a more humane prison environment. In this light, we should give the public what it wants.

Recommendation 5: Make Wardens Accountable for Correcting Offenders

Many obstacles exist to the effective delivery of treatment services to inmates, including, for example, prison crowding, budget constraints, and a lack of qualified treatment professionals. Still, the source of this failure can be traced to a more fundamental factor: "correctional officials *get paid to maintain order and not to rehabilitate*" (Cullen and Gilbert 1982, p. 267, emphasis in original). This prioritization of incentives is not new, and historically it has limited the therapeutic potential of institutions. Writing about the corruption of "conscience" in the progressive era, Rothman (1980, p. 157) notes that "in the end, it was security that counted, not rehabilitation and the prison administrators knew it, fashioned their routine accordingly, and survived in power."

Wardens and other prison officials could be expected to oppose being held accountable for inmate recidivism. Two likely objections would be that they do not have sufficient funding to provide adequate treatment to all offenders and that they do not control what occurs after inmates are released. Still, the current state of affairs in which they accept *no accountability* for offender reform and public safety is indefensible. Even if their impact on recidivism has limits, this does not mean that their actions make no difference whatsoever—especially when offenders are under their supervision for years on end (see DiIulio 1987). Further, developments in law enforcement are instructive. Police managers no longer deny accountability for crime rates but often embrace it. A new era of policing innovation—under such names as Compstat, problem-oriented policing, and hot spots policing—has spread across the United States and elsewhere (Weisburd and Braga 2006). These managers face obstacles, not the least of which is that they do not control the root causes of crime in their communities. But they have rejected the idea that offender decisions are unaffected by police strategy, deployment, and practices. Although eliminating crime is utopian, the aspiration to make communities safer has led to police reforms that have had demonstrable effects.

Accountability in prisons is likely to have positive effects (Cullen et al. 2012). First, it will compel the development of an information system that typically does not exist. To hold officials accountable, it will be necessary to calculate, taking inmates' risk levels into consideration, rates of recidivism by correctional institution, by time spent in different facilities, by treatment program participation, and by the communities into which prisoners were released. Second, once this information is compiled, wardens and other officials will need to meet to discuss areas of success and areas in need of improvement. It might then be possible to identify best practices and to create a knowledge base for organizational reform. Similar to policing, an impetus for innovation might well emerge as some prisons outperform others, with effective models disseminated to other jurisdictions. More experimentation on how to create a prison that cures might be forthcoming. Officials would also have an incentive to hire staff with treatment expertise, to lobby for funds to institute more effective programs, and to call for accountability for community corrections agencies that are failing at prisoner reentry.

Accountability requires consequences, but this does not mean that wardens and other correctional officials and staff should have their heads placed on the chopping block (Cullen et al. 2012). As with offenders, harsh threats and punishments perceived to be unfair are likely to produce defiance (Braithwaite 2002; Sherman 1993). In the end, if wardens or others prove particularly recalcitrant and inept, their removal will be justified. But the task is not to precipitate an oppositional culture but a culture of success in which positive steps are supported and rewarded. Corporate sales departments, for example, regularly establish annual goals and reward high performance with honors (e.g., employee of the year), vacations (e.g., to Hawaii), bonuses, raises, and promotions. It would be possible to allocate rewards to wardens, staff, and/or units in a prison.

This last observation is important. Although this recommendation focuses on wardens' responsibility for recidivism, it would be advisable to seek to broaden the culture and practice of accountability to include all employees. Although the goal of reducing crime among reentering inmates should never be attenuated, it would be possible to develop a range of performance standards within the prison. These might include reducing inmates' victimization and disciplinary infractions, increasing attainment in educational programs, and delivering higher quality medical care. Again, the challenge is to create a system that monitors outcomes and provides meaningful, positive incentives for meritorious staff performance.

Intervene Effectively with Prisoners

Recommendation 6: Use the RNR Model to Rehabilitate Offenders

The risk–need–responsivity model of offender rehabilitation—known as the RNR model—is based on three core principles (for more detailed discussions, see Andrews and Bonta 2010; Smith 2013). First, the risk principle (R) argues that treatment programs should be targeted for higher risk offenders, with the level of risk determined by an actuarial assessment instrument that measures the criminogenic needs of offenders. Second, the need principle (N) proposes that interventions should target for change those dynamic risk factors that are the strongest predictors of recidivism. For example, antisocial attitudes or cognitions are both dynamic (unlike age, they can be changed) and are strongly related to reoffending. Third, the responsivity principle (R) asserts that treatment modalities should be used that are capable of changing criminogenic needs (e.g., use of cognitive-behavior therapy to change antisocial attitudes). Substantial evidence exists that programs adhering to these principles achieve meaningful reductions in recidivism (Andrews and Bonta 2010; Gendreau et al. 2006; Smith et al. 2009).

Prison rehabilitation programs should be based on the RNR model. This approach makes considerable sense. It argues that treatment should be focused on offenders with the highest propensity to recidivate, should target for change the empirically demonstrated predictors of recidivism, and should employ modalities capable of changing these predictors or criminogenic needs. Why would an intervention focus on low-risk offenders who have little wrong with them, target predictors unrelated to recidivism, or use modalities incapable of changing these sources of reoffending? The key to the RNR model, however, is not just its sensible internal logic. Its appeal also lies in its advocates' commitment to rooting the paradigm in a wealth of scientific data. Once a much slimmer volume, the 5th edition of Andrews and Bonta's (2010) *The Psychology of Criminal Conduct*—the RNR model's criminological bible—now runs to 672 pages (Cullen 2012).

To be sure, other rehabilitation perspectives are gaining supporters, especially those that seek to reduce recidivism by bolstering offenders' strengths rather than trying to fix their deficits or criminogenic needs (for discussions, see Brayford et al. 2010; Craig et al. 2013; Raynor and Robinson 2009). Developed by Tony Ward and others, the most sophisticated of these new strategies is the Good Lives Model, now known by its acronym of the GLM (see, in particular, Ward and Maruna 2007). Rooted in positive psychology, the GLM emphasizes the importance of motivating offenders to visualize and then accomplish the changes needed to avoid crime and live a "good life". It rejects the RNR model's focus on targeting and treating criminogenic needs (also called dynamic risk factors) as too narrow (Willis and Ward 2013; for a response, see Andrews, Bonta, and Wormith 2011). "From a GLM perspective," note Carich, Wilson, Carich, and Calder (2010, p. 193), "it is not sufficient to teach skills or to reduce or manage risk. Instead, the task of achieving and maintaining behaviour change needs to be meaningfully embedded within the notions of personal well-being, personal identity and a positive lifestyle." More popular outside than inside North America, the GLM and similar approaches should not be dismissed. If found to reduce recidivism, they should be added to the treatment repertoire—alongside the RNR model—available to prison staff. At this point, however, the empirical support for the GLM, though promising, remains in its beginning stages (Willis and Ward 2013). Accordingly, using GLM programs in place of RNR programs potentially has substantial opportunity costs (Cullen 2012). Why rely on a plausible intervention based on modest or scant evidence (GLM programs) as opposed to a more proven intervention strategy (RNR model programs)?

Finally, in its full elaboration, the RNR model has 15 principles (Andrews and Bonta 2010, pp. 46–47). Because the perspective was developed by psychologists (Andrews, Bonta, Gendreau, and others), the first principle is "respect for the person and the normative context" (2010, p. 46). Thus, Andrews and Bonta assert that services are to be "delivered with respect for the person, including respect for personal autonomy, being humane, ethical, just, legal, decent, and being otherwise normative" (p. 46). The model emphasizes "the principle of human service," arguing that it "is through human, clinical, and social services that the major causes of crime may be addressed" (p. 47). By contrast, the model rejects "getting mean, getting even, and getting justice" because punitive legal sanctions are both ineffective and often unethical (p. 477). Thus, on both normative and scientific grounds, the RNR model provides a compelling justification for transforming prisons from coercive and custodial environments into therapeutic communities that place the delivery of targeted human services at their core.

Recommendation 7: Teach Prison Officers to Be Change Agents

Within probation and parole, an important line of inquiry has emerged that is exploring how the nature of supervision affects offender recidivism. Although office meetings between supervising officers and probationers or parolees are often limited (i.e., a half hour or less), the nature of these interactions can have a meaningful impact on supervision success or failure. Rather than assume that these appointments are too brief to matter, research now indicates that officers can use these interactions to be change agents and reduce recidivism (Kennealy et al. 2012; Manchak et al. 2014; Raynor et al. 2014; Raynor and Vanstone 2015). In fact, programs have been developed that have successfully trained supervising officers to use office visits for therapeutic purposes (Andrews and Bonta 2010; Bonta et al. 2011; Lowenkamp et al. 2014; Robinson et al. 2012; Smith et al. 2012).

In general, effective supervision conforms to the "core correctional staff practices" based on the RNR model (Andrews and Bonta 2010, p. 47). As identified by Dowden and Andrews (2004, pp. 204–205), there are "five dimensions of effective correctional practice" (CCP): (1) the "effective use of authority" by dealing with offenders in a "firm but fair" manner; (2) "appropriately modeling and reinforcing anticriminal attitudes and behaviors through directive positive and/or negative reinforcement"; (3) "teaching concrete problem-solving skills to the offender"; (4) using community resources effectively, such as job referrals and medical referrals; and (5) maximizing therapeutic influence by creating "open, warm, and enthusiastic communication" so as to develop "mutual respect and liking between the offender and correctional staff member." According to Dowden and Andrews (2004, p. 205), the "fifth and final component of CCP, relationship factors, is also arguably the most important" (see also Manchak et al. 2014). Notably, traditional supervision approaches, including intensive control-oriented supervision, have little impact on reoffending (Bonta et al. 2008; Petersilia and Turner 1993).

Trice (2014) has proposed that prison officers (or correctional officers as they are called in the United States) be trained in the RNR model and core correctional practices to deliver effective supervision. Challenges exist to transferring treatment technology from a community to an institutional setting. Probation and parole officers have the luxury of meeting with an individual offender for a short period of time during a scheduled appointment that supervisees must attend. By contrast, prison officers must supervise tens of inmates for an eight-hour shift within the context of a crowded and potentially dangerous prison (Conover 2000; Page 2011). They have no assigned official therapeutic duties, and a close relationship with an inmate can be exploited and put them in jeopardy of corruption. Still, sending officers into the prison marginally trained to manage inmates, presumably with a tradition-based custodial approach, is a recipe for potential failure. By contrast, line staff have the potential, through their interactions with prisoners, to use core correctional practices to manage offenders and effect behavioral change during incarceration and perhaps beyond. The CCP approach values procedural justice (being firm but fair) and the use of skills to guide offenders to make better decisions. Quality relationships based on trust and respect, as opposed to mistrust and disrespect, can be a conduit through which more effective supervision can be accomplished.

Would prison officers want to expand their role from custodian to include being a change agent? It would be foolish to expect that all officers would embrace such a role. Research shows that some officers possess a clear custodial orientation and harbor negative sentiments toward inmates (see, e.g., Lambert et al. 2014; Misis et al. 2013). However, three considerations are relevant. First, although undoubtedly varying by context, prison officers show support for rehabilitation (Blevins et al. 2007; Cullen et al. 1989). If there is a difficulty, it is that they tend to underestimate coworkers' professional attitudes and overestimate their embrace of custody (Cook and Lane 2014; Klofas and Toch 1982; Toch and Klofas 1982). Second, encouraging a treatment orientation may have positive effects, given that officers' support for rehabilitation is associated with better inmate relations, lower levels of stress, higher job satisfaction, and more commitment to organizational citizenship (Lambert et al. 2014; Misis et al. 2013). Third, although dated, Toch and Klofas (1982, p. 41) found a "desire for job enrichment" among prison officers that would include moving beyond a concern over custody and security to include showing an interest in offenders, at times becoming a father figure, and providing counseling.

Successfully encouraging officers to become behavior change agents is likely to hinge on developing quality CCP training applicable to a prison setting, strong supervisory support that includes incentives for positive performance, and the creation of a therapeutic organizational culture in which all prison staff see offender reform as a valued goal. At the very least, experiments in officers' use of core correctional practices should be undertaken and used to inform reforms in other prison settings.

Conclusion: Toward a Criminology of Imprisonment

By their very nature as total institutions used by the state as an instrument of punishment, prisons are restrictive and potentially damaging. As Sykes (1958) taught us more than a half century ago, a penal institution is a "society of captives," not of free of citizens, and exposes its members to an array of pains of imprisonment. Indeed, "keeping men confined," observed Sykes (1958, p. 130), "is a complex and difficult task." But he cautioned against pessimism and inaction. "The greatest naïveté," he noted, "perhaps lies in those who believe that because progress in methods of reforming the criminal has been so painfully slow and uncertain in the past, little or no progress can be expected in the future" (pp. 133–134). In fact, whether a "prison social system works in the direction of the prisoner's deterioration rather than his rehabilitation" is an issue that confronts "us and not the recalcitrance of the individual inmate" (p. 134).

As with most other organizations, the future of any given prison is not foreordained but, to an important degree, chosen by those with stewardship over it (DiIulio 1987). At its founding, the penitentiary was a source of national pride (Rothman 1971), and into the 1960s correctional systems such as California's were trumpeted for their commitment to research and therapeutic innovation (McKelvey 1977; Petersilia 2008). In choosing the future ahead, we could do worse than to return to the aspiration for correction to have a positive social purpose. In doing so, we would be wise to avoid the excessive optimism that hubris and good intentions have, in the past, encouraged and left unfulfilled. But with a more sober and evidence-based perspective, it might well be possible to improve life within, and the ultimate effects of, prisons.

We have suggested a roster of recommendations that might contribute to an effort to make prisons work better than they do now. Although the seven recommendations are distinct, they coalesce into a coherent strategy for reform. The first task at hand is to make prisons smaller and thus closer in size to their designed capacity. Reducing crowding should be part of a more general strategy to improve the quality of the institutional environment by making it more rewarding and encouraging of positive coping. The second task is to follow the public will by placing rehabilitation at the center of the correctional enterprise and by holding wardens and other officials accountable for treating inmates and reducing their recidivism upon release. And the third task is to rely on the best evidence available to equip those staff dealing with inmates with the knowledge and skills to achieve offender change.

These recommendations, however, should be the beginning, not the end, of theory and research on how best to make prisons work more effectively. Criminologists have a long and valuable tradition of peering into the society of captives and unmasking the disquieting conditions and damaging practices that otherwise would remain hidden from public view. But showing what does not work is not enough to improve the lives of inmates and ultimately to increase public safety. At this point, we need a *criminology of imprisonment* that is devoted to *knowledge construction*—that is, to creating an evidence-based tool kit that prison wardens and staff can use to do their jobs more effectively (see Gleicher et al. 2013). Although the role of critic should never be abandoned, the time has come for scholars to forge an alliance with practitioners to achieve the mutually valued goal of moving beyond the mean season of mass imprisonment and toward a correctional era where stark, custodial, harmful prisons are no longer tolerated.

References

Allen, F. A. (1981). *The decline of the rehabilitative ideal: Penal policy and social purpose*. New Haven: Yale University Press.

Alter, A. (2013). *Drunk tank pink: And other unexpected forces that shape how we think, feel, and behave*. New York: Penguin Group.

Alvarez, G. G., & Avas, N. T. (2004). The impact of daily sleep duration on health: A review of the literature. *Progress in Cardiovascular Nursing, 19*, 56–59.

Andrews, D. A., & Bonta, J. (2010). *The psychology of criminal conduct* (Vol. 5). New Providence: Anderson/LexisNexis.

Andrews, D. A., Bonta, J., & Wormith, S. (2011). The risk-need-responsivity (RNR) model: Does adding the good lives model contribute to effective crime prevention? *Criminal Justice and Behavior, 38*, 735–755.

Applegate, B. K. (2001). Penal austerity: Perceived utility, desert, and public attitudes toward prison amenities. *American Journal of Criminal Justice, 25*, 253–268.

Ashcraft v. *Tennessee* (1944) 322 U.S. 143.

Aviram, H. (2015). *Cheap on crime: Recession-era politics and the transformation of American punishment.* Berkeley: University of California Press.

Babin, B. J., Hardesty, D. M., & Suter, T. A. (2003). Color and shopping intentions: The intervening effect of price fairness and perceived affect. *Journal of Business Research, 56*, 541–551.

Baldwin, J. M. (2013). *Veterans treatment courts: Studying dissemination, implementation, and impact of treatment-oriented criminal courts.* Unpublished Ph.D. dissertation, University of Florida.

Banks, S., Van Dongen, H. P. A., Maislin, G., & Dinges, D. F. (2010). Neurobehavioral dynamics following chronic sleep restriction: Does-response effects of one night for recovery. *Sleep, 33*, 1013–1026.

Beebe, D. W., Rose, D., & Amin, R. (2010). Attention, learning, and arousal of experimentally sleep-restricted adolescents in a simulated classroom. *Journal of Adolescent Health, 47*, 523–525.

Bennett, W. J., DiIulio Jr., J. J., & Walters, J. P. (1996). *Body count: Moral poverty and how to win America's war against crime and drugs.* New York: Simon and Shuster.

Benzel, J., & A. Stanley. (1990, December 30). The Agony of Ecstasy. *New York Times.* Retrieved from http://www.nytimes.com/1990/12/30/arts/1990-the-agony-and-the-ecstasy.html

Billiard, M., & Bentley, A. (2004). Is insomnia best categorized as a symptom or disease? *Sleep Medicine, 5*, S35–S40.

Blevins, K. R., Cullen, F. T., & Sundt, J. L. (2007). The correctional orientation of 'Child savers': Support for rehabilitation and custody among juvenile correctional workers. *Journal of Offender Rehabilitation, 45*(3–4), 47–83.

Bonta, J., Rugge, T., Scott, T.-L., Bourgon, G., & Yessine, A. K. (2008). Exploring the black box of community supervision. *Journal of Offender Rehabilitation, 47*, 248–270.

Bonta, J., Bourgon, G., Rugge, T., Scott, T.-L., Yessine, A. K., Gutierrez, L., et al. (2011). An experimental demonstration of training probation officers in evidence-based community supervision. *Criminal Justice and Behavior, 11*, 1127–1148.

Bosch, S. J., Cama, R., Edelstein, E., & Malkin, J. (2012). *The application of color in healthcare settings.* Concord: The Center for Health Care Design Inc..

Bottoms, A. E. (1999). Interpersonal violence and social order in prisons. In M. H. Tonry & J. Petersilia (Eds.), *Prisons* (Vol. 26 of Crime and justice: A review of research). Chicago: University of Chicago Press.

Braithwaite, J. (2002). *Restorative justice and responsive regulation.* New York: Oxford University Press.

Brayford, J., Cowe, F., & Deering, J. (Eds.) (2010). *What else works? Creative work with offenders.* Cullompton: Willan.

Bureau of Justice Assistance (2004). *Prison industry enhancement certification program.* Washington, DC: Bureau of Justice Assistance, U.S. Department of Justice.

California Department of Corrections and Rehabilitation. (2013). *Month report of population as of midnight September 30, 2013.* Sacramento: Data Analysis Unit, California Department of Corrections and Rehabilitation.

Carich, M. S., Wilson, C., Carich, P. A., & Calder, M. C. (2010). Contemporary sex offender treatment: Incorporating circles of support and the good lives model. In J. Brayford, F. Cowe, & J. Deering (Eds.), *What else works? Creative work with offenders.* Cullompton: Willan.

Clarke, R. V. (1992). *Situation crime prevention: Successful case studies.* New York: Cambridge University Press.

Clarke, R. V., & Cornish, D. B. (1985). 'Modeling offenders' decisions: A framework for research and policy. In M. Tonry & N. Morris (Eds.), *Crime and justice: An annual review of research* (Vol. 6). Chicago: University of Chicago Press.

Clear, T. R. (2007). *Imprisoning communities: How mass incarceration makes disadvantaged neighborhoods worse.* New York: Oxford University Press.

Clear, T. R., & Frost, N. A. (2014). *The punishment imperative: The rise and failure of mass incarceration in America.* New York: New York University Press.

Commission on Sex in Prison. (2014). *Women in prison: Coercive and consensual sex—Briefing paper 2.* London: The Howard League for Penal Reform.

Conover, J. (2000). *Newjack: Guarding Sing Sing.* New York: Random House.

Cook, C. L., & Lane, J. (2014). Professional orientation and pluralistic ignorance among jail correctional officers. *International Journal of Offender Therapy and Comparative Criminology, 58*, 735–757.

Cornish, D. B., & Clarke, R. V. (2003). Opportunities, precipitators, and criminal decisions: A reply to Wortley's critique of situational crime prevention.

In M. Smith & D. Cornish (Eds.), *Theory for practice in situational crime prevention* (Vol. 16). Monsey: Criminal Justice Press.

Craig, L. A., Dixon, L., & Gannon, T. A. (Eds.) (2013). *What works in offender rehabilitation: An evidence based approach to assessment and treatment*. London: Wiley-Blackwell.

Cullen, F. T. (2012). Taking rehabilitation seriously: Creativity, science, and the challenge of offender. *Punishment and Society, 14*, 94–114.

Cullen, F. T. (2013). Rehabilitation: Beyond nothing works. In M. Tonry (Ed.), *Crime and justice in America, 1975–2025* (Vol. 36 of Crime and justice: a review of research). Chicago: University of Chicago Press.

Cullen, F. T., & Gendreau, P. (2001). From nothing works to what works: Changing professional ideology in the 21st century. *The Prison Journal, 81*, 313–338.

Cullen, F. T., & Gilbert, K. E. (1982). *Reaffirming rehabilitation*. Cincinnati: Anderson.

Cullen, F. T., & Gilbert, K. E. (2013). *Reaffirming rehabilitation* (2nd ed.). Waltham: Anderson/Elsevier.

Cullen, F. T., & Jonson, C. L. (2011). Rehabilitation and treatment programs. In J. Q. Wilson & J. Petersilia (Eds.), *Crime and public policy*. New York: Oxford University Press.

Cullen, F. T., & Travis III, L. F. (1984). Work as an avenue of prison reform. *New England Journal of Criminal and Civil Confinement, 10*(1), 45–64.

Cullen, F. T., Lutze, F. E., Link, B. G., & Wolfe, N. T. (1989). The correctional orientation of prison guards: Do officers support rehabilitation? *Federal Probation, 53*(1), 33–42.

Cullen, F. T., Fisher, B. S., & Applegate, B. K. (2000). Public opinion about punishment and corrections. In M. Tonry (Ed.), *Crime and justice: A review of research* (Vol. 14). Chicago: University of Chicago Press.

Cullen, F. T., Pealer, J. A., Fisher, B. S., Applegate, B. K., & Santana, S. A. (2002). Public support for correctional rehabilitation in America: Change or consistency? In J. V. Roberts & M. Hough (Eds.), *Changing attitudes to punishment: Public opinion crime and justice*. Cullompton: Willan.

Cullen, F. T., Jonson, C. L., & Nagin, D. S. (2011). Prisons do not reduce recidivism: The high cost of ignoring science. *The Prison Journal, 91*, 48S–65S.

Cullen, F. T., Jonson, C. L., & Eck, J. E. (2012). The accountable prison. *Journal of Contemporary Criminal Justice, 28*, 77–95.

Cullen, F. T., Jonson, C. L., & Stohr, M. K. (Eds.) (2014). *The American prison: Imagining a different future*. Thousand Oaks: Sage.

Currie, E. (2013). *Crime and Punishment in America* (rev. and updated ed.). New York: Metropolitan.

Custodial Review. (2013). The unexpected effect on inmates of changing to LED lighting. *Custodial Review, 68*, 22–23.

Deurveiher, S., Ryan, N., Burns, J., & Semba, K. (2013). Social and environmental contexts modulate sleep deprivation-induced C-Fos activation in rats. *Behavioural Brain Research, 256*, 238–249.

Deweerdt, S. (2013). Mood disorders: The dark night. *Nature, 497*, S14–S15.

DiIulio Jr., J. J. (1987). *Governing prisons: A comparative study of correctional management.* New York: The Free Press.

DiIulio Jr., J. J., & Logan, C. H. (1992). Ten myths about crime and prisons. *Wisconsin Interest, 1*(1), 21–35.

DiIulio Jr., J. J., & Piehl, A. P. (1991). Does prison pay? The stormy national debate over the cost-effectiveness of imprisonment. *The Brookings Review, 9*(4), 28–35.

Dowden, C., & Andrews, D. A. (2004). The importance of staff practice in delivering effective correctional treatment: A meta-analytic review of core correctional practice. *International Journal of Offender Therapy and Comparative Criminology, 48*, 203–214.

Durose, M. R., Cooper, A. D., & Snyde, H. N. (2014). *Recidivism of prisoners released in 30 states in 2005: Patterns from 2005 to 2010.* Washington, DC: Bureau of Justice Statistics, U.S. Department of Justice.

Eastridge, B. J., Hamilton, E. C., O'Keefe, G. E., Rege, R. V., Valentine, R. J., Jones, D. J., et al. (2003). Effect of sleep deprivation on performance of simulated laparoscopic surgical skill. *The American Journal of Surgery, 186*, 169–174.

Eck, J. (2006). Preventing crime at places. In L. W. Sherman, D. P. Farrington, B. C. Welsh, & D. L. MacKenzie (Eds.), *Evidence-based crime prevention.* London: Routledge.

Foucault, M. (1977). *Discipline and punish: The birth of the prison.* New York: Plenum.

French, S. A., & Gendreau, P. (2006). Reducing prison misconducts: What works! *Criminal Justice and Behavior, 33*, 185–218.

Garland, D. (2001). *The culture of control: Crime and social order in contemporary society.* Chicago: University of Chicago Press.

Gendreau, P., Goggin, C. E., & Law, M. A. (1997). Predicting prison misconduct. *Criminal Justice and Behavior, 24*, 414–431.

Gendreau, P., Smith, P., & French, S. A. (2006). The theory of effective correctional intervention: Empirical status and future directions. In F. T. Cullen,

J. P. Wright, & K. R. Blevins (Eds.), *Taking stock: The status of criminological theory* (Vol. 15 of *Advances in criminological theory*). New Brunswick: Transaction.

Gildner, T. E., Liebert, M. A., Kowal, P., Chatterji, S., & Snodgrass, J. J. (2014). Associations between sleep duration, sleep quality, and cognitive test performance among older adults from six middle income countries: Results from the study on global ageing and adult health. *Journal of Clinical Sleep Medicine, 10*, 613–621.

Gleicher, L., Manchak, S. M., & Cullen, F. T. (2013). Creating a supervision toolkit: How to improve probation and parole. *Federal Probation, 77*(1), 22–27.

Goffman, E. (1961). *Asylums: Essays on the social situation of mental patients and other inmates*. Garden City: Doubleday.

Golden, T. (2006, September 17). The battle for Guantánamo. *New York Times Magazine*, pp. 60–71. Available on-line: http://www.nytimes.com/2006/09/17/magazine/17guantanamo.html?pagewanted=all&_r=0

Gottschalk, M. (2006). *The prison and the gallows: The politics of mass incarceration in America*. New York: Cambridge University Press.

Gottschalk, M. (2015). *Caught: The prison state and the lockdown of American politics*. Princeton: Princeton University Press.

Gutheil, T. G., & Daly, M. (1980). Clinical considerations in seclusion room design. *Hospital and Community Psychiatry, 31*, 268–270.

Harrison, Y., & Horne, J. A. (2000). Sleep loss and temporal memory. *The Quarterly Journal of Experimental Psychology, 53A*, 271–279.

Hemmens, C., & Stohr, M. K. (2014). The racially just prison. In F. T. Cullen, C. L. Jonson, & M. K. Stohr (Eds.), *The American prison: Imagining a different future*. Thousand Oaks: Sage.

Hirsch, L. E. (2007). Weaponizing classical music: Crime prevention and symbolic power in the age of repetition. *Journal of Popular Music Studies, 19*, 342–358.

Holsinger, K. (2014). The feminist prison. In F. T. Cullen, C. L. Jonson, & M. K. Stohr (Eds.), *The American prison: Imagining a different future*. Thousand Oaks: Sage.

Ireland, J. L., & Culpin, V. (2006). The relationship between sleeping problems and aggression, anger, and impulsivity in a population of juvenile and young offenders. *Journal of Adolescent Health, 38*, 649–655.

Jalil, N. A., Yunus, R. M., & Said, N. S. (2011). Environmental colour impact upon human behaviour: A review. *Social and Behavioral Sciences, 35*, 54–62.

Jonson, C. L. (2010). *The impact of imprisonment on reoffending: A meta-analysis.* Unpublished Ph.D. dissertation, University of Cincinnati.

Jonson, C. L., & Cullen, F. T. (2015). Prisoner reentry programs. In M. Tonry (Ed.), *Crime and justice: A review of research* (Vol. 44). Chicago: University of Chicago Press.

Jonson, C. L., Cullen, F. T., & Lux, J. L. (2013). Creating ideological space: Why public support for rehabilitation matters. In L. A. Craig, L. Dixon, & T. A. Gannon (Eds.), *What works in offender rehabilitation: An evidence based approach to assessment and treatment.* London: Wiley-Blackwell.

Jonson, C. L., Eck, J. E., & Cullen, F. T. (2014). The small prison. In F. T. Cullen, C. L. Jonson, & M. K. Stohr (Eds.), *The American prison: Imagining a different future.* Thousand Oaks: Sage.

Jonson, C. L., Eck, J. E., & Cullen, F. T. (2015). Putting a price on justice: How to incentivize prison downsizing. *Victims and Offenders, 10*(4), 452-476.

Kamphuis, J., Meerlo, P., Koolhaas, J. M., & Lancel, M. (2012). Poor sleep as a potential causal factor in aggression and violence. *Sleep Medicine, 13*, 327–334.

Karlin, B. E., & Zeiss, R. A. (2006). Best practices: Environmental and therapeutic issues in psychiatric hospital design: Toward best practices. *Psychiatric Services, 57*, 1376–1378.

Keenan v. Hall (1996). 83 F.3d 1083 (9th Cir.)

Kennealy, P. J., Skeem, J. L., Manchak, S. M., & Louden, J. E. (2012). Firm, fair, and caring officer-offender relationships: Protect against supervision failure. *Law and Human Behavior, 36*, 496–505.

Killgore, W. D. S. (2010). Effects of sleep deprivation on cognition. In G. A. Kerkhof & H. P. A. Van Dongen (Eds.), *Progress in brain research* (Vol. 185). London: Elsevier.

Kling, J. R., & Krueger, A. B. (1999). Costs, benefits and distributional consequences of inmate labor. *Analysis Prepared for the National Symposium on the Economics of Inmate Labor Force Participation*, May, Washington, DC.

Klofas, J., & Toch, H. (1982). The guard subculture myth. *Journal of Research in Crime and Delinquency, 19*, 238–254.

Knutson, K. L., Spiegel, K., Peney, P., & Van Cauter, E. (2007). The metabolic consequences of sleep deprivation. *Sleep Medicine Review, 11*, 163–178.

Kovensky, J. (2014). It's time to pay prisoners the minimum wage: Paying just $2 a day hurts our economy and punishes families. *The New Republic.* Retrieved from http://www.newrepublic.com/article/119083/prison-labor-equal-rights-wages-incarcerated-help-economy

Kruttschnitt, C., & Gartner, R. (2005). *Marking time in the Golden State: Women's imprisonment in California*. New York: Cambridge University Press.

Kwallek, N. (2005). Color in office environments. *Implications, 5*(1), 1–6.

Lambert, E. G., Barton-Bellessa, S. M., & Hogan, N. L. (2014). The association between correctional orientation and organizational citizenship behaviors among correctional staff. *International Journal of Offender Therapy and Comparative Criminology, 58*, 953–974.

Langan, P. A., & Levin, D. J. (2002). *Recidivism of prisoners released in 1994*. Washington, DC: Bureau of Justice Statistics, U.S. Department of Justice.

Latessa, E. J., & Smith, P. (2011). *Corrections in the community* (Vol. 5). Burlington: Anderson.

Latessa, E. J., Listwan, S. J., & Koetzle, D. (2014). *What works (and doesn't) in reducing recidivism*. Waltham: Anderson.

Listwan, S. J., Sullivan, C. J., Agnew, R., Cullen, F. T., & Colvin, M. (2013). The pains of imprisonment revisited: The impact of strain on inmate recidivism. *Justice Quarterly, 30*, 144–168.

Lowenkamp, C. T., Alexander, M., & Robinson, C. (2014). Using 20 minutes wisely: Community supervision officers as agents of change. In M. S. Crow & J. O. Smykla (Eds.), *Offender reentry: Rethinking criminology and criminal justice*. Burlington: Jones and Bartlett Learning.

Maconochie, A. (1851). *On reformatory discipline in county and borough prisons*. Birmingham: William Gren and Son.

Malik, S. (2012, August 8). Prisoners paid £3 a day to work at call centre that has fired other staff. *The Guardian*. Retrieved from http://www.theguardian.com/society/2012/aug/08/prisoners-call-centre-fired-staff

Manchak, S. M., Kennealy, P. J., & Skeem, J. L. (2014). Officer-offender relationship quality matters: Supervision process as evidence-based practice. *Perspectives, 38*(2), 56–70.

Martinson, R. (1974). What works?—Questions and answers about prison reform. *The Public Interest, 35*(2), 22–54.

McKelvey, B. (1977). *American prisons: A history of good intentions*. Montclair: Patterson Smith.

Mears, D. P., & Cochran, J. C. (2015). *Prisoner reentry in the era of mass incarceration*. Thousand Oaks: Sage.

Mears, D. P., Cochran, J. C., & Cullen, F. T. (Forthcoming). Incarceration heterogeneity and its implications for assessing the effectiveness of imprisonment on recidivism. *Criminal Justice Policy Review*, 26(7), 691-712.

Merritt v. Hawk (2001). 153 F. Supp. 2d 1216.

Milewski, M. D., Skaggs, D. L., Bishop, G. A., Pace, J. L., Ibrahim, D. A., Wren, T. A. L., et al. (2014). Chronic lack of sleep is associated with increased sports injuries in adolescent athletes. *Journal of Pediatric Orthopaedics, 34,* 129–133.

Misis, M., Kim, B., Cheeseman, K., Hogan, N. L., & Lambert, E. G. (2013). The impact of correctional officer perceptions of inmates on job stress. *SAGE Open* (April–June), 1–13. Available on-line at doi:10.1177/2158244013489695.

Mitchell, O. (2011). Drug and other specialty courts. In M. Tonry (Ed.), *The Oxford handbook of crime and criminal justice.* New York: Oxford University Press.

Morris, N. (2002). *Maconochie's gentlemen: The story of Norfolk Island and the roots of modern prison reform.* New York: Oxford University Press.

Nagin, D. S., Cullen, F. T., & Jonson, C. L. (2009). Imprisonment and reoffending. In M. Tonry (Ed.), *Crime and justice: A review of research* (Vol. 38). Chicago: University of Chicago Press.

Page, J. (2011). *The toughest beat: Politics, punishment, and the prison officers in California.* New York: Oxford University Press.

Petersik, T. (2000). *The economics of inmate labor force participation.* Retrieved at http://www.correction.org/Secondary%20Pages/InmateLabor.html

Petersilia, J. (2008). California's correctional paradox of excess and deprivation. In M. Tonry (Ed.), *Crime and justice: A review of research* (Vol. 37). Chicago: University of Chicago Press.

Petersilia, J., & Cullen, F. T. (2015). Liberal but not stupid: Meeting the promise of downsizing prisons. *Stanford Journal of Criminal Law and Policy, 2,* 1–43.

Petersilia, J., & Turne, S. (1993). Intensive probation and parole. In M. Tonry (Ed.), *Crime and justice: A review of research* (Vol. 17). Chicago: University of Chicago Press.

Physicians for Human Rights. (2007). *Leave no marks: Enhanced interrogation techniques and the risk of criminality.* Washington, DC: Physicians for Human Rights.

Pratt, T. C. (2009). *Addicted to incarceration: Corrections policy and the politics of misinformation in the United States.* Thousand Oaks: Sage.

Raynor, P., & Robinson, G. (2009). *Rehabilitation, crime and justice* (rev. and updated edn.). Hampshire: Palgrave Macmillan.

Raynor, P., & Vanstone, M. (2015). Moving away from social work and half way back again: New research on skills in probation. *British Journal of Social Work.* Available on-line at doi:10.1093/bjsw/bcv008.

Raynor, P., Ugwudike, P., & Vanstone, M. (2014). The impact of skills in probation work: A reconviction study. *Criminology and Criminal Justice, 14,* 235–249.

Robinson, C. R., Lowenkamp, C. T., Holsinger, A. M., Van Benshoten, S., Alexander, M., & Oleson, J. C. (2012). A random model of staff training aimed at reducing re-arrest (STARR): Using core correctional practices in probation interaction. *Journal of Crime and Justice, 35,* 67–88.

Rothman, D. J. (1971). *The discovery of the Asylum: Social order and disorder in the new republic.* Boston: Little, Brown.

Rothman, D. J. (1980). *Conscience and convenience: The Asylum and its alternatives in progressive America.* Boston: Little, Brown.

Schauss, A. G. (1979). Tranquilizing effect of color reduces aggressive behavior and potential violence. *Journal of Orthomolecular Psychiatry, 8,* 218–220.

Sherman, L. W. (1993). Defiance, deterrence, and irrelevance: A theory of the criminal sanction. *Journal of Research in Crime and Delinquency, 30,* 445–473.

Simon, J. (1993). *Poor discipline: Parole and the social control of the underclass, 1890–1990.* Chicago: University of Chicago Press.

Simon, J. (2014). *Mass incarceration on trial: A remarkable court decision and the future of prisons in America.* New York: The New Press.

Singh, S. (2006). Impact of color on marketing. *Management Decision, 44,* 783–799.

Smith, P. (2006). *The effects of incarceration on recidivism: A longitudinal examination of program participation and institutional adjustment in federally sentenced adult male offenders.* Unpublished Ph.D. dissertation, University of New Brunswick, Canada.

Smith, P. (2013). The psychology of criminal conduct. In F. T. Cullen & P. Wilcox (Eds.), *The oxford handbook of criminological theory.* New York: Oxford University Press.

Smith, C. J., Bechtel, J., Patrick, A., Smith, R. R., & Wilson-Gentry, L. (2006). *Correctional industries preparing inmates for re-entry: Recidivism and post-release employment, final report.* Washington, DC: U.S. Department of Justice.

Smith, P., Gendreau, P., & Swartz, K. (2009). Validating the principles of effective intervention: A systematic review of the contributions of meta-analysis in the field of corrections. *Victims and Offenders, 4,* 148–169.

Smith, P., Schweitzer, M., Labrecque, R. M., & Latessa, E. J. (2012). 'Improving probation officers' supervision skills: An evaluation of the EPIC'S model. *Journal of Crime and Justice, 35,* 189–199.

Spruyt, K., Molfese, D. L., & Gozal, D. (2011). Sleep duration, sleep regularity, body weight, and metabolic homeostasis in school-aged children. *Pediatrics, 127*, 345–352.

Steiner, B., & Meade, B. (2014). The safe prison. In F. T. Cullen, C. L. Jonson, & M. K. Stohr (Eds.), *The American prison: Imagining a different future*. Thousand Oaks: Sage.

Stohr, M. K., Jonson, C. L., & Lux, J. L. (2015). Understanding the female prison experience. In F. T. Cullen, P. Wilcox, J. L. Lux, & C. L. Jonson (Eds.), *Sisters in crime revisited: Bringing gender into criminology*. New York: Oxford University Press.

Sundt, J., Cullen, F. T., Thielo, A. J., & Jonson, C. L. (2015). Public willingness to downsize prisons: Implications for Oregon. *Victims and Offenders*, 10, in press.

Sykes, G. M. (1958). *The society of captives: A study of a maximum security prison*. Princeton: Princeton University Press.

Telzer, E. H., Fuligni, A. J., Lieberman, M. D., & Galvan, A. (2013). The effects of poor quality sleep on brain function and risk taking in adolescence. *NeuroImage, 71*, 275–283.

Thielo, A. J., Cullen, F. T., Cohen, D. M., & Chouhy, C. (2015). *Rehabilitation in a Red State: Public support for correctional reform in Texas*. Unpublished paper, University of Cincinnati.

Timberg, S. (2005, February 15). Classical music as a crime stopper. *Los Angeles Times*.

Toch, H., & Klofas, J. (1982). Alienation and desire for job enrichment among correction officers. *Federal Probation, 46*(1), 35–44.

Tonry, M. (2004). *Thinking about crime: Sense and sensibility in American penal culture*. New York: Oxford University Press.

Tonry, M. (2011). *Punishing race: A continuing American dilemma*. New York: Oxford University Press.

Trice, S. (2014). *CBT and EPICS in the training of custodial officers: Potential effects on officer beliefs, behaviors, and officer/offender conflict rates*. Unpublished paper, University of Cincinnati.

Turley, L. W., & Milliman, R. E. (2000). Atmospheric effects on shopping behavior: A review of the experimental evidence. *Journal of Business Research, 49*, 193–211.

Villettaz, P., Gilliéron, G., & Killias, M. (2015). *The effects on re-offending of custodial vs. non-custodial sanctions an updated systematic review of the state of knowledge*. Philadelphia: Campbell Collaboration Crime and Justice Group.

Von Dongen, H. P., Maislin, G., Mullington, J. M., & Dinges, D. F. (2003). The cumulative cost of additional wakefulness: Does-response effects on neurobehavioral functions and sleep physiology from chronic sleep restriction and total sleep deprivation. *Sleep, 26,* 117–126.

Wansink, B., & van Ittersum, K. (2012). Fast food restaurant lighting and music can reduce calorie intake and increase satisfaction. *Psychological Reports, 111,* 228–232.

Ward, T., & Maruna, S. (2007). *Rehabilitation: Beyond the risk paradigm.* London: Routledge.

Weisburd, D., & Braga, A. E. (Eds.) (2006). *Police innovation: Contrasting perspectives.* New York: Cambridge University Press.

Welsh, B. C., & Farrington, D. P. (2008). *Closed circuit television surveillance on crime.* Oslo: The Campbell Collaboration.

Whitman, J. Q. (2003). *Harsh justice: Criminal punishment and the widening divide between America and Europe.* New York: Oxford University Press.

Willis, G. M., & Ward, T. (2013). The good lives model: Does it work? Preliminary evidence. In L. A. Craig, L. Dixon, & T. A. Gannon (Eds.), *What works in offender rehabilitation: An evidence-based approach to assessment and treatment.* Chichester: John Wiley.

Wilson, J. Q. (1975). *Thinking about crime.* New York: Vintage.

Wortley, R. (2001). A classification of techniques for controlling situational precipitators of crime. *Security Journal, 14,* 63–82.

Wortley, R. (2002). *Situational prison control: Crime prevention in correctional institutions.* Cambridge: Cambridge University Press.

Wright, K. N. (1994). *Effective prison leadership.* Binghamton: William Neil.

www.anchortex.com (Website).

www.derbyindustries.com (Website).

www.northwestwoolen.com (Website).

Yalch, R. F., & Spangenberg, E. R. (2000). The effects of music in a retail setting on real and perceived shopping times. *Journal of Business Research, 49,* 139–147.

Zimbardo, P. G. (2007). *The Lucifer effect: Understanding how good people turn evil.* New York: Random House.

8

Five Steps Towards a More Effective Global Drug Policy

Caroline Chatwin

Introduction

We are at an interesting global juncture for drug policy, with an increasing volume of literature critiquing a zero tolerance approach, arguing that it has made little impression on either the production or consumption of illegal substances, and has caused a number of serious unintended consequences for both drug users and the societies in which they live. At the same time, increasingly liberal systems of drug policy have emerged. Portugal, for example, decriminalised the possession of all drugs for personal use in 2001. More recently, in the United States, Colorado and Washington have already established fully regulated cannabis markets. Alaska, Oregon and Washington DC have emerging regulated markets; and others such as Nevada, California, Arizona and Maine are widely expected to propose similar systems by 2016. Similarly, in Uruguay, legislation has been approved which will provide the first nationwide regulated cannabis market, and the pressure for international treaty reform

C. Chatwin (✉)
University of Kent, Canterbury, UK

© The Editor(s) (if applicable) and The Author(s) 2016
R. Matthews (ed.), *What is to Be Done About Crime and Punishment?*,
DOI 10.1057/978-1-137-57228-8_8

from Latin American governments in general is growing. Nevertheless, Reuter (2011) has noted the difficulties that any government has in breaking out of the traditional drug policy mould. Any significant change requires the employment of sometimes radical new solutions which, if not found to be successful, would amount to political suicide for those involved in having pushed through their implementation. Thus, global drug policy often appears to be in a position of stalemate—the evidence of failure mounts, but the appetite for alternatives remains muted. This chapter offers five steps that we need to take if we are to effect any substantial change in drug policy on a global scale, and produce policies that are both more effective and more humane.

Acknowledge the Limitations of a War on Drugs Strategy, and the Unintended Consequences it Has Produced

Until the early 1900s, few countries in the world had any form of national drug legislation; the use of specific substances—such as cocaine or opium—was not likely to be considered either unduly harmful to the individual, or worthy of the intervention of national or international governments. This, however, was to radically change from the date of the first international opium convention, held in Shanghai in 1909 at the behest of the Americans, which saw the birth of an international approach to drug policy, as well as the emergence of prohibition style policy as the accepted way to deal with drug problems (Bruun et al. 1975). The 1909 Shanghai Convention was to become the first in an increasingly influential series of international agreements on the topic of drugs, the most important of which was the 1961 Single Convention on Narcotic Drugs. The 1961 convention commits all signatories to the recognition that 'addiction to narcotic drugs constitutes a serious evil for the individual and is fraught with social and economic danger' (United Nations 1961: 1). On these grounds, the manufacture, import, export and possession of substances such as cannabis, cocaine and opium, must be prohibited, and is usually criminalised. Ultimately, the policy of prohibition aims to deliver a drug-free world operating under the assumption that 'criminalization deters drug use, and therefore reduces harm to health' (Mena and Hobbs 2010: 61).

The policy of prohibition enshrined in the international conventions has, since the outset, been championed most heavily and most consistently by America. In 1971 President Richard Nixon escalated the nature of American national drug policy to that of a 'war on drugs'. Drugs were designated as the number one public enemy, a state of national emergency was declared, and mandatory sentences and a huge increase in federal funds were implemented (Woodiwiss 1988). This initial declaration of war was intensified, first by Ronald Reagan who declared drugs a national security threat (inspired by the crack cocaine epidemic), and then by George Bush senior who shifted the focus to countries that supply drugs and channelled American efforts into curbing drug production (Bullington 2000). These successive strategies have drawn much of the rest of the world into the war on drugs and ensured that the stringently prohibitionist aim of a drug-free world has been the continued focus of global drug policy.

More recently, general recognition of the limitations of the war on drugs strategy has grown in certain circles. In the first instance, the available evidence suggests that the number of drug users, rather than being eradicated or significantly reduced, has grown significantly since the 1960s, and now remains at a consistently high rate (EMCDDA 2015; UNODC 2014). Alongside this, global data reports that drugs have become increasingly easy to obtain over the years and prices have generally decreased (EMCDDA 2015; UNODC 2014). The lofty aims of a drug-free world, or a significant reduction in the use and supply of drugs, have therefore come to seem a distant possibility, in favour of the emergence of a multi-billion dollar market for illegal substances which remains in the hands of criminals. This failure to make headway in the war on drugs has been accompanied by a growing awareness of the unintended and harmful consequences that it can bring. Kebhaj et al. (2013) report on significant increases in the number of people being arrested and incarcerated for drug offences which leads to an overall increase in the number of people, particularly young people, being criminalised, and clogs up the courts and the prisons. The link between contact with the criminal justice system and race is now well documented (Alexander 2010; Provine 2007), resulting in disproportionate numbers of black men being sanctioned for these offences. An overriding emphasis on prohibition has ensured that funding goes to law enforcement efforts rather than treatment, and means that the actual users of drugs have become a group who are 'criminalised, marginalised and stigmatised' (Global Commission on Drug Policy 2011: 9), and who remain at significant risk of drug related disease and/or death. These problems can be seen most starkly in America where prohibition has been stringently interpreted, but can also be seen to a greater or lesser extent in most other nations characterised as net consumers of drugs.

There are even more devastating consequences for countries which are characterised as the traditional producers of drugs. Bush senior conceptualised the drugs issue as a problem that was external to America—if other countries weren't producing and marketing these products, then vulnerable Americans wouldn't be lured into becoming dependent on them. This is a line of argument that has been generally adopted wholesale throughout the Western world in relation to producer countries, and has resulted in the implementation of extremely harmful policies. These harms include: the corruption of governments in countries where organised criminals are better resourced than the governments themselves; rising levels of drug use; significantly increased levels of violence; armed violence and homicide; environmental problems caused by, for example, aggressive crop spraying programmes; and human-rights abuses, such as the routine shooting of child cannabis farmers in Iran (Amnesty International 2011; Bowling 2011; Mena and Hobbs 2010). In spite of these efforts, Youngers and Roisin (2005) report that, globally, levels of coca production have remained steady. Many (Bowling 2010; Costa 2008) have attributed this to the phenomenon of displacement, whereby efforts concentrated against drug production in a particular geographical location can be effective in the short term, but ultimately lead to a displacement of activity to a different geographical location, which then also experiences the problems brought by illegal drug production. Bowling (2011), inspired by the work of Jock Young in 1971 on drug control and deviancy amplification, has conceptualised the situation described above as an example of iatrogenic harm, whereby the drug problems have worsened, not in spite of prohibition policies, but, in some cases, because of them—in other words, the countries which have implemented these policies have themselves become the producers of harm.

There is increasing evidence of disillusionment with the war on drugs policy: President Obama publicly abandoned the term in 2005; regulated cannabis markets are being trialled in some US states and Uruguay; there are increasing calls for reform of the UN international drug conventions; and the heads of some drug producing countries are beginning to speak out about the role of consumer countries in contributing to the problem. There is also much to suggest, however, that a stringent interpretation of prohibition continues to persist. For example, a United Nations General Assembly special session on drugs in 1998 recommitted to the goal of a drug-free world by 2008 and, when this date was reached without success, only modified the aim to a world in which the use and supply of drugs was significantly reduced. Similarly, successive European Union drug strategies and action plans have consistently maintained their primary aims as the significant reduction of drug use and drug supply. Finally, global reaction to the recent emergence of new psychoactive substances (NPS) has almost universally been to implement war on drugs style emergency legislation and, in Poland, Ireland and the UK, to introduce blanket bans, in what Stevens and Measham (2014) have referred to as a 'drug policy ratchet'.

While we continue to cling to these extreme versions of prohibition that prioritise law enforcement efforts over all other types of intervention, we cannot see real progress in global drug policy. In order to improve the way that we control the use of illicit substances, the first step ought, therefore, to be to accept the limitations of the war on drugs strategy, and to acknowledge the many harms that it has produced. Such an acknowledgement does not mean the end of prohibition—reducing the demand for and supply of illicit substances is still a worthy goal. There are, however, many ways of implementing prohibition based policies that do not make enemies out of the users, suppliers and producers of illegal substances, and which rather seek to achieve these goals without producing further harm or contravening human rights legislation.

Recognise the Importance of Reducing Drug Related Harm, of Upholding Human Rights, and of Giving Public Health a More Prominent Role in the Formulation of Policy

The problems with a war on drugs strategy and an exclusive focus on law enforcement have been outlined above. As we have seen, waging war on the supply of drugs can do much to damage vulnerable people in producer countries, and waging war on the demand for drugs can criminalise, stigmatise and marginalise the users of drugs. It is not enough, however, to question these strategies; we need to develop alternatives for controlling illicit substances that can be employed alongside, or in place of, law enforcement strategies. These alternative strategies should aim to reduce or minimise the harm done to the users and producers of drugs, to promote and protect public health, and to uphold the human rights of those who use drugs.

Harm reduction is broadbrush terminology which describes 'interventions, programmes and policies that seek to reduce the health, social and economic harms of drug use to individuals, communities and societies' (Rhodes and Hedrich 2010: 21). The over-arching aim of a utopian 'drug free society' (de Jarlais 1995) is replaced by an acceptance that illicit drug use is part of our world, and a primary goal of reducing the harm done by the use of drugs (Lenton and Single 1998). These may be the primary harms caused by the use of drugs themselves, or, more usually, the secondary harms that are done to the users and suppliers of drugs because of the policies that have been put in place to control the criminalised substances. For example, one of the strategies to control the use of injecting heroin has been to limit access to the needles which are used to inject the drug. This strategy, however, has caused considerable harm in that users of heroin have often, due to their scarcity, shared needles, opening themselves up to increased rates of infection from serious diseases such as HIV, AIDS and Hepatitis C. Hawks and Lenton (1998) suggest that most drug policy initiatives have been implemented without due consideration of the harms or unintended consequences that they may cause, and harm reduction can thus be conceptualised as an attempt to remedy that by retrospectively revisiting drug policy initiatives to reduce those harms that have been caused.

Harm reduction is by no means a new concept within the drugs field: in the 1920s addicts in the UK were prescribed heroin and/or morphine (Spear 1994); in the 1960s methadone maintenance treatment was introduced in the United States (Erickson 1999); and in the early 1980s groups of Dutch drug users came together to form the *Junkiebond*, campaigning for the rights of dependent drug users to both needle exchange services and substitution treatment (Chatwin 2010a). In particular, throughout the 1980s, the value of harm reduction strategies was highlighted in response to the threat of AIDS (Hunt 2004). Due, in part, to the sharing of needles and the unsanitary injecting practices of many heroin addicts, levels of HIV and AIDS infection were relatively high amongst the dependent drug using population. At this time, many dependent drug users also worked as prostitutes to fund their drug habit, and thus the infection rate was at risk of spreading to the general population. Services which provided addicts with clean needles and, in some cases, actually supplied drug users with 'safer' versions of their drugs (such as methadone maintenance programmes) were therefore authorised on a fairly widespread scale, in an effort to reduce or minimise the harm done by the criminalisation of drugs.

In these early beginnings—providing drug addicts with needles to inject their drugs, or giving them access to versions of the drugs themselves through substitution treatment—were seen as rather controversial and in direct contradiction to the main aim of global drug policy, that of prohibiting the use and supply of drugs. Now, however, needle exchange programmes and substitution treatment are relatively standard provisions in consumer countries throughout the Western world. To become a member state of the European Union, for example, it is now necessary to show that you have implemented both of these harm reduction strategies (Rhodes and Hedrich 2010). New harm reduction approaches have since developed, such as street level nursing (showing injecting drug users the safest ways to inject), the provision of drug consumption rooms (safe places to use drugs), the provision of heroin to the most severely addicted users, the testing of pills and powders, and the decriminalisation of cannabis. These newer measures are more controversial and do not yet enjoy widespread implementation. For example, the International Narcotics Control Board (1999) has deemed the provision of drug consumption rooms as being against the terms of the international conventions on drug control. Others, however, argue that much of the world could do more to provide even basic harm reduction measures. MacGregor (2011), for example, suggests that more harm reduction work is urgently needed on a global scale in relation to the prevention of hepatitis and the reduction of drug-related harm for vulnerable groups, such as those working in prostitution, migrant populations and people in prison.

Harm reduction has been hampered by a persistent perception that it condones and, in some cases, enables, the use of illegal drugs (Rehm et al. 2010), and has long been, wrongly, associated with the legalisation movement. Governments are thus consistently worried that it 'sends out the wrong message' (DuPont 1996). On the other side of the coin, Bourgois and Schonberg (2009) contest that harm reduction resonates well with middle-class users but actually alienates street users as they are incapable of incorporating harm reduction practices into their daily routines. He invokes Foucault's ideas about a 'discourse of science' to explain how drug users can become further marginalised by well meaning harm reduction practices as they publicly fail to discipline their abnormality. There are also problems surrounding the definition of harm which can make it difficult to effectively evaluate initiatives (Hall 2007). Finally, criticisms have been made about the ideological limitations of harm reduction as being restricted to policies that reduce the harm of other, already existing, policies (Keane 2003).

Because of these long standing critiques, Hall (2007) suggests that we should move away from harm reduction terminology and, instead, attempt to implement an approach that is based on the principles of public health more broadly, allowing the introduction of strategies that are concerned with improving health from the outset, rather than as an antidote to a law enforcement oriented policy. In this way, the values of public health can underlie drug policy in the provision of a four pillar system of drug control comprising prevention, treatment, enforcement and harm reduction. Stevens (2011a) further suggests that drug use disproportionately affects vulnerable people and is often rooted in inequality, and that this would continue to be the case even if drugs were decriminalised or legalised. Even public health policies can ignore these wider inequalities and Strang et al. (2012: 71) have therefore introduced the concept of public good, which suggests that effective drug policy 'should aim to promote the public good by improving individual and public health, neighbourhood safety, and community and family cohesion, and by reducing crime'.

Despite the growing academic appetite for basing drug policies on principles of harm reduction, public health and public good, Portugal remains one of the only countries in the world to have designed their national drug policy centring on these concepts. Portuguese policy has been promoted as humanistic and pragmatic (Council of Ministers 1999), and encompasses not only the decriminalisation of the possession of all drugs for personal consumption, but also the provision of treatment for all who seek it, the extension of harm reduction programmes, the reintegration of dependent drug users into society and, where possible, the abandonment of imprisonment as a punishment for drugs use (van het Loo et al. 2002; Chatwin 2011). Elsewhere, harm reduction and public health/good strategies have gained ground, but have ultimately been limited to 'add ons' to the primary law enforcement orientated policies, and have often been viewed as being in direct conflict with, and secondary to, the aims of significant reduction in the supply and demand of drugs.

Alongside these developments, but receiving much less attention, has been the recognition of the importance of human rights in the development of drug policy. Every UN member state has now ratified nine human-rights treaties (Jensema 2015) which promote and encourage respect for human rights and for fundamental freedoms for all without distinction. This means that everyone involved in the illicit drugs market is protected by human-rights laws and any drug control measure 'that violates their basic human rights is illegitimate' (Jensema 2015: 1). Numerous examples, however, can be found of drug control policies throughout the world that do violate human rights: military operations against farmers who produce drugs; the chemical spraying of swathes of crops in attempts to eradicate drugs; the use of the death penalty for those involved in the drugs trade; and racial discrimination within systems of drug control.

Bartilow (2014) describes how counternarcotics policies often work towards actually increasing human-rights abuses. For example, aid coming from the US and Europe has been used to fund the Nigerian Drug Law Enforcement agency, which engages in inhumane practices such as 'routine shooting of cannabis farmers and the standard arrest of drug offenders deported after completing their prison sentences in other countries' (Klein 2011: 225). Amnesty International has drawn attention to the executions in 2011 of 488 people, including children, for drug trafficking offences in Iran (Amnesty International 2011), which has been assisted in its war on drugs by significant amounts of aid from the EU. As Barrett (2010: 142) comments, the drug conventions 'cannot displace human rights law' or put themselves above it, and by tolerating or knowingly ignoring abuses, international systems of drug control become complicit in human-rights violations (Mena and Hobbs 2010).

In order, then, to move forward in a more effective global drug policy, we need to move beyond the kind of prohibition which invokes a war on drugs, towards the kind of prohibition which is linked to and tempered by the promotion of harm reduction, public health and public good. A good starting place for incorporating these philosophies into drug policy is by seeking to reduce the harm done to drug users, predominantly by stringent enforcement strategies. Drug policy, however, should ultimately aim to evolve from this position to one where the intrinsic values of public health and public good are used as the building blocks for drug policies. It is not enough to include these strategies as an adjunct to law enforcement oriented policies—they must be given equal footing, or even placed at the centre, as we have seen is the case in Portugal. Furthermore, aims must not be limited to the promotion of harm reduction and public health/good goals; discussions must also be framed in terms of fundamental human rights (Bewley-Taylor 2005).

Encourage the Development of Innovative Strategies of Drug Policy Control

As part of the effort to implement additions to prohibition, it is important to recognise that there is 'considerable room for manoeuvre' (Bewley-Taylor and Jelsma 2011: 9) under the international treaties in the way that individual nations respond to many aspects of drug control, particularly around the field of drug use and drug users. Given that, to date, no strategy of drug control that has been employed anywhere across the globe has been unilaterally successful in eradicating the drug problem, or even in significantly reducing the use and/or supply of drugs, in many ways it makes sense to allow a diversity of innovative drug policy strategies to bloom in the effort to find effective ways to reduce the harm caused by drug use and the policies employed to control them. Rather than seeking to close down the available drug policy options, international drug policy regimes ought to be concerning themselves with opening 'up the possibility of policy experimentation at the national level or … at subnational levels' (Room and Mackay 2012: 8). These sentiments were echoed at the recent Cartagena summit in Colombia in 2012, at which Latin American leaders called for 'open and frank discussions of alternatives to US drug enforcement' (Bartilow 2014: 42).

The most well known 'innovative' alternative to a war on drugs approach to the control of drugs is the decriminalisation, depenalisation or regulation of certain drugs in certain situations. These terms are often used interchangeably, but actually represent distinct points on a drug policy continuum from criminalisation to legalisation: depenalisation denotes a policy where a particular behaviour (e.g. use of cannabis) remains criminal but the punishment of imprisonment has been removed; decriminalisation denotes a policy where a behaviour is no longer criminalised but punishments (e.g. fines, warnings) can still be applied; and regulation denotes a policy where a behaviour is not criminalised and cannot be punished, but where certain restrictions apply (as is the case for use of alcohol and tobacco). These 'decriminalisation' options are not new strategies—Rosmarin and Eastwood (2012) describe how some countries never criminalised drug use and possession in the first place and others have had decriminalisation policies in place since the early 1970s.

In the past fifteen years, however, many more countries have moved towards the decriminalisation model, mainly in relation to cannabis, but sometimes in relation to the possession of all drugs for personal use. Within Europe for example, Belgium and Luxembourg have effectively removed criminal sanctions for the possession of cannabis for personal use. Germany, Estonia and Lithuania, meanwhile, have written into their penal codes the possibility of waiving prosecution in the case of small amounts of any drug for personal use. Spain, the Czech Republic and Latvia have gone one step further in making administrative sanctions the norm for possession of small amounts of illegal drugs for personal use (Chatwin 2010b). Elsewhere Armenia, Chile and Mexico have all adopted some form of decriminalisation policy as part of this new wave. Perhaps the most well known recent example of decriminalisation comes from Portugal where the possession of all drugs for personal use was decriminalised in 2001 as part of the overhaul of national drug laws to align them with public health principles.

An important point to note here is that different countries have interpreted decriminalisation in radically different ways. Thus, in contrast to Portugal, the coffee shop model, which developed in the Netherlands in the 1970s, is only concerned with the decriminalisation of cannabis in an effort to 'separate the market' (Boekhout van Solinge 1999) for this drug from other more harmful ones. To this end, coffee shops provide a semi-legal environment in which the sale and purchase of cannabis is tolerated on a small scale, but, rather confusingly, no provision is made for the legal supply of coffee shops themselves (Korf 2008) leaving the whole-sale end of the market firmly in criminal hands. Different again are the newer systems of 'cannabis clubs' (Decorte 2014), originating in Spain but quickly being adopted elsewhere, which take advantage of national legislative loopholes tolerating the growth of one or two cannabis plants for personal consumption, to allow the collective production of much larger amounts of cannabis.

In the last couple of years, some countries have taken even more innovative steps in relation to their cannabis policies, surpassing the decriminalisation of this drug by implementing fully regulated markets. Although the American systems share the general aim of creating a regu-lated cannabis market, there are important differences in how they have implemented this legislation (see Room 2014 for a discussion of these), lending an exploratory nature to the venture of finding a workable alter-native to criminalisation. Different again is the more paternalistic and less commercialised (Room 2014) situation in Uruguay.

While there is little indication that this kind of policy will be extended to drugs other than cannabis, a range of potential options for creating regu-lated markets for all prohibited drugs have been developed (Rolles 2009).

Indeed, many of these options are already being partially incorporated in various parts of the world. For example, one option for developing a regulated market for very harmful drugs such as heroin, would be to provide access to them via prescription. This could be either for them to take home to consume later (as practised in Britain from the 1920s to 1960s) or to consume on specially provided premises (as trialled recently in Switzerland and the Netherlands). Another option, perhaps suitable for some stimulant drugs, would be to adapt pharmacies to be able to sell these substances under strict regimes, controlling amounts and providing medical advice. The regulated cannabis market in Uruguay will partially operate under such a system. Finally, those drugs perceived to be less harmful could be sold either by those holding licences granted by the government (as is the case with alcohol and tobacco) or in licensed premises (as with coffee shops in the Netherlands or drug consumption rooms around the world).

The main point to emphasise from this discussion is that this diversity of strategy in dealing with either the decriminalisation of drugs in general, or the regulation of cannabis in particular, should be seen as a strength. In relation to the different developments in cannabis policy, Uchtenhagen (2014: 357) suggests that a 'policy allowing for experimentation alongside credible documentation and evaluation of effects not only improves the chances for evidence-based decisions, but also the chances for public acceptance'. In other words, it is only through experimentation with innovative policy options that we will discover effective and appropriate drug policy solutions. International systems of drug control should therefore seek to open up the existing drug policy options and 'somehow show more flexibility in order to allow this irreversible dynamic of reform to influence, adapt and modernise the system' (Vasconi 2013: 23).

Ensure that Drug Policy Innovations are Evaluated and Evidence on Their Effectiveness is Shared Widely

As Uchtenhagen (2014) argues above, drug policy innovations are only useful in a system that also allows for evaluation of novel strategies and which has the resources to disseminate the results widely. Traditionally, the gap between evidence and policy has been particularly striking in the field of drug policy, with war on drugs policies continuing to operate in stark contrast to the significant evidence that has been gathered about their ineffectiveness (Wood et al. 2010). Recent years have seen much discussion of the importance of 'evidence-based policy' in building effective drug control strategies (Boaz and Pawson 2005), alongside a counter debate about the low value that is usually placed on evidence in drug policy making (Stevens 2011b). Most research in this area now suggests that 'good policy is presumed to be based on a solid evidence base' (Ritter 2007: 70), with the caveat that evidence must also compete with political and public opinion in the actual implementation of policy. More specifically, Wood et al. (2010: 311–12) suggest that 'reorienting drug policies towards evidence-based approaches that respect, protect, and fulfil human rights has the potential to reduce harms deriving from current policies and would allow for the redirection of the vast financial resources to where they are needed most: the implementation and evaluation of evidence-based prevention, regulatory, treatment, and harm-reduction interventions'.

In global terms, both the United Nations Office on Drugs and Crime (UNODC) and the European Monitoring Centre for Drugs and Drug Addiction (EMCDDA) have concerned themselves with the collation and dissemination of statistical information on the nature of the illicit drug situation in different countries and global regions, in an effort to improve the evidence base on which drug policy is founded. Typically, data is collected by individual countries in areas such as the number of drug users and the frequency of use, drug related deaths and disease, and the number of police arrests and drug seizures. This data is then collated and disseminated widely. This is important work, but there is much that could be done to improve it were evidence gathering prioritised and resources made available.

Cross-national comparative research conducted on this scale is often hampered by different research methods and cultures (Galtung 1990; Hakim 2000). Additional problems include scarce data of poor quality from many countries and the inherent problems faced when attempting to uniformly define complex concepts such as drug-related death, disease or crime (MacCoun and Reuter 2001). Another problem arises because there are no universally accepted indicators of success by which to judge individual drug strategies (Flynn 2001). This point can be illuminated by considering the respective evaluations of Swedish and Dutch drug policies. In Sweden, for example, the generally low levels of prevalence of drug use (EMCDDA 2015) have been attributed to the uniformity and totality of their zero-tolerance approach to illicit drugs, which have been deemed to be a strong indication of the 'success' of their policy in global terms (UNODC 2007). In the Netherlands meanwhile, where levels of prevalence are generally higher, the decreasing number of dependent drug users and the health and longevity of those who are dependent on drugs (EMCDDA 2015), have been similarly drawn upon to indicate the 'success' of the Dutch approach (Grund and Breeksema 2013). Furthermore, while the evaluation of drug demand reduction initiatives is now well established, there has been very little attempt to evaluate the impact of supply reduction initiatives. Traditionally, initiatives directed towards disrupting the supply of drugs have been presumed to be necessary and effective in controlling the drug market, but there is no shared understanding of what defines 'success' in this field (Stevens 2011c) and no concrete evidence that a net benefit is being achieved from these policies. A recent external evaluation of European drug policy describes a 'lack of progress' (Rand 2012: 59) in developing these indicators.

If we want to be able to use this kind of data to make informed decisions about what kinds of policy interventions are likely to be successful in specific circumstances, we need to invest more time and resources in producing common definitions of drug related problems, common indicators by which to judge the success of initiatives, and common methods and practices for data collection. We could also do more to improve the ways that we share and disseminate this information on a global scale. Rather than aiming to 'discover' the best overall method of drug control and then forcing its worldwide implementation, we could accept that there is often little relationship between style of drug policy and nature of the drug problem (Reinarman et al. 2004). Instead, dissemination efforts could focus on encouraging policy emulation: by making existing robust policies available to new locations experiencing similar problems; by making incidences of best practice and national drug strategy evaluations widely available; and by bringing networks of experts together, for example from consumer and producer countries, to discuss issues of common interest.

Standring (2012) provides evidence to suggest that Europe, via the EMCDDA, is starting to take this kind of data dissemination seriously, but it is not yet a global practice and it is in danger of becoming under-funded. The value of the innovative drug strategies outlined above depends on this kind of research commitment. Innovations must not be produced in isolation but must be implemented within a framework that allows for their thorough evaluation and which brings networks of experts together to discuss their efficacy. Under such a regime, we can begin to build up a picture of which strategies are appropriate in which different locations and situations. So, just as the rethinking of the war on drugs requires an alternative aim of drug policy to fill the vacuum (commitment to harm reduction, public health and human rights), so must the encouragement of a variety of innovative drug strategies be underpinned by the provision of a framework that improves both evidence building and the way in which we share information.

Broaden the Horizons of the Drug Policy Debate

The final piece in the puzzle to determine what we should do about drugs, is recognising the need to broaden our horizons in terms of what is considered a relevant part of the drug policy debate today. Much of this chapter has described the tensions between the drug problems as perceived by predominantly Western consumer countries, and predominantly producer countries from the rest of the world. The war on drugs approach has long encouraged the US, and by extension the UK and much of Europe, to conceptualise illicit drugs as a problem that is coming from the outside, and which is perpetuated by poor control strategies in those countries from which drugs often originate, such as West Africa and Latin America. This chapter has described a growing involvement in global drug policy debates from, in particular, Latin American heads of state who often put forward the viewpoint that many drug related problems present in producer countries are caused, at least in part, by overwhelming demand from consumer countries in the West. There is a growing sense within the field of criminology in general that much of the academic body of knowledge in this field comes from a Westerncentric viewpoint (Aas 2007), and this debate has been readily extended to the illegal drugs field (Youngers and Roisin 2005). In order to produce a more effective global drug policy, this problem must be overcome and effective strategies must be implemented within a global framework that considers the problems of both producer and consumer countries, and which designs strategies that can bridge them both.

It is not, however, only a greater variety of geographical locations which need to be given an equal footing in drug policy debates. It is arguably no longer appropriate to base discussions around the usual substances (e.g. cannabis, MDMA, cocaine, heroin, crack cocaine, amphetamines). For a long time there have been calls to consider legal substances, namely alcohol and tobacco, alongside illegal substances (Gable 2004; NICE 2010). Professor David Nutt, formerly head of the UK's Advisory Committee on the Misuse of Drugs (ACMD), has done much work on this issue. Together with a range of scientific colleagues and experts, Nutt has produced evidence in support of these calls by developing a scale of harm that considers the physical harms (damage to organs and bodily systems, toxicity, route of administration, immediate and chronic health problems), the dependence harms (addictive qualities including psychological dependence, withdrawal symptoms) and the social harms (harm to families and societies, costs to systems of health care, social care and police) of different substances in an effort to produce a universal classification of substances by harm (Nutt et al. 2007, 2010).

Alongside illegal substances, both alcohol and tobacco are also considered, and the latest research (Nutt et al. 2010) has alcohol at the top of the list as the most harmful substance, while tobacco is placed sixth out of twenty. Cannabis appears around the middle of the scale of harmful substances, while LSD, ecstasy and magic mushrooms, usually classified as very harmful drugs, are at the bottom. These findings lend support to the idea that alcohol and, to a lesser extent, tobacco, ought to be targeted at least as hard as illegal substances under harm reduction/public health oriented strategies, and that the various systems of drug harm classification ought to be updated and based on scientific evidence. It is perhaps unsurprising that Professor Nutt was summarily sacked as head of the ACMD by the Tory party for producing this evidence and expounding his view that the use of ecstasy is less harmful, to both individuals and society, than popular sporting activities such as horse riding (Nutt 2009).

The last decade has revealed, therefore, that we need to broaden our horizons by recognising the relative harm of alcohol and tobacco in comparison to illegal substances. The latest phenomenon to catch the attention of drug policy makers and practitioners around the globe has been the rise in the popularity, availability and use of NPS—a catch all term for chemical compounds that have been modified and developed to mimic the effects of drugs that are already prohibited. Latest figures from the EMCDDA indicate that more than 280 potentially harmful NPS and more than 690 online sites and headshops are now being monitored in Europe (EMCDDA and Europol 2012), leading the European commission to claim that NPS 'are emerging at an unprecedented rate' (European Commission 2011). On a global scale, the International Narcotics Control Board (INCB) has declared that this situation is causing 'increasing concern' (INCB 2011: 97) and UNODC is in the process of developing an early warning advisory (EWA) to share information on NPS on a global scale (UNODC 2013).

Also relevant to ongoing debates are other kinds of substances often broadly described as human enhancement drugs (HEDs), although these substances have received much less popular and academic attention. Evans-Brown et al. (2012) describe how these are divided into six categories: muscle drugs such as steroids; weight loss drugs; image enhancing drugs (e.g. Melanotan); sexual enhancers; cognitive enhancers (e.g. Ritalin); and mood and behaviour enhancers (e.g. Diazepam). The increasing range and scope of development of these substances has huge implications for the kind of policies that can be implemented, and also adds to the evidence that prohibition based policies can have significant unintended consequences. For example, the ease of developing NPS, has meant that national governments have had to think of new strategies to supplement traditional systems of legislation that list prohibited substances one by one via a lengthy and bureaucratic process. Going forward from this point, it seems sensible to include a much greater range of substances than the traditional illegal drugs, even with alcohol and tobacco added in, when implementing holistic substance use policies.

Finally, in another example of the limited ability of prohibition policies to effectively control drugs, drug markets have changed radically, with the advent of internet markets for not yet criminalised NPSs and HEDs. While the development of these kinds of novel substances is not a new problem *per se* it is generally accepted that the internet has played a significant role in their marketing and distribution (Seddon 2014), which has led to an increase in their 'range, potency, profile and availability' (Winstock and Ramsey 2010: 1685). Over and above this significant development, has been the rise of the darknet as an illegal drug marketplace, accessible through Tor anonymising software which encrypts computer IP addresses (Barratt 2012; van Hout and Bingham 2013a). Van Hout and Bingham (2013b: 389) have described accessing darknet drug marketplaces (e.g. Silk Road, Agora) as 'a joyful child in a sweet shop type experience by virtue of its host of quality products and vendors, and its capacity to offer an anonymous, safe, and speedy transactioning without any of the risks associated with street drug sourcing'. Taken together, these significant changes in types of substance available and types of markets in operation have meant that there is much to do in terms of adding to the body of knowledge in these areas, as well as considering intersections between the old and new, exploring how these developments change our understandings of traditional drug markets, and inspiring appropriate lines of policy improvement.

Conclusion

The discussion above therefore provides a clear outline of the steps that must be taken by global drug policy if it is to become a more effective and humane process. The first step must be to acknowledge the limitations of the war on drugs approach to drug policy, and the many unintended consequences that it has caused. Once this has been acknowledged, we can move forward in implementing new aims in global drug policy to sit alongside, or in place of, stringent law enforcement strategies: the reduction of the harm caused by either drug use itself, or the policies employed to control drug use; the implementation of strategies that promote public health or public good; and the importance of operating within the terms of human-rights legislation. At the same time, we should be opening up drug policy possibilities and seeking to employ experimental or innovative strategies of drug control in an effort to become more efficient and effective in our pursuit of these aims. These drug policy innovations must be underpinned by robust frameworks for evaluation and the networks must be in place to ensure that the results can be easily and widely shared. In this way, countries, regions or localities, will all be able to peruse the range of strategies being employed across the globe and pick those most likely to provide successful outcomes for their particular situation. Finally, all this must be done while keeping in mind the need to focus the debate on both producer and consumer countries, on alcohol and tobacco as well as illegal substances, on the new range of semi-legal substances—such as new psychoactive substances and human enhancement drugs—and on emerging markets, such as those provided by the clearweb and the darkweb.

References

Aas, K. F. (2007). *Globalization & crime*. London: Sage Publications.

Alexander, M. (2010). *The new Jim Crow: Mass incarceration in the age of colorblindness*. New York: The New Press.

Amnesty International. (2011). *Addicted to death: Executions for drug offense in Iran*. London.

Barratt, M. J. (2012). Silk Road: Ebay for drugs. *Addiction, 107*, 83–84.

Barrett, D. (2010). Security, development & human rights: Normative, legal and policy challenges for the international drug control system. *International Journal of Drug Policy, 21*, 140–144.

Bartilow, H. A. (2014). Drug wars collateral damage: US counternarcotic aid and human rights in the Americas. *Latin American Research Review, 49*(2), 24–46.

Bewley-Taylor, D. (2005). Emerging policy contradictions between the United Nations drug control system and the core values of the United Nations. *International Journal of Drug Policy, 16*, 423–431.

Bewley-Taylor, D., & Jelsma, M. (2011). *Fifty years of the 191 single convention on narcotic drugs: A reinterpretation*. TNI: series on legislative reform of drug policies. Retrieved from http://www.tni.org

Boaz, A., & Pawson, R. (2005). The perilous road from evidence to policy: Five journeys compared. *Journal of Social Policy, 34*, 175–194.

Boekhout van Solinge, T. (1999). Dutch drug policy in a European context. *Journal of Drug Issues, 20*, 511–528.

Bourgois, P., & Schonberg, J. (2009). *Righteous dopefiend.* Berkeley: University of California Press.

Bowling, B. (2010). *Policing the Caribbean: Transnational security cooperation in practice.* Oxford: Oxford University Press.

Bowling, B. (2011). Transnational criminology and the globalisation of harm production. In M. Bosworth & C. Hoyle (Eds.), *What is criminology?* Oxford: Oxford University Press.

Bruun, K., Pan, L., & Rexed, I. (1975). *The gentleman's club.* Chicago/London: University of Chicago Press.

Bullington, B. (2000). America's drug war: Fact or fiction. In R. Coomber (Ed.), *The control of drug use and drug users.* Amsterdam: Harwood Academic Publishers.

Chatwin, C. (2010a). User involvement in the illegal drugs field: What can Britain learn from European experiences. *Safer Communities, 9*, 51–60.

Chatwin, C. (2010b). Have recent evolutions in European governance brought harmonisation in the field of illicit drugs any closer? *Drugs and Alcohol Today, 10*, 26–32.

Chatwin, C. (2011). *Drug policy harmonization and the European Union.* London: Palgrave Macmillan.

Costa, A. (2008). *Making drug control 'fit for purpose': Building on te UNGASS decade.* Vienna: Commission on Narcotic Drugs.

Council of Ministers. (1999). *National drug strategy*, Resolution of hte Council of Ministers No. 46/99 www.drugtext.org

de Jarlais, D. C. (1995). Editorial: Harm reduction—A framework for incorporating science into drug policy. *American Journal of Public Health, 85*(1), 10–12.

Decorte, T. (2014). Cannabis social clubs in Belgium: organisational strengths and weaknesses, and threats to the model. *International Journal of Drug Policy, 26*(2), 122–130.

Dupont, R. (1996). Harm reduction and decriminalisation in the United States: A personal perspective. *Substance Use and Misuse, 31*, 1929–1945.

EMCDDA. (2015). *European drug report* 2015. Retrieved from http://www.emcdda.europa.eu

EMCDDA & Europol. (2012). *New drugs in Europe*, 2012. Retrieved from http://www.emcdda.europa.eu

Erickson, P. (1999). Introduction: The three phases of harm reduction. An examination of emerging concepts, methodologies and critiques. *Substance Use and Misuse, 34*(1), 1–7.

European Commission. (2011). *Towards a stronger European drug policy.* Brussels: COM (2011) 689 final.

European Monitoring Centre for Drugs and Drug Addiction. (2015). *European drug report 2015*: *Trends and developments.* Retrieved from http://www.emcdda.eu.org

Evans-Brown, M., McVeigh, J., Perkins, C., & Bellis, M. A. (2012). *Human enhancement drugs: The emerging challenges to public health.* Liverpool John Moores University: North West Public Health Observatory.

Flynn, P. (2001). *Social consequences of and responses to drug misuse in member states.* Social, Health and Family Affairs Committee, Parliamentary assembly. Luxembourg: Office for Official Publications of the European Communities.

Gable, R. S. (2004). Comparison of acute lethal toxicity of commonly abused psychoactive substances. *Addiction, 99*, 686–696.

Galtung, J. (1990). Theory formation in social research: A plea for pluralism. In E. Oyen (Ed.), *Comparative methodology.* London: Sage.

Global Commission on Drug Policy. (2011). *War on drugs*: *Report of the Global Commission on Drug Policy.* Retrieved from http://www.globalcommission-ondrugs.org

Grund, J. P., & Breeksema, J. (2013). *Coffeeshops and compromise*: *Separated illicit drug markets in the Netherlands.* Open Society Foundations, Retrieved from http://www.opensocietyfoundations.org

Hakim, C. (2000). *Research design: Successful designs for social and economic research* (2nd ed.). London: Lynne Reiner Publishers.

Hall, W. (2007). What's in a name. *Addiction, 102*, 691–692.

Hawks, D., & Lenton, S. (1998). Harm minimisation: A basis for decision making in drug policy? *Risk Decision Policy, 3*, 157–163.

Hunt, N. (2004). Public health or human rights: What comes first? *International Journal of Drug Policy, 15*, 231–237.

INCB. (2011). *Report of the International Narcotics Control Board for 2011.* Retrieved from http://www.unodc.org

Jensema, E. (2015). Human rights and drug policy. Transnational Institute www.tni.org

Keane, H. (2003). Critiques of harm reduction: Morality and the promise of human rights. *International Journal of Drug Policy, 14*(3), 227–232.

Kebhaj, S., Shahidinia, N., Testa, A., & Williams, J. (2013). Collateral damage & the war on drugs: Estimating the effect of zero tolerance policies on drug arrest rates, 1975–2002. *The Public Purpose, XI*, 1–25.

Klein, A. (2011). Written evidence to the House of Lords' enquiry into the European drug strategy. In House of Lords *The EU drugs strategy: oral and written evidence*. Home Affairs Subcommittee of the European Select Committee. http://www.parliament.co.uk

Korf, D. J. (2008). An open front door: The coffeeshop phenomenon in the Netherlands. In S. Rodner, B. Sznitman, B. Olsson, & R. Room (Eds.), *A cannabis reader: Global issues and local experiences—Perspectives on cannabis controversies, treatment and regulation in Europe*. Luxembourg: Office for Official Publications of the European Communities. EMCDDA monograph no. 8.

Lenton, S., & Single, E. (1998). The definition of harm reduction. *Drug and Alcohol Review, 17*, 213–220.

MacCoun, R., & Reuter, P. (2001). *Drug war heresies: Learning from other vices, times and places*. Cambridge, UK: Cambridge University Press.

MacGregor, S. (2011). Oral evidence to the House of Lords' enquiry into the European drug strategy. In House of Lords *The EU drugs strategy: Oral and written evidence*. Home Affairs Subcommittee of the European Select Committee. http://www.parliament.co.uk

Mena, F., & Hobbs, R. (2010). Narcophobia: Drugs prohibition and the generation of human rights abuses. *Trends in Organised Crime, 13*(1), 674.

NICE. (2010). *Alcohol-use disorders: Preventing the development of hazardous and harmful drinking*. London: National Institute for Health and Clinical Excellence.

Nutt, D. J. (2009). Equasy—An overlooked addiction with implications for the current debate on drug harms. *Journal of Psychopharmacology, 23*(1), 3–5.

Nutt, D. J., King, L. A., Saulsbury, W., & Blakemore, C. (2007). Development of a rational scale to assess the harm of drugs. *The Lancet, 369*, 1047–1053.

Nutt, D. J., King, L. A., & Phillips, L. D. (2010). Drug harms in the UK: A multicriteria decision analysis. *The Lancet, 376*, 1558–1565.

Provine, D. M. (2007). *Unequal under law: Race in the war on drugs*. Chicago/London: University of Chicago Press.

RAND. (2012). *Assessment of the implementation of the EU drugs strategy and its action plans*. www.rand.org

Rehm, J., Fischer, B., Hickman, M., Ball, A., Atun, R., Kazalchkine, M., Southwell, M., Fry, C., & Room, R. (2010). Perspectives on harm reduction—What experts have to say. In EMCDDA's (Ed.), *Harm reduction: Evidence, impact and challenges*. www.emcdda.europa.eu

Reinarman, C., Cohen, P., & Kaal, H. (2004). The limited relevance of drug policy: Cannabis in Amsterdam and San Francisco. *American Journal of Public Health, 94*, 836–842.

Reuter, P. (2011). *Options for regulating new psychoactive drugs: A review of recent experiences.* UK Drug Policy Commission.

Rhodes, T., & Hedrich, D. (2010). Harm reduction and the mainstream. In European Monitoring Centre for Drugs and Drug Addiction's *Harm reduction: Evidence, impacts and challenges.* www.emcdda.europa.eu

Ritter, A. (2007). How do drug policy makers access research evidence? *International Journal of Drugs Policy, 20,* 70–75.

Rolles, S. (2009). *After the war on drugs: Blueprint for regulation.* Transform Drug Policy Foundation, Retrieved from http://www.tdpf.org.uk

Room, R. (2014). Legalising a market for cannabis for pleasure: Colorado, Washington, Uruguay and beyond. *Addiction, 109*(3), 345–351. doi:10.111/add/12355.

Room, R., & MacKay, S. (2012). *Roadmaps to reforming the UN drug conventions.* A Beckley Foundation report. Retrieved from http://www.beckleyfoundation.org

Rosmarin, A., & Eastwood, N. (2012). *A quiet revolution: Drug decriminalisation policies in practice across the globe.* www.release.org

Seddon, T. (2014). Drug policy and global regulatory capitalism: The case of new psychoactive substances (NPS). *International Journal of Drug Policy, 25,* 1019–1024.

Spear, B. (1994). The early years of the 'British System' in practice. In J. Strang & M. Gossop (Eds.), *Heroin addiction and drug policy.* Oxford: Oxford University Press.

Standring, A. (2012). *An ever closer union—Towards the 'soft' convergence of European*

Stevens, A. (2011a). *Drugs, crime and public health: The political economy of drug policy.* London: Routledge-Cavendish.

Stevens, A. (2011b). Telling policy stories: An ethnographic study of the use of evidence in policy-making in the UK. *Journal of Social Policy, 40,* 237–255.

Stevens, A. (2011c). Oral evidence to the House of Lords' enquiry into the European drug strategy. In House of Lords *The EU drugs strategy: Oral and written evidence.* Home Affairs Subcommittee of the European Select Committee. http://www.parliament.co.uk

Stevens, A., & Measham, F. (2014). The 'drug policy ratchet': Why do sanctions for new psychoactive drugs typically only go up? *Addiction, 109*(8), 1226–1232.

Strang, J., Babor, T., Caulkins, J., Fischer, B., Foxcroft, D., & Humphreys, K. (2012). Drug policy and the public good: Evidence for effective interventions. *The Lancet, 379,* 71–83.

Uchtenhagen, A. (2014). Some critical issues in cannabis policy reform. *Addiction*, *109*(3), 356–358. doi:10.111/add.12455.

United Nations. (1961). *Single convention on narcotic drugs*, 1961. Retrieved from http://www.druglibrary.org/schaffer/legal

United Nations Office on Drugs and Crime. (2014). *World drug report*. Retrieved from http://www.unodc.org

UNODC. (2007). *Sweden's successful drug policy: A review of the evidence*. Retrieved from http://www.unodc.org.

UNODC. (2013, March). *The challenge of new psychoactive substances*. Global Smart Programme.

van het Loo, M., van Beusekom, I., & Kahan, J. (2002). Decriminalisation of drug use in Portugal: the development of a policy. *Annals of the American Academy of Political and Social Science, 582*, 49–63.

van Hout, M. C., & Bingham, T. (2013a). Surfing the Silk Road: A study of users' experiences. *International Journal of Drug Policy, 24*, 524–529.

van Hout, M. C., & Bingham, T. (2013b). Silk Road, the virtual drug market-place: A single case study of user experiences. *International Journal of Drug Policy, 24*, 385–391.

Vasconi, C. (2013). *Where next for Europe on drug policy reform?*. Expert seminar, Lisbon, Portugal, 20–21 June 2013. Transnational Institute, Retrieved from http://www.tni.org

Winstock, A., & Ramsey, J. (2010). Legal highs and the challenges for policy makers. *Addiction, 105*(10), 1685–1687.

Wood, E., Werb, D., Kazatchkine, M., Kerr, T., Hankins, C., Gorna, R., et al. (2010). Vienna declaration: A call for evidence-based drug policies. *The Lancet, 376*, 310–312.

Woodiwiss, M. (1988). *Crime, crusades and corruption: Prohibitions in the United States, 1900–1987*. London: Pinter.

Young, J. (1971). *The drugtakers: The social meaning of drug use*. London: McGibbon & Kee.

Youngers, C., & Roisin, E. (Eds.) (2005). *Drugs and democracy in Latin America: The impact of US policy*. London: Lynne Reinner.

9

Taming Business? Understanding Effectiveness in the Control of Corporate and White-collar Crime

Fiona Haines

The harms generated by business activity are undeniable and their persistence, despite efforts at their control, striking. Criminologists, amongst others, have documented the range of these harms[1] from financial (Snider 2007), to the deaths and injuries of workers (Tombs and Whyte 2007) and of the public (Hutter 2001), devastation of the environment (Beirne and South 2007), the abuse of market system ideals through insider trading (Polk and Weston 1990, cf. Bhidé 2009) and market manipulation (Punch 1996). The focus of this chapter is to analyse critically the possibilities of

F. Haines (✉)
University of Melbourne, Melbourne, VIC, Australia

[1] This chapter uses the terms corporate and white-collar crime and corporate and white-collar harm interchangeably. It is not important to the arguments in this chapter to define what is meant by the term corporate or white-collar crime as neither a restrictive nor an expansive definition assists in understanding the central challenges of control. Further, I have argued elsewhere that categorisations and classifications of the forms of white-collar and corporate crime obscure the ambiguities in these classifications (see e.g. Haines and Beaton-Wells 2012; Haines 2014). What is important in this chapter is an interrogation of the economic and political influences that shape what is, and what is not, considered harmful or unacceptable and by whom and how those influences also shape control.

I would like to thank Subvina Monir Chithi for her invaluable research assistance with this chapter. All errors remain my own.

control and reduction of these harms by placing them in their economic and political context. It argues that control measures are best understood when framed not only around the methods of control (punishment or persuasion) but also around the degree to which they explicitly attempt to reshape who can and should influence business behaviour and the institutional conditions under which business activity occurs.

A Brief Political Economy of the Control of Corporate and White-collar Crime

The first step to understanding control might seem somewhat paradoxical but is important, namely, to pay attention to the benefits of (and who benefits from) the current economic system. The benefits of a capitalist economy are felt broadly (Bhagwati 2004) and are experienced not only in material forms, jobs, goods and services for the citizenry, but also ideologically in the form of cultural myths and expectations built into versions of the American Dream (Wyatt-Nichol 2011). States, and by extension capital P Politics, are linked symbiotically to these benefits. Direct revenue for governments (through taxation and royalties) depends on an economy (Habermas 1979) that is tied to the legitimacy this revenue confers by virtue of the services provided (health, education and so on). Without these benefits that accrue to both government and the broader public from business activity the elimination of harm would be much more straightforward since businesses point to these benefits to limit regulatory controls, arguing that too tight a control will threaten the economy and with it jobs, services and well-being (Wynne 2010; Haines 2011).

The second step, well noted by critical criminologists amongst others, is a recognition that the benefits generated by the current capitalist system are also characterised by significant inequalities. Unequal distribution is evident in terms of the concentration of economic benefit to those with capital (Picketty 2014). Contributive justice, that is the right to a meaningful and fulfilling life, is also unequally shared (Sayer 2011). Further, the burden of unwanted risks is borne by those with the least access to resources and political influence (Gilbert and Russell 2002; Marmot et al. 2008) as globalisation alters the boundaries and nature of vulnerability (Murphy 2001; Kirby 2006). The harms that businesses generate are embedded in a complex suite of unequally distributed benefits. In certain times and places, these inequalities lead to significant protests and demands for protection from these harms, thereby threatening the legitimacy of governments (Haines 2011).

Ultimately, governments within a capitalist system need to respond not only to the demands of business to facilitate economic activity but also to promise security and protection from harm to the citizenry, including that wrought by business itself. The resulting dynamic between a tighter and looser control of business activity emanates from the tension between legitimation and capital accumulation, a tension long debated in its implications for the willingness or capacity of the state to exert control over business (see for example Block 1981, 2001; Gulalp 1987).

Notwithstanding the challenges this dynamic poses, the analysis below suggests it is possible to control at least some of the harms generated by business conduct. This chapter uses three *frames,* or ideal types, to analyse the variety of methods that have been used in an attempt to control corporate harm and make comments about their effectiveness. The first understands regulatory methods as discrete and instrumental controls that aim to surgically remove corporate harm from the underlying capitalist economic system. The second frame may employ many of the same methods, but emphasises the needs of those affected as a priority for action rather than a reliance on either law, criminal or otherwise, or corporate self-regulation. In particular, disciplining business into serving the public good requires the empowering of third-party actors so that they are able to have a significant and lasting impact on the rules by which businesses compete. Third are the more radical options that replace, to a smaller or greater extent, capitalist forms of exchange. They combine both the use of law and scepticism about it, together with transnational advocacy to push for a more thoroughgoing institutional reform to empower local labour and communities. Here, the emphasis is not necessarily on a single instance of harm but may seek to address multiple related harms that accrue from a capitalist system. Within this third frame, a change in the character of socio-economic relationships can take place in quite localised settings or be attempted at a broader national level. Examples in the former range from the growth of cooperatives and sharing economies through to, in the latter case, changing measures of well-being away from GDP to a more holistic understanding of national wealth.

A focus on methods of control of corporate and white-collar crime analysed within these frames needs to be met with an interrogation of the substance of the harm and the context within which the method is used. So, methods may be shared between the first two frames but *what comprises corporate harm and how human economic relations are perceived* differs. In the first, any intervention should be measured to ensure that the benefits of the capitalist system in terms of entrepreneurialism and economic growth are not negatively affected. In the second, interventions should be directed towards problem-solving and empowerment, building regulatory processes that can mitigate the harms generated by business. The third would tend to see those discrete interventions that do not challenge or reorientate existing power relations in any substantial way as seriously problematic. Here the focus is on institutions that can act as a bulwark against the iatrogenic problems within a capitalist economy, or on a redistribution of power so that social and environmental concerns of marginalised communities govern how business is conducted.

Controls as Discrete Interventions

The first frame understands the controls on corporate and white-collar crime as legal, quasi-legal and non-legal instruments designed to be used where the philosophical orientation is towards maintaining the economic benefits of a capitalist system by removing specific and identified harm. Here the aim is to discipline regulation so that it does as little damage as possible to that underlying system. A preference is for those controls that intrude less on business activity and private forms of regulation are preferred over state control; self-regulation and 'nudge' (Baldwin 2014) are preferred over direct government intervention. Much literature on the effective control of business harm implicitly sits within this paradigm in the sense that it either does not explicitly look beyond the control of the particular harm to demand broader institutional changes or it is designed with the maintenance of the economic system at the forefront of concern.

A basic assumption here is that significant attention should be paid to preserving the underlying economic system. Regulation that deters economic activity should be resisted. One striking example of a regulatory concept that enshrines this philosophical orientation towards the market as a primary concern is *over-deterrence*. Criminologists will be familiar with specific and general deterrence but perhaps less so with over-deterrence. In the context of white-collar and corporate crime this is regulatory activity in pursuit of that crime which has a chilling effect on beneficial economic activity (Yeung 2004). Yet, over-deterrence only makes sense when corporate harm is seen as embedded within a broader benefit that accrues from the capitalist system. Here, both regulation and enforcement *themselves* need to be disciplined to ensure they do not intrude too much on the creativity and productivity of the capitalist market. Perhaps the most prominent example of this, in the context of enforcement, was the statement by US Attorney General Eric Holder, in the wake of the financial crisis, that he feared vigorous enforcement of those responsible might have a negative effect on the economy, creating further hardship (Taibbi 2014). In the context of regulatory regimes more generally a large body of writing examines the proliferation of mechanisms that try to rein in and reduce regulations specifically because they are seen to impede entrepreneurial activity and economic growth. Here we see a rapid development of 'meta-regulation', the regulation of regulation (Morgan 2003) within the bureaucracy. An array of policies is promoted, aimed at limiting what is seen as the rising tide of regulation: regulatory impact statements; one-in one-out policies; and a variety of red/green tape reduction schemes.

Notwithstanding the preference for less rather than more, the mechanism of control can be varied with vigorous debates about which methods are warranted in any particular case, namely those with a more punitive orientation (criminal and civil penalties including fines, imprisonment and licence revocation) or compliance approaches (audits, warnings, improvement notices). A variety of approaches is often promoted, however there are significant differences about the weighting that should be given to punishment over persuasion. For example, the prominent approach in responsive regulation argues for a mix, with persuasive tactics giving way to more punitive measures when persuasion fails (Braithwaite 2002). Others have argued for a 'regulatory mix', where different techniques can be used at the same time rather than sequentially (Gunningham and Grabosky 1998).

Critically, the type of harm also matters. Criminalisation of particular forms of corporate crime *can* fit within this frame, particularly those forms of harm that are seen to threaten the market system. The call for a greater emphasis on criminalisation and punishment, drawing attention to the pusillanimous approach of many regulatory agencies, is not entirely absent here. Indeed, Sutherland's seminal work on white-collar crime, for example, is not inconsistent with this orientation. He argued there was a normative consensus around the benefits of the American way of life, a life predicated on capitalist advancement (Sutherland 1983, p. 45). White-collar crime could be defined by reference to how it harms that way of life. For this reason, white-collar crime included what was seen as taking an unfair advantage over market transactions. It is interesting that the criminalisation of harms against the market—such as insider trading and what in the USA is called anti-trust (elsewhere anti-competitive) conduct—has a long history of being understood as part of the criminal law within the United States, but less so elsewhere. Recently, there has been a concerted effort by the United States to encourage trading partners to embrace the criminalisation of market misconduct and, in particular, cartel conduct (Beaton-Wells and Haines 2009; Haines and Beaton-Wells 2012). This has met with some success in both the UK and in Australia, but has been eschewed in some European countries, such as Sweden.

Vigorous regulation of anti-competitive conduct, though, can create problems for other regulatory regimes. The economic logic underpinning competition law may support vigorous enforcement of that law, but is much less sanguine about other forms of regulation. From the logic of those who push for a more rigorous approach to the pursuit of anti-competitive conduct, other regulatory regimes can risk economic health.[2] The reason for this is that what might loosely be termed social regulation (health and safety and environmental regulation) advantages those larger businesses with greater resources to comply with

---

[2] It is intriguing to note that the economist's term regulatory capture describes this situation, where larger businesses use regulations to squeeze smaller businesses out of the market. This concept of regulatory capture differs markedly from the criminological use of the same term. Here, the emphasis is on weak enforcement, where the regulatory enforcement inspector sees the world too much from the perspective of the particular business and so fails to enforce properly (for a more complete description of the complexities here see Haines 2011, p. 19).

that regulation.[3] Small businesses often struggle with the weight of regulatory demands placed upon them since they have fewer resources with which to comply with regulatory demands. Further, the different logic of the harm (individual competitiveness for the former and care for others in the latter) means that an overweening emphasis on a stringent pursuit of anti-competitive conduct can create challenges for business to comply with other forms of regulation, such as occupational health and safety (Haines and Gurney 2003).

The point here is that the particular regulatory technique or enforcement orientation, in and of itself, should not be the sole focus of criminological attention, important as they may be. There should be an equal interrogation into the *substance* of the harm and the *purpose* of the enforcement.

Further, when attention is given to the breadth of efforts to control *different* forms of corporate harm a complex picture emerges, one that has created some debate in the academic literature. It is possible to observe both a proliferation of regulation and enforcement and areas of significant regulatory weakness. The proliferation of regulation at the same time as the broader penetration of capitalist economic globalisation has been termed by some as 'regulatory capitalism' (Braithwaite 2008; Levi-Faur 2005), to distinguish these observations from the conclusion of others that we live in a neoliberal era, one characterised by deregulation. Those arguing the regulatory capitalist view point not only to increases in some forms of regulatory controls (such as competition law) but also to the increase in regulatory controls that stems from the privatisation of public services. Privatisation generates regulation in the form of regulatory control of electricity and other essential services. Other regulations are also involved, such as: the steep increase in those aimed at preventing money laundering and shoring up national security; regulation that comes in the form of censorship; and increasing requirements for private businesses to retain information on consumers and to pass that information on to governments (The Economist 2015). In this process businesses are drawn into a regulatory network as

---

[3] Whether they do so, of course, is an entirely different question. The irony here is that larger businesses can find it easier to comply with competition regulations and indeed to use those regulations to demonstrate their compliance with the law (see Parker 2012).

regulators (rather than regulated entities), for example in an extension of government policies aimed at promoting national security. Yet, there are also significant areas of deregulation and weak regulation in health and safety, the environment and finance (Gunningham 2009; Tombs and Whyte 2007). In short, there is evidence of both the regulatory capitalist and neoliberal viewpoints.

Weaknesses are well illustrated by the regulatory responses to the financial crisis of 2008. Despite the significance of the crimes and harms that were uncovered by that financial crisis, the reforms in the United States to rein in the problem of shadow banking (a major cause of the problem) remain weak (Rixen 2013). Rixen's analysis of the reasons behind this weakness are revealing in light of the discussion at the beginning of this chapter. He argues that this weakness is borne of two separate but intersecting dynamics. The first is global competition between countries to attract financial activity. The finance sector and national governments see it as important that national regulation should not be anti-competitive in the global race to attract finance. These pressures are met by a national dynamic which comprises local financial institutions influencing regulatory reforms that suit their purpose whilst, at the same time, government responds to public demand for stronger regulation in the wake of the crisis. The government response to this was symbolic reform that gives the perception of improvement, but little of the substance. Second, at the level of enforcement, an allied piece of legislation aimed at constraining speculation on commodity futures has increased the demands on regulators, in this case the Commodities Futures Trading Commission, to produce evidence of illegality through precise quantification of what constitutes *excess* speculation. Such a high bar limits the discretion of enforcers (Williams 2015), so financial regulation and financial regulatory enforcement are compromised.

But there are some intriguing successes, one in the form of the Foreign Account Tax Compliance Act (FATCA)[4] enacted in the United States in the wake of high-profile scandals around tax avoidance by US citizens hiding their money offshore. FATCA requires foreign financial institutions (FFIs) to enter into an agreement with the internal revenue

---

[4] I am grateful to my master's student, Diane Jaio, for bringing this to my attention.

service (IRS), the US tax authority, whereby it agrees to provide information about accounts held by US citizens. Those institutions that do not enter into such agreements are subject to punitive levels of withholding tax—essentially freezing them out of the lucrative US market (Woldeab 2015). Put simply, the cost for an FFI of not complying with FATCA significantly outweighs the benefits of providing tax havens for wealthy US citizens offshore. So far, efforts to repeal the law have not been successful, although there remains significant opposition to it. The *harm* of this particular form of tax avoidance has been addressed, but it impinges on *benefits* and opposition to it is based on the impact of the law on the right to privacy and the rights of US citizens living overseas (Woldeab 2015). How enduring it will be, given these criticisms, remains to be seen.

There is a logic to when effective regulatory reform is likely to be forthcoming and when it is not. I have argued elsewhere that the enactment of effective legislation to control corporate harm requires a circumstance in which political legitimacy is enhanced through the implementation of an effective regulatory measure (Haines 2011). Political legitimacy is not negotiable, effective measures cannot be implemented if they seriously risk that legitimacy. It is critical, though, that public disquiet not be assuaged by symbolic yet ineffective measures. The periods under which these propitious political conditions are in place are few and far between. The aftermath of disaster and scandal can be one such time, as illustrated by FATCA, but as the reforms in the wake of the financial crisis show, a crisis alone does not generate effective reform.

There is one final point of importance here. That is, business and wealthy individuals can generate significant harm that is perfectly legal. Any amount of rigorous enforcement is unlikely to solve this problem. There are two dynamics at play here. The first as explained above is pressure on government to pass weak or ineffective law. This is the reason why a focus on reform is equally as important to criminologists as a study of enforcement (Aubert 1952; Carson 1980). Weak environmental legislation, for example, provides little challenge in terms of business compliance but harms can be significant (see e.g. King et al. 2013). But there is a second challenge, namely the challenge within law itself. Law provides the means by which business can act legally but continue to perpetrate harm.[5] The binary nature of the law enables creative compliance, compliance with the letter of the law but abusing the spirit. Tax is one of the best examples here. It has been well documented that the very wealthy, both individuals and corporations, can avoid paying their fair share of tax quite legally. In a number of cases, this means paying no tax at all (Braithwaite 2003). For this reason, it is critical to take a broader view of what is needed to control corporate crime beyond the passing of individual laws and individual examples of enforcement.

Ultimately, the complex dynamism that characterises the control of corporate and white-collar crime demonstrates the way the benefits of the capitalist system and its significant harms compete for political attention. The regulatory successes are shaped through a concern to preserve the capitalist market (e.g. anti-competition law), to use businesses to enhance security (e.g. counterterrorism measures including money-laundering) and security to bolster political legitimacy. The analysis above shows how a focus on generic enforcement methods, whether criminalisation or persuasion, cannot be divorced from the broader economic and political context that shapes what law reform is forthcoming. The control of corporate and white-collar harm can never be merely a technical—or law enforcement—exercise. What the law demands, as well as whether or how it is enforced, and against what kind of harm, all demand criminological attention.

The Second Frame: Beyond the Law?

The philosophical underpinning of the second framework that shapes the control of corporate and white-collar crime is focused on measures that attempt to reshape the premises under which businesses compete and redefine who should be brought in to control corporate and white-collar crime. A particular focus here is inclusion of those affected by corporate activity to civilise the business impulse to amass profits by avoiding responsibility for harm. There may be less reliance on individual laws or

---

[5] My late colleague and friend, Adam Sutton, likened using the law to try and control corporate crime as akin to trying to drown a fish in water.

regulatory agencies as capable in and of themselves of controlling capital. There can be significant variation within this second frame: from efforts to push business beyond the merely legal, for it to embrace the spirit of the law or embrace human rights more broadly; to a *problem-based* approach to reducing harm; and finally to the ongoing presence of actors (such as unions) who can provide a counterweight to the narrow self-interested imperatives of business for profit maximisation.

Responsive regulation has already been alluded to above in the context of the first frame, the instrumental targeting of specific regulatory regimes, and mainly in the context of the enforcement pyramid. A broad appreciation of responsive regulation and related approaches in the new governance field, though, goes beyond a focus on the enforcement pyramid or the particular dynamic of the relationship between the regulator and regulated business. Arguably, the most radical elements of responsive regulation involve bringing those affected by the harmful activities of business in to the regulatory equation (Haines 1997). Responsive regulation and related approaches argue that workers need to be empowered to protect their own health and safety work (Rees 1988), nursing home residents have a right to be heard about the conditions of their home (Braithwaite 1993) and local communities to have a say on environmental controls (Gunningham et al. 2004). Social pressure can push company behaviour beyond legal requirements (Gunningham et al. 2004). Responsive regulation in its comprehensive sense is far from the 'light touch' approach that neoliberals might desire (Haines 2011). It is rooted philosophically within republicanism which entails obligations on citizens, including businesses, to advance positive conceptions of liberty rather than a neoliberal frame of negative liberty and freedom from intervention (Ayres and Braithwaite 1992 see especially p. 18). Related new governance approaches are similar in the sense that they look to building the capacity of those who are harmed to negotiate directly with those who have abused their rights (Simon 2004).

Conflating these second-frame elements with a capitulation of the control of corporate crime to the vicissitudes of the market arguably misses much of the insight to be gleaned here. A significant benefit of drawing in third parties is the capacity to overcome the strategic manipulation of compliance to ensure its legality but not its morality. An emphasis on the right of those affected to have access to critical information that affects them is also important. The need for greater flexibility in providing redress to those harmed, beyond what the law requires, can be effective. A focus on local resolution, which brings tangible benefits to those most at risk or most egregiously harmed, is also important to recognise. An executive in jail does not provide material forms of redress for those who are harmed. The capacity of these and related approaches to get companies to go *beyond compliance* deserves attention. It points to the importance of broadening our understanding of who can, and has the right to, control business conduct. A responsive approach, even in the context of enforcement, and particularly when those affected are brought in to a relationship with businesses, has the potential to engender a greater commitment to improving standards than an immediate assumption that the behaviour causing the harm is criminal and intentional. Defiance can create additional problems of 'gaming' the law (Braithwaite 2009).

Criticisms of responsive regulation are also important to understand. These highlight the need for effective control to be situated within an institutional environment to counter an overabundance of optimism in the beneficial outcomes of capitalist enterprises. Any analysis of the benefits of a *responsive* interaction needs to be complemented by an appreciation of the broader context or history within which regulation takes place (cf Mills 1959). A history that points to the way corporate harm can be framed as 'non-intentional' so watering down its significance and impact (Carson 1980). Problems arise, too, in the way that ideas of the new governance and responsive regulation are translated into practice. The superficial similarities between how responsive and *light-touch* regulation are used can legitimate a light-touch approach as being consistent with responsive regulation even in the face of significant harm. A half-hearted implementation of a responsive approach can provide legitimacy to a regime more accurately characterised as lax (Mascini 2013; Tombs and Whyte 2013).

The global character of corporate harm also requires attention. Many prominent examples of corporate and white-collar crime are international in reach and recently there has been considerable effort to put in place a range of controls, independently of state regulation, to prevent the reoccurrence of disasters (for example in the wake of the collapse of the Rana

Plaza complex in Bangladesh), and to provide redress for those who have suffered. In important respects, these initiatives reflect a second-frame orientation on shaming business into provide redress for those harmed and for enhanced controls to be put in place to avoid future harm, to be shaped by local actors (or, more accurately, advocacy-based NGOs and unions) in concert with the businesses themselves. Consistent with this, a long drawn-out process through the United Nations has seen the development of the United Nations Guiding Principles on Business and Human Rights (hereafter Guiding Principles). These principles determine that whilst it is a state responsibility to protect human rights, there is a business obligation to respect those rights and a joint obligation for redress (United Nations 2011). These principles have been accompanied by a range of different initiatives based on 'soft law', or problem-solving processes, aimed at improving the behaviour of multinational enterprises and the businesses that comprise their supply chain.

The diversity of these approaches is significant. There are company-based codes of conduct (often couched within a framework of Corporate Social Responsibility), industry-based schemes (such as the International Council on Mining and Minerals) and initiatives associated with international organisations (such as the OECD guidelines for Multinational Enterprises and the United Nations Global Compact). Finally, there are a range of multi-stakeholder initiatives, some of which are specific to a particular industry (such as the Roundtable on Sustainable Palm Oil, RSPO) and others broader in application (such as the Ethical Trading Initiative). Multi-stakeholder initiatives involve not only governments and companies but also NGOs and unions. The advantage here is the increased level of independence that NGOs and unions can bring to ensure more robust procedures for the protection of local communities.

Research on the efficacy of these approaches is, not surprisingly given their diversity, mixed. There is some evidence that the most robust of these initiatives can reduce levels of corporate harm. For example, research on the Forest Stewardship Council suggests some benefits (Meidinger 2006). The development of the Kimberley Process in ensuring the diamond trade is not funding entrenched conflicts has also seen some success (Haufler 2009). Evidence on multi-stakeholder and related initiatives, however, highlight the challenges in ensuring communities at the ground level are protected. For example, the complex nature of, and conflicts involved in, land grabs associated with palm oil means that the RSPO struggles to ensure high ethical standards in the industry (Köhne 2014). Further, there is a significant challenge in competing schemes that cover the same kinds of harm. In some cases, when multiple schemes have developed alongside each other this can lead to pressure to improve their standards in a push for greater legitimacy (Overdevest 2010), yet the challenges of a sustained improvement and avoiding a race to the bottom remain significant (Macdonald 2013).

For many, this approach of persuasion and shaming is destined to fail (Shamir 2010). Much of the criticism has been levelled at company and industry-based schemes which are argued to be motivated as much by an attempt to stall tougher measures as they are aimed at improving corporate practice (Shamir 2004, 2010). The response of advocacy groups—including NGOs, unions, and southern states—to approaches shaped by the Guiding Principles is that there should be a renewed effort towards a more binding treaty on business and human rights. Ecuador and South Africa, with a separate proposal by Norway, were instrumental in this latest effort to bring about a more binding treaty approach, but the path is difficult. There is a significant challenge in motivating states to engage with the new treaty process. Another obstacle is a demand by southern states that the treaty should only cover multinational enterprises and not local businesses. This position is acceptable neither to northern states nor NGOs. Then there is the problem of responsibility for enforcement. It is most likely that states would be required to enforce Treaty provisions (Ruggie 2014a), but this raises the problem of a lack of capacity and willingness of some states to enforce even their own laws, let alone those required through a treaty process. For John Ruggie, who chaired the UN committee that developed the Guiding Principles, previous experiences of failure in treaty negotiations prior to the development of the guiding principles, together with current conflicts around the renewed push, mean that the focus should remain on ensuring as complete an implementation as possible of those principles (Ruggie 2014b).

A critical area for analysis in the context of multinational businesses and corporate crime is the need for redress of those affected. Indeed, one of the strengths of the Guiding Principles is this focus on redress.

A team of researchers in Australia, including myself, has been focused on taking seriously the Guiding Principles' requirement for adequate redress where there has been human-rights abuse by multinational enterprises. The research has analysed the effectiveness of a range of redress schemes, including the Compliance Advisor Ombudsman (hereafter CAO) associated with the International Finance Corporation, the National Contact Point scheme associated with OECD member countries, and multi-stakeholder schemes covering tea, palm oil and textile clothing and footwear. These multi-stakeholder schemes also range from the relatively large Ethical Trading Initiative, based in the UK, to the RSPO and the Freedom of Association Protocol, a much smaller initiative based in Indonesia with a strong focus on local engagement. Our research has been designed to understand the conditions under which redress is more likely through an analysis of the schemes themselves complemented by ten in-depth case studies based in agribusiness, mining and textile clothing and footwear in India and Indonesia.

This research highlights the importance of understanding which elements of new governance or responsive regulation are negotiable in these redress processes. As highlighted above, problem-solving and mediation are only two of a number of elements that characterise these approaches. Other elements it is important to acknowledge include: the need for a diversity of voices to be heard (in particular those who have been aggrieved); an informality in the approach to achieve more effective justice; an emphasis on dialogue and a capacity for creativity in outcomes; a commitment to transparency of information; continuous learning; and close attention to the resolution of grievances at the most local level. Finally, these approaches depend on the adequacy of institutional resources so that the grievance process can be sustained in the long term (for an overview of these elements see Simon 2004). Our research suggests that good outcomes in mediation depend on a robust adherence by the grievance mechanisms to elements other than problem-solving and mediation, in particular the need for a diversity of voices that include a long-term commitment to those most aggrieved as well as significant institutional resources to ensure mechanisms are not dependent on intermittent funding (for an overview see Haines 2015). These institutional resources include not only adequate financing of the mechanism but also access to skilled and dedicated staff to bring the parties together and a commitment to ensuring that those at local level are able to press their claims in an effective manner. A determination to continue with mediation and problem-solving in the absence of a genuine commitment to dialogue on both sides, where there is strategic manipulation of information or where resourcing is inadequate, risks making a dire situation worse (Balaton-Chrimes and Haines 2015).

What was striking in this research was that the CAO grievance process generated the most tangible outcomes of all those we studied and enshrined most completely those elements of new governance seen as important in bringing about effective change. This suggests that a focus on the problem-solving or mediation process used in pursuing a just outcome needs to be matched with an equal interrogation of which elements surround that process. Few of the required elements suggest a higher likelihood of a worse outcome for local communities.

However, the research suggested that these non-judicial mechanisms, taken as a whole and including the CAO, failed to bring about an adequate resolution more often than they succeeded. These failures stemmed from companies manipulating jurisdiction so they no longer needed to respond to the grievance claim, inadequate resourcing of the grievance mechanism and poor employment of those resources, although they did have to ensure the most effective outcome possible. In the case of multi-stakeholder initiatives a concern to retain company membership of the scheme could also militate against the development of robust procedures. Finally, non-judicial redress processes predominantly resided within a philosophical worldview that promoted the benefits of capitalist industrialisation, which made them reluctant to prevent projects proceeding even where there was significant resistance by local communities. Notwithstanding the potential for new governance-style approaches to counter the capitalist impulse to visit harm on the most vulnerable, there was little evidence of this in practice.

In similar fashion to the first-frame approaches, the economic and political context surrounding non-judicial, or second-frame efforts, matter. In our case studies the following all generated better outcomes: local organising anchored in local protests tied to the Communist Party in India (Balaton-Chrimes 2015); tribal peoples who could gain leverage within Indian law (Macdonald et al. 2015); a robust union presence that could inject into multi-stakeholder initiatives and an enduring commitment to local concerns (Rennie and Connor 2015). Other examples outside of our own research also attest to the importance of a history of local organising for success in campaigns for redress (Simmons 2014). The concerted efforts of networked actors can achieve greater leverage to bring redress (Burris et al. 2005).

Also important is a history of organising that leads to more sustained change in institutional arrangements, ensuring benefits generated by business activity are shared more broadly. Such change does have the potential to shift the ground rules that underpin business activity in a progressive manner and to counter the inequalities both in the burden of risk and the sharing of benefit (in the context of occupational health and safety see Walters and Nichols 2009). This suggests that second-frame approaches that also address inequalities in power and influence between the company and those affected are likely to be more successful. However, any institutional arrangement brings with it potential weaknesses and requires careful interrogation. In the case of unions, questions need to be asked about their independence and their commitment to the well-being of their members rather than to their own political advancement (Fry 2014; Curran 1993).

The Third Frame: Changing the Premises of Control

The third frame, those initiatives that seek a fundamental reorientation of economic and political power, extends from the adversarial edge outlined in some of the initiatives above. Just as the first and second frames could share legal or regulatory techniques, the second and third frames share a commitment to a more *socialised* vision of economic life. The difference between the second and the third frame of reference is twofold: firstly, the unwillingness of those within a third frame to compromise, where compromise would undermine fundamental values; and secondly, a commitment to counter-hegemony that actively resists the proliferation of individualism and market-based forms of exchange. Pragmatic compromise is jettisoned where it would reinscribe existing inequalities.

Initiatives that emanate from this third frame draw strength from an understanding of inequality as relative and not absolute. That is, human flourishing can only be possible where there is a central commitment to human and social well-being, not just one that is an accidental side-effect of market processes based on greed and self-interest. There is an attempt to 'see through' institutionalised forms that generate and sustain inequality. Law, property, labour and money itself can be rendered suspect where they are used to perpetuate victimisation and injustice (cf. Bourdieu 2001). As with the first two frames, examples of third-frame approaches are diverse and broad (de Sousa Santos and Rodríguez-Garavito 2005). An intriguing example is the Mathadi Boards that are used to protect 'headload' workers in Maharashtra, India (Marshall 2013). Shelley Marshall's (2013) work points to the way these boards created a totally different working environment for workers required to carry material in the port area. Prior to the introduction of the boards, headload workers were the most vulnerable of contingent workers dependent on piece rates. There was no guarantee of work, no base rate of pay, they simply waited for a chance to earn some money. It was fiercely competitive. In the wake of significant protest, the boards were set up not only to regulate work, but also to provide for health, safety and welfare and reduce the chance of unemployment. Registration to the boards is required both for those needing workers and those needing work. The boards also require 'employers' to pay a levy that is used to pay for Social Security and other benefits. The boards have also set up hospitals to provide medical care to workers and their families. This reorientation has more than a passing similarity to the welfare state, but the initiative is on a local rather than national scale. The emphasis is no longer on solving a single problem generated by the market (in this instance intense competition from an oversupply of workers, leading to dire poverty) but rather a complete reorientation that puts the well-being of the workers at the centre, rather than the periphery, of concern.

The cooperative movement serves as another example, one of the most well-known being the Mondragon cooperative in northern Spain. Similar to the Mathadi boards, their emphasis is on providing a living wage and stable work, but with an added emphasis on democratising the control of the businesses and their operation. Cooperative members, or *socios,* run the businesses. There are over 50 businesses in the Mondragon cooperative itself, many of which have been in operation for a number of decades. There is a probation period before a person is accepted into the cooperative, but once they are accepted they are guaranteed work, and support if work is not available. The difference between the wages of the lowest and highest paid is in multiples of three to five, to a maximum of eight in some cases. Where there is not enough work in one business, a person can be asked to travel to another. Periods of not working are rotated to ensure that work is shared and the benefits that come from working, in terms of relationships and self-esteem, are maintained. The success of this cooperative is based on both its structure and its socialisation processes (Redondo et al. 2011). The relevance of this example for the control of corporate and white-collar crime is the way the cooperative is based on a different socio-economic relationship. The harms generated by businesses are not tackled on a case-by-case basis but rather reconstituted into a different way of working, premised on democratic control.

Many examples of initiatives that fall within this third frame come from the literature on 'globalisation from below', which combines social movement and post-colonialism in what Sousa Santos and Rodrigues-Garavito (2005) label a 'subaltern cosmopolitan legality'. The starting point is solidarity with those most marginalised by economic globalisation, premised on free trade and with a focus on strategy and protest:

> [this approach] entails inquiring into the combination of legal and illegal (as well as non-legal) strategies through which transnational and local movements advance their causes. Rallies, strikes, consumer boycotts, civil disobedience, and other forms of (oftentimes illegal) direct action are part and parcel of counter-hegemonic movements that simultaneously pursue institutional avenues such as litigation and lobbying. (Sousa Santos and Rodríguez-Garavito 2005, p. 15).

Networked resistance is driven by empowering workers and communities at the most local level (Rodríguez-Garavito 2005). Ultimately, resistance to, and rejection of, industrialisation is accompanied by a restructuring of the ways industrialisation takes place. The successes that are borne of a conscious and strategic use of multiple means to reach a desired goal range from gender empowerment (Rusimbi and Mbilinyi 2005) to more affordable medical treatment in the case of HIV AIDS (Klug 2005). Like the Mathadi boards and the Mondragon cooperatives the focus is on the most vulnerable in capitalist economic systems. This orientation not only identifies specific problems in a particular market but should change its institutional structure and premises of operation. There may be a particular concern that animates protest, for example privatisation of water, but there can also be an attempt to change the premise by which economic benefits are shared. New forms of budgeting emerge, such as gender budgeting, which include those often sidelined through dominant accounting processes (Rusimbi and Mbilinyi 2005).

Grievance processes, described in the section above, can also form one of the strategies in a broad-based campaign for more radical change. Resistance to mining by the Dongria Kondh tribal peoples in Odisha, India, included: multiple protests and campaigns; legal cases brought at both Indian state and federal levels; international campaigns targeting the UK, where Vedanta (the mining company concerned) was domiciled, including a grievance claim laid against Vedanta taken to the National Contact Point; campaigns in Norway and France to push for divestment in the project. Mining in an area sacred to the Dongria Kondh was finally halted through a decision of the Indian High Court, which emerged from the multiple and varied campaigns and from the communal strength of the Dongria Kondh themselves (Macdonald et al. 2015).

As with the first two frames, none of these third-frame initiatives are problem free. Santos and Rodríguez-Garavito (2005) recognise that many are 'fragile' and struggle to maintain a counter-hegemonic presence. Resistance to mining in one region can result in it shifting to another. Counter-hegemonic activism saps resources, both material and emotional. Heavy repression can take its toll (Connor and Haines 2013). The Mathadi boards, too, are restricted in their operation and do not cover the vast number of informal workers still found in India (Marshall 2013). Cooperatives have been criticised for their undermining of unions and international solidarity (for a discussion see Heras-Saizarbitoria 2014). Other problems with well-established cooperatives that have overcome the problem of fragility, such as the Mondragon cooperative, are also instructive. Recent research into the Mondragon cooperative shows how the goals and aspirations of the cooperative movement have gradually moved away from the lived reality of the everyday cooperative member (Heras-Saizarbitoria 2014). But these approaches do show that a different logic can be applied to the problems generated by corporations, local and global businesses. Different rules that govern the conditions under which businesses ply their trade can be put in place, rules that take greater account of those most marginalised by dominant economic systems. Approaches that fall under the third frame point to viable alternatives to capitalist industrialisation. They allow us to imagine different futures that explicitly recognise both social and environmental harms, harms often normalised within current dominant economic systems.

Conclusion

This chapter has undertaken a critical analysis of controls on white-collar and corporate harm. It started from the premise that these harms, at least within a capitalist system, are embedded in both material and ideological benefits. The material benefits are unequally shared, yet the promise of a better future in terms of employment, wealth and consumption exercise considerable leverage over both governments and the broader public. The analysis above parsed control of corporate and white-collar harm into three basic frames, or ideal types, that differ in their orientation to this system. The first of these prioritises the capitalist market as needing protection to nurture its creative capacity; controls are narrowly targeted and framed so as to impinge as little as possible on the market itself, with the possible exception of those initiatives aimed at generating competitive pressures, such as anti-trust measures. The prioritisation of the market, though, is countered by pressures on government to protect their citizens. The need for governments to nurture their political legitimacy requires them to respond when the harms wrought by business threaten that legitimacy, a response that can bring about effective change, but only where there is sustained public pressure on the substance of the harm, pressure that will not be assuaged by ineffective reform. Criminalisation may be an effective and just response to some harm but it can also be a distraction from critiquing assumptions about corporate harm as stemming from corporate deviance rather than as an inevitable reflection of a normal state of affairs under capitalist industrialisation. The second frame turned out attention to an interrogation of the philosophical and social underpinnings of control. A focus on methods of control like responsive regulation are anchored in philosophies which, when taken at full value, do not equate to deregulation or light-handed regulation. Nonetheless, approaches premised on a pragmatic response to repairing harm might be more effective if they remained committed to their own philosophical vision: the need for access by those most affected; effective institutional resources provided for problem-solving and mediation; and a transparent process that engenders commitment from all sides. A narrow focus promoting mediation or problem-solving at all costs risks reinscribing existing inequalities. Finally, the third frame turned out attention to alternative economic and social orderings; methods of control that fundamentally reorder the way in which businesses ply their trade (Mathadi Boards), who they are controlled by (in the case of cooperatives), or whose interests are being served (subaltern cosmopolitan legalities).

In each of the three frames attention was drawn to the way that institutional settings necessarily create their own set of unique problems. Well-canvassed in criminology are those associated with a neoliberal market ordering. It is critical to understand the problems within these markets and their control, particularly given their hegemonic status. But students of the control of corporate and white-collar crime would do well not to gloss over the problems associated with controls under both the second and third frames. This is not to say that their advantages should not be promoted, they should, particularly the third frame in the context of significant challenges associated with a distribution of risks to the most marginalised and to the environment. But we need to become more skilled at understanding the iatrogenic properties of all forms of control so that we are better equipped to shape economic, political and social institutions so they are better able to serve the interests of humanity and the globe.

References

Aubert, W. (1952). White collar crime and social structure. *American Journal of Sociology, 58*, 263–271.

Ayres, I., & Braithwaite, J. (1992). *Responsive regulation: Transcending the deregulation debate.* New York: Oxford University Press.

Balaton-Chrimes, S. (2015). *POSCO's Odisha project: OECD National Contact Point complaints and a decade of resistance.* Available from http://www.deakin.edu.au/__data/assets/pdf_file/0008/385838/POSCO-report-FINAL.pdf. Accessed 28 Aug 2015.

Balaton-Chrimes, S., & Haines, F. (2015). The depoliticisation of accountability processes for land-based grievances, and the IFC CAO. *Global Policy, 6*(4), 446-454.

Baldwin, R. (2014). From regulation to behaviour change: Giving nudge the third degree. *The Modern Law Review, 77*(6), 831–857.

Beaton-Wells, C., & Haines, F. (2009). Making cartel conduct criminal: A case study of ambiguity in controlling business conduct. *Australian and New Zealand Journal of Criminology, 42*(2), 218–243.

Beirne, P., & South, N. (2007). *Issues in green criminology: Confronting harms against environments, humanity and other animals.* Cullompton/Portland: Willan.

Bhagwati, J. (2004). Corporations: Predatory or beneficial? In *Defense of globalization* (pp. 162–195). New York: Oxford University Press.

Bhidé, A. (2009). An accident waiting to happen. *Critical Review, 21*(2–3), 211–247.

Block, F. (1981). The fiscal crisis of the capitalist state. *Annual Review of Sociology, 7*, 1–27.

Block, F. (2001). Introduction. In K. Polanyi (Ed.), *The great transformation: The political and economic origins of our time* (pp. xviii–xxxviii). Boston: Beacon Press.

Bourdieu, P. (2001). *Practical reason.* Cambridge: Blackwell.

Braithwaite, J. (1993). The nursing home industry. In M. Tonry & A.J. Reiss (Eds.), *Beyond the law: Crimes in complex organizations* (Crime and justice: A review of research, Vol. 18, pp. 11–54). Chicago: University of Chicago.

Braithwaite, J. (2002). *Restorative justice and responsive regulation.* New York: Oxford University Press.

Braithwaite, J. (2003). Through the eyes of the advisors: A fresh look at high wealth individuals. In V. Braithwaite (Ed.), *Taxing democracy: Understanding tax avoidance and tax evasion* (pp. 245–268). Aldershot: Ashgate.

Braithwaite, J. (2008). *Regulatory capitalism: How it works, ideas for making it work better*. Cheltenham: Edward Elgar.

Braithwaite, V. (2009). *Defiance in taxation and governance: Resisting and dismissing authority in a democracy*. Cheltenham: Edward Elgar.

Burris, S., Drahos, P., & Shearing, C. (2005). Nodal governance. *Australian Journal of Legal Philosophy, 30,* 30–58.

Carson, W. G. (1980). The institutionalization of ambiguity: Early British factory acts. In E. Stotland & G. Geis (Eds.), *White collar crime: Theory and research* (pp. 142–173). Beverly Hills: Sage.

Connor, T., & Haines, F. (2013). Networked regulation as a solution to human rights abuse in global supply chains? The case of trade union rights violations by Indonesian sports shoe manufacturers. *Theoretical Criminology, 17*(2), 197–214.

Curran, D. J. (1993). *Dead laws for dead men: The politics of federal coal mine health and safety legislation*. Pittsburgh: University of Pittsburgh Press.

de Sousa Santos, B., & Rodríguez-Garavito, C. A. (2005). Law, politics, and the subaltern in counter-hegemonic globalization. In B. d. S. Santos & C. A. Rodríguez-Garavito (Eds.), *Law and globalization from below: Towards a cosmopolitan legality* (pp. 1–26). Cambridge: Cambridge University Press.

Fry, R. (2014). Dissent in the coalfields: Miners, federal politics, and union reform in the United States, 1968–1973. *Labor History, 55*(2), 173–188.

Gilbert, M. J., & Russell, S. (2002). Globalization of criminal justice in the corporate context. *Crime, Law & Social Change, 38*(3), 211–238.

Gulalp, H. (1987). Capital accumulation, classes and the relative autonomy of the state. *Science & Society, 51*(3), 287–313.

Gunningham, N. (2009). Environmental law, regulation, governance: Shifting architectures. *Journal of Environmental Law, 21*(2), 179–212.

Gunningham, N., & Grabosky, P. (1998). *Smart regulation: Designing environmental policy*. Oxford: Clarendon Press.

Gunningham, N., Kagan, R. A., & Thornton, D. (2004). Social license and environmental protection: Why businesses go beyond compliance. *Law & Social Inquiry, 2,* 307–341.

Habermas, J. (1979). *Legitimation crisis*. London: Heinemann.

Haines, F. (1997). *Corporate regulation: Beyond 'punish or persuade'*. Oxford: Clarendon Press.

Haines, F. (2011). *The paradox of regulation: What regulation can achieve and what it cannot*. Cheltenham: Edward Elgar.

Haines, F. (2014). Corporate fraud as misplaced confidence? Exploring ambiguity in the accuracy of accounts and the materiality of money. *Theoretical Criminology, 18*(1), 20–37.

Haines, F. (2015). Realising justice for corporate crime? Exploring the impact of non-judicial redress mechanisms for human rights abuse by multi-national corporations. *3rd Annual Crime, Justice and Social Democracy Conference*, Brisbane, QUT.

Haines, F., & Beaton-Wells, C. (2012). Ambiguities in criminalizing cartels: A political economy. *British Journal of Criminology, 52*(5), 953–973.

Haines, F., & Gurney, D. (2003). The shadows of the law: Contemporary approaches to regulation and the problem of regulatory conflict. *Law & Policy, 25*(4), 353–380.

Haufler, V. (2009). The Kimberley process certification scheme: An innovation in global governance and conflict prevention. *Journal of Business Ethics, 89*, 403–416.

Heras-Saizarbitoria, I. (2014). The ties that bind? Exploring the basic principles of worker-owned organizations in practice. *Organization, 21*(5), 645–665.

Hutter, B. M. (2001). *Risk and regulation*. Oxford: Oxford University Press.

King, J., Alexander, F., & Brodie, J. (2013). Regulation of pesticides in Australia: The great barrier reef as a case study for evaluating effectiveness. *Agriculture Ecosystems & Environment, 180*, 54–67.

Kirby, P. (2006). Theorising globalisation's social impact: Proposing the concept of vulnerability. *Review of International Political Economy, 13*(4), 632–655.

Klug, H. (2005). Campaigning for life: Building a new transnational solidarity in the face of HIV/AIDS and TRIPS. In B. de Sousa Santos & C. A. Rodrigues-Garavitos (Eds.), *Law and globalization from below: Towards a cosmopolitan legality* (pp. 118–139). Cambridge: Cambridge University Press.

Köhne, M. (2014). Multi-stakeholder initiative governance as assemblage: Roundtable on sustainable palm oil as a political resource in land conflicts related to oil palm plantations. *Agriculture & Human Values, 31*(3), 469–480.

Levi-Faur, D. (2005). The rise of regulatory capitalism: The global diffusion of a new regulatory order. *The Annals of the American Academy of Political and Social Science, 598*(1), 12–32.

Macdonald, K. (2013). *The politics of global supply chains*. Cambridge, UK: Polity.

Macdonald, K., Marshall, S., & Balaton-Chrimes, S. (2015). Demanding rights in company-community resource extraction conflicts: Examining the cases of POSCO and Vedanta in Odisha, India. In J. Nem Singh et al. (Eds.), *Demanding justice in the global south*. London: Palgrave Macmillan Press.

Marmot, M., Friel, S., Bell, R., Houweling, T. A. J., & Taylor, S. (2008). Closing the gap in a generation: Health equity through action on the social determinants of health. *The Lancet, 372*(9650), 1661–1669.

Marshall, S. (2013). Institutional change in practice: Experimental displacement and complementary layering in labour law reform. SSRN- Social Science Research Network. Available from http://papers.ssrn.com/sol3/papers.cfm?abstract_id=2342453

Mascini, P. (2013). Why was the enforcement pyramid so influential? And what price was paid? *Regulation & Governance, 7*(1), 48–60.

Meidinger, E. E. (2006). The administrative law of global private-public regulation: The case of forestry. *European Journal of International Law, 17*, 47–87.

Mills, C. W. (1959). *The sociological imagination.* Oxford/New York: Oxford University Press.

Morgan, B. (2003). The economization of politics: Meta-regulation as a form of nonjudicial legality. *Social & Legal Studies, 12*(4), 489–523.

Murphy, R. (2001). Nature's temporalities and the manufacture of vulnerability: A study of a sudden disaster with implications for creeping ones. *Time and Society, 10*(2/3), 329–348.

Overdevest, C. (2010). Comparing forest certification schemes: The case of ratcheting standards in the forest sector. *Socio-Economic Review, 8*(1), 47–76.

Parker, C. (2012). Economic rationalities of governance and ambiguity in the criminalization of cartels. *British Journal of Criminology, 52*(5), 974–996.

Picketty, T. (2014). *Capital in the twenty first century.* Cambridge, MA: The Belknap Press of Harvard University Press.

Polk, K., & Weston, W. (1990). Insider trading as an aspect of white collar crime. *Australian and New Zealand Journal of Criminology, 28*(1), 29–38.

Punch, M. (1996). *Dirty business: Exploring corporate misconduct: Analysis and cases.* London/Thousand Oaks: Sage Publications.

Redondo, G., Santa Cruz, I., & Rotger, J. M. (2011). Why Mondragon? Analyzing what works in overcoming inequalities. *Qualitative Inquiry, 17*(3), 277–283.

Rees, J. V. (1988). *Reforming the workplace: A study of self regulation in occupational safety.* Philadelphia: University of Pennsylvania Press.

Rennie, S., & Connor, T. (2015). *The freedom of association protocol: A worker empowerment model for increasing respect for human rights in global supply chains* (report on file with author).

Rixen, T. (2013). Why reregulation after the crisis is feeble: Shadow banking, offshore financial centers, and jurisdictional competition. *Regulation & Governance, 7*(4), 435–459.

Rodríguez-Garavito, C. A. (2005). Global governance and labor rights: Codes of conduct and anti-sweatshop struggles in global apparel factories in Mexico and Guatemala. *Politics & Society, 33*, 203–333.

Ruggie, J. (2014a). A UN business and human rights treaty? *Issues Brief,* Harvard Kennedy School. Available from http://www.hks.harvard.edu/m-rcbg/CSRI/UNBusinessandHumanRightsTreaty.pdf. Accessed 28 Aug 2015.

Ruggie, J. (2014b) International legalization in business and human rights. John F Kennedy School of Government: Harvard Kennedy School. Available from http://www.hks.harvard.edu/m-rcbg/CSRI/research/WFLS.pdf. Accessed 28 Aug 2015.

Rusimbi, M., & Mbilinyi, M. (2005). Political and legal struggles over resources and democracy: Experiences with gender budgeting in Tanzania. In B. de Sousa Santos & C. A. Rodrigues-Garavito (Eds.), *Law and globalization from below: Towards a subaltern cosmopolitan legality* (pp. 283–309). Cambridge: Cambridge University Press.

Sayer, A. (2011). Habitus, work and contributive justice. *Sociology, 45*(1), 7–21.

Shamir, R. (2004). The re-radicalization of corporate social responsibility. *Critical Sociology, 30*(3), 669–689.

Shamir, R. (2010). Capitalism, governance, and authority: The case of corporate social responsibility. *Annual Review of Law and Social Science, 6*(1), 531–553.

Simmons, E. (2014). Grievances do matter in mobilization. *Theory and Society, 43*(5), 513–546.

Simon, W. H. (2004). Solving problems vs. claiming rights: The pragmatist challenge to legal liberalism. *William & Mary Law Review, 46*(1), 127–212.

Snider, L. (2007). 'This time we really mean it!' Cracking down on stock market fraud. In H. N. Pontell & G. Geis (Eds.), *International handbook of white-collar and corporate crime* (pp. 627–647). New York: Springer.

Sutherland, E. H. (1983). *White collar crime: The uncut version.* New Haven: Yale University Press.

Taibbi, M. (2014). *The divide: American injustice in the age of the wealth gap.* Brunswick: Scribe.

The Economist. (2015). A fearful number: Banks and money-laundering. *The Economist,* Economist Intelligence Unit N.A. Incorporated. 67 Available from http://www.economist.com/news/finance-and-economics/21653673-bank-rejects-american-accusations-it-abetted-financial-crime-fearful. Accessed 28 Aug 2015.

Tombs, S., & Whyte, D. (2007). *Safety crime.* Cullompton: Willan.

Tombs, S., & Whyte, D. (2013). Transcending the deregulation debate? Regulation, risk, and the enforcement of health and safety law in the UK. *Regulation & Governance, 7*(1), 61–79.

United Nations. (2011). Guiding principles of business and human rights: Implementing the United Nations 'Protect, Respect and Remedy' framework. New York/Geneva: Office of the High Commissioner, Human Rights. Available from http://www.ohchr.org/Documents/Publications/GuidingPrinciplesBusinessHR_EN.pdf. Accessed 28 Aug 2015.

Walters, D., & Nichols, T. (Eds.) (2009). *Workplace health and safety: International perspectives on worker representation*. Basingstoke: Palgrave Macmillan.

Williams, J. W. (2015). Dodging Dodd-Frank: Excessive speculation, commodities markets, and the burden of proof. *Law & Policy, 37*(1–2), 119–152.

Woldeab, Y. (2015). 'Americans: We love you, but we can't afford you': How the costly U.S.-Canada FATCA agreement permits ciscrimination of Americans in violation of international law. *American University International Law Review, 30*, 611–647.

Wyatt-Nichol, H. (2011). The enduring myth of the American dream: Mobility, marginalization, and hope. *International Journal of Organization Theory & Behavior (PrAcademics Press), 14*(2), 258–279.

Wynne, B. (2010). Strange weather, again: Climate science as political act. *Theory, Culture & Society, 27*(2–3), 289–305.

Yeung, K. (2004). *Securing compliance: A principled approach*. Oxford: Hart.

10

Cybercrime 4.0: Now What Is to Be Done?

Michael R. McGuire

Introduction

There has been widespread agreement about the scale of the cybercrime problem—that it represents one of the most serious of all contemporary criminal threats (Cabinet Office 2011; Cowley 2012). From the mid-1990s onwards this conclusion has driven significant shifts in legislation, policing powers and policy across most national jurisdictions. But how effective have these been? Perhaps more significantly, do these responses offer any kind of template for dealing with future developments in the cybercrime threat? In this chapter I review the health of our defences against online offending in the light of what may be its latest mutation, an emerging complex of technical opportunity which, for convenience, will be termed Cybercrime 4.0. I ask if what worked in previous contexts is likely to continue to work, or if this latest shift represents another permutation of the old maxim that crime control is always one step behind the (cyber)criminal.

M. McGuire (✉)
University of Surrey, Guildford, Surrey, UK

© The Editor(s) (if applicable) and The Author(s) 2016
R. Matthews (ed.), *What is to Be Done About Crime and Punishment?*,
DOI 10.1057/978-1-137-57228-8_10

Cybercrime 1.0–3.0

The usual rationale for distinguishing cybercrime from 'traditional' criminal offences centres upon the role played by technology (specifically information technology) in furthering it (though for an alternative view see McGuire 2007). Either traditional crime is 'enhanced' in some way by technology, or technology serves to shape altogether new forms of criminality. This rationale implies an obvious framework for evaluating where we have come from, where we are now and how successful our efforts have been against cybercrime. This is to periodise its development in terms of certain technological shifts and to then test the relative success of responses against these shifts. Whilst there are clearly different ways in which such a periodisation might be conceptualised, one very minimal, but plausible, approach would be to identify three foundational moments in this process of change.

What we might call Cybercrime 1.0 would extend from the origins of modern computing in the 1940s, right through to the late 1980s. At worst this phase offered little more than a kind of 'beta' version of cybercriminality. For though there was speculation about what computer crime might entail (Parker 1976; Bequai 1987), actual instances were minimal. In his seminal text *Crime by Computer*, Donn Parker argued that, by 1976, there had been just 374 computer-related offences, with many of these simply involving the theft of a computer. The reason for such a low frequency of offending is obvious enough. At the time Parker was writing there were no more than around 150,000 computers in existence (1976, p. 15), most of these were large corporate or government owned mainframe devices and none were connected together in any very useful way. Under these conditions, whatever the speculation, there were few practical possibilities for enacting anything like what we now think of as computer crime. Towards the end of the 1.0 era (around the mid-1980s) when the advent of desktop, or PC, versions of computing devices began to expand the user base, opportunities for criminal exploitation also began to expand. But the isolation of these devices from each other remained a major obstacle. The limited connections that were available—largely through copying of disks or programs—created some precedents for future misuse,[1] but cybercrime 1.0 was little more than a prelude of what was to come.

Cybercrime 2.0 had a far shorter lifespan than 1.0—arguably extending only from the early 1990s to the mid-2000s. The technical shifts which distinguished this phase include the mass proliferation of personal computing devices and (of course) their global networking into the internet via the development of the HyperText, URI and HTTP system, better known as the world wide web. In a sense, cybercrime 2.0 remains the basic template for all cybercriminality, for it suffices to provide for its key requirements, a network of social relations where most of the crimes familiar within everyday life—theft, sexual misconduct, antisocial behaviour and more—can be perpetrated. Two things lent cybercrime 2.0 its sense of novelty: first, that crimes could be committed 'at a distance'; and second, the unique criminal possibilities created by ICT itself—the so-called, pure or cyberdependent crimes, such as malware creation and distribution. Though it caught many off guard, the explosive growth associated with 2.0 ought not to have been any more surprising than previous surges in offending driven by new technologies. For example, the huge rises in intellectual property theft which followed the advent of the printing press (McGuire 2007).

If technological change offers a suitable framework for evaluating changes to the cybercrime threat then shifts in the mid-2000s offer good grounds for identifying a further transition—to cybercrime 3.0. Like 2.0 this reconfiguration rested upon a further acceleration in the scope of connectivity, this time provided by the advent of mobile computing. Just how quickly this shift occurred can be seen in the fact that by 2006 around 93 % of UK households had acquired a mobile connection—for the first time exceeding households with a fixed connection (90 %) (Ofcom 2007). In the same year, 3G connections grew by over 70 %, resulting in 7.8 million subscribers. Only five years later 4G had become the 'new normal' for connectivity, with active subscriptions in the UK alone rising from 318,000 in early 2013 to over six million by 2014 (Ofcom 2015). And just as smartphone take-up in the UK expanded from 51 % to around 61 % between 2013 and 2014, 'traditional' desktop PC ownership continued to decline rapidly (down from 44 % in 2012 to

---

[1] Computer viruses offer one example, piracy and illicit copying provide another.

35 % in 2014), (Ofcom 2014). When considered at the global level these trends are even more pronounced. There were one billion unique mobile subscribers across the globe in 2003 (just under one in six people) but within ten years this had more than trebled to over 3.4 billion (GSMA 2014). The majority of the world's population (56 %) are likely to have their own mobile subscription by 2020, (ibid). This exponential leap in global connectivity brought enough new and distinctive vulnerabilities to suggest that a qualitatively (and quantitatively) new criminal landscape had indeed emerged. As early as 2004 the world's first mobile malware was detected—the Cabir internet worm, which targeted the Nokia Series 60 (Schmidt et al. 2009; Fortinet 2013). Though this had a relatively innocuous outcome (the word Caribe appearing on the screen of infected phones), mobile malware had become a far more serious problem by 2014, affecting over 16 million phones (Spencer 2015). In the same year, over 38 % of smartphone users were reporting being a victim of cybercrime, typically via phishing and spam attacks (Norton 2014). As with cybercrime 2.0 a key problem was user awareness and a failure to appreciate the nature of the shift. Even now, under 50 % of wireless users do not use passwords or PINs (personal identification numbers) on their handsets (CTIA 2013). Still fewer use any security software when using their smartphones to access online banking details (ibid).

Cybercrime 4.0?

In the 1950s, when Moore's Law of computing development was first formulated,[2] no one imagined that computer crime might follow a similar pattern of sustained acceleration (cf. Tuomi 2002). Thus, almost before there has been any time to acknowledge the criminal assemblage that is cybercrime 3.0, a new mutation is arguably already underway. Whether it is premature to think of this is in terms of a cybercrime 4.0 is not yet clear. But, given the failure to anticipate previous criminal adaptations to changes in information technology, it would seem to be wise to take any prospect of such a change very seriously. At least three factors seem likely to be constitutive of this latest shift.

---

[2] This suggests that computing power roughly doubles every two years.

(i) *Network multiplication* and *bodily embeddedness* The much vaunted Internet of Things is just one aspect of a vastly more connected network. Within this, not only do more and more everyday objects, like fridges, become linked together but even the body itself—for example through 'always on' wearable devices.

(ii) *Shifts towards remote/proprietary service delivery* A major shift away from user-centred ownership of computing power towards large scale, remote delivery of resources and storage, via the Cloud, is underway. Whether it is SaaS (software as a service) or PaaS (platform as a service), cloud technologies offer new ways of using computing resources. Paralleling this is a related change, sometimes referred to as appification—where our 'traditional' way of accessing the web—via (passive) websites is replaced by function oriented, independently owned varieties of web resources—the app.

(iii) *Device autonomy* and '*intelligent*' *interactivity* Beyond predictive texting or sites which 'recognise' you, a whole new era of online intelligence has begun. Whilst online assistants like Google Now or Siri already mimic AI, far more powerful varieties of online intelligence are beginning to emerge from the increasing plurality of links which now exist.

Taken together, these shifts do not just represent a sea change in how we use and experience connectivity, but imply some equally significant transitions in how this can be misused. Whilst it is impossible to be sure about the scope of this new criminality, we can certainly reflect upon how effective responses to previous versions of cybercrime have been and their likely impact upon this new configuration. In the following sections I try to work through what this might mean.

Cybercrime 1.0–3.0 Precedents and Portents: What Happened

The widespread assumption that cybercriminals are always one step ahead of the authorities, may have been plausible for most of the Cybercrime 2.0 period, but how far does it continue to hold? If we are to make any progress in saying what works and what does not in fighting cybercriminality, it is not only clarity about some of the key challenges that remain which is required, but also sober reflection upon previous successes. For, in spite of all the pessimism, there is a reasonable case to be made that concerted action has resulted in significant progress in curbing cybercrime.

How to measure this is of course a difficult question since an obvious metric—comparisons between arrests/prosecutions and material reductions in cybercrime—is made difficult by the lack of robust, cybercrime-specific data across most jurisdictions. Insofar as any answers can be given, evaluating success has usually come down to using one or more of the following measures.

- (I) *Prevalence*—what has gone down (or up) according to key indicators. Rises or falls in the prosecution or conviction of cybercrime offences is, as we have just seen, one such obvious indicator. In isolation however this metric cannot offer any guarantee that a particular response has 'worked', since other factors might also be responsible. For example, suppose the prevalence of a less serious category of cybercrime fell substantively, whilst another more serious variety rose slightly. Would that mean certain countermeasures have been successful, or unsuccessful? Such reflections point to the major problem with the use of prevalence measures in social science, they tell us little about *causation*, that is, which responses might be responsible for any changes in prevalence levels. Nonetheless, in spite of these limitations, prevalence metrics tend to remain the most common descriptor of cybercrime trends.
- (II) *Cost effectiveness*—There have been numerous attempts to indicate how serious cybercrime is by estimating how much it 'costs' particular economies or institutions (cf. Cabinet Office 2011; CSIS/ Mcafee 2014; Anderson et al. 2012). An obvious suggestion for measuring the possible success or failure of a measure would therefore be to look at the ratio between *expenditure* on this and its effectiveness in curbing the problem. The problem is that this not only presupposes what 'effective' means (which begs the original question), but that it is possible to meaningfully cost cybercrime—an assumption which has proved highly controversial (cf McGuire and Dowling 2013; Maass and Rajagopalan 2012)

- (III) *Public confidence* and *participation*—Irrespective of how well a
  set of countermeasures might (or might not) appear to be working,
  there will be continued questions about their utility if they fail to
  create a sense of security in the public. And such insecurity may
  actually undermine countermeasures if it results in a failure to cooperate or support the fight against cybercrime

At minimum then, such metrics need plausible correlations with
specific countermeasures if they are to be of any use in evaluating how
successful (or unsuccessful) these may have been. At present, countermeasures have fallen into three broad categories:

- (R1) Network security/technical responses
- (R2) Criminal justice based responses
- (R3) Educational and prevention oriented responses

Whilst these responses may clearly dovetail in various ways—for example collecting forensic digital evidence combines R1 and R2—I will, for
the most part, ignore these additional complexities. However, more comprehensive evaluations of cybercrime countermeasures will clearly need
to consider such overlaps.

As suggested, a relative, if limited measure of success in responding
to cybercrime can be seen in prevalence metrics linked specifically to
offending. For, in spite of continuing concerns, we have actually seen
many offences considered to represent key varieties of cybercriminality falling or levelling off. Take for example losses from UK card fraud,
which stood at around £479 million for 2014 (FFA 2014). Though there
have been slight rises over the past three years this figure represents an
overall ten-year decline from the £504 million which was lost in 2004.
Given that card use has increased substantially over this period (from
10.5 billion transactions in 2008 alone to over 15 billion in 2014) this
fall is all the more impressive. Similar reductions can be found across
most of the key varieties of digital fraud. For example, since its peak in
2008 counterfeit card fraud (a classic cybercrime involving the cloning or
skimming of cards) has dropped by nearly 75 % in the UK—from losses
of £169 m to just £48 m in 2014. Similarly, card ID theft (another category which regularly attracts alarmist headlines) fell from around £47 m
of losses in 2008 to £30 m in 2014. ATM or cash machine fraud (also

a common marker of cybercriminality) has fallen by nearly two thirds over this period—from £77 m of losses in 2004 to just 27 m in 2014 (ibid). Phishing websites targeting UK banks and financial institutions have also significantly declined, from the 2011 high of 286,995 to just 23,729 in 2014 (ibid). Online banking and internet commerce frauds (goods bought and sold on the internet) represent some of the only fraud categories where there have been rises in loss prevalence, the former up from £12.2 m of losses to £60.4 m over this period and the latter up to £217 m in 2015 compared to £117 m in 2004 (FFA 2014). However, both rises need to be seen in the light of the major increases in online banking and purchasing activity since the 1990s.

The picture is a little more ambiguous with another high-profile cyber-crime—sexual grooming, especially of children. UK police data suggests that the offence peaked in 2009 with 393 recorded offences and has remained around or below this level since then (McGuire and Dowling 2013). Ministry of Justice data suggests a more definitive upward trend, doubling from 37 individuals sentenced in 2006 to 72 individuals in 2012 (ibid). Since UK sentencing data does not distinguish between online or offline grooming offences, it is also possible that the prevalence of such offending may be higher, because it is recorded under different legislation or, more simply, because it goes unreported. Equally, this rise may be deceptive, reflecting more sophisticated policing provisions of the kind provided by agencies like CEOP (Child Exploitation and Online Protection Centre), or the more vigorous arrest and prosecution options available since the 2005 Sexual Offences Act. Either way, despite the lurid media reporting of online grooming and repeated warnings by experts, available controls appear to have restricted its prevalence to levels lower than might have been expected. This more sober conclusion is corroborated by one of the most comprehensive pieces of research in this area, the EU Kids Go Online survey, which sampled over 25,000 European 9–16-year-olds in 2010. Its findings suggested that just 0.1 % of the 9 % who followed up an online encounter with a stranger with an offline meeting had subsequent sexual contact—and, of course, it is entirely possible that many of these meetings did not involve coercive grooming but simply young people meeting other young people to explore their sexuality. Prevalence metrics also suggest progress with another high-profile sexual cybercrime— the creation, use and distribution of IIOC (indecent images of children).

Over 16,000 individuals were charged with making an indecent image of a child in 2010, a figure which fell to around 14,000 in 2012/13 (McGuire and Dowling 2013). This trend was paralleled in data from the UK watchdog, the Internet Watch Foundation, which suggested a downward global trend in URLs including images with criminal child sexual abuse content—from around 13,000 in 2011 to just under 10,000 in 2012 (Internet Watch Foundation 2012).

Using prevalence measures to evaluate success against other 'typical' cybercrime offences is more ambiguous given the poverty of good data. In particular, success against computer-dependent forms of offending, such as malware distribution, remains very hard to assess. One familiar problem here is the notorious tendency of software security firms, who hold a lot of the key data, to report regular—often huge—annual increases in computer misuse. But simply looking at the prevalence of malware in circulation, the frequency of data breaches or the quantity of DDos (distributed denial of service) attacks could never be a reliable indicator of success (or failure). One strain of virus may have many variants, and volume in isolation tells us nothing about the real issue of how much damage actually results. Measuring success in terms of the *impact* of responses—i.e. how they limit what cyberdependent attacks are intended for—offers a more promising option. For example, the reductions in digital fraud noted above could suggest that cybersecurity has been successful in limiting the use of standard techniques for effecting this, such as phishing mails or keylogging software.

Evaluation becomes far more uncertain when assessing responses to one of the most pernicious varieties of cybersecurity incident—espionage and state-sponsored cyberattacks. Prima facie, there appears to be a clear upward trend here, with US research indicating that the 50 attacks on US companies per week in 2010, rose to 72 in 2011 and over 102 by 2012 (Ponemon 2010–2014). The sophistication of the attacks is certainly increasing. In 2014–15 alone a range of very high-profile US government computers were breached, whilst in June 2015 personal data from over four million federal employees was obtained illicitly (Reuters 2015). Though the Pentagon has specifically identified China as the source of many of these attacks (Sanger 2013), there is no confirmation of this, nor what it was that failed in US network protections.

Cybercrime 1.0–3.0 Precedents and Portents: What Was Done and What Has Worked?

Technical responses have seemed to be the most obvious ingredient of any crime control solution aimed at a technology-based offence like cybercrime. And the relative success of technical measures like chip and pin against card fraud, or filters and firewalls against IIOC appears to support their efficacy. As does the fact that the highest levels of fraud against UK cards used abroad are reported in jurisdictions where there are no such protections, like the USA (nearly a quarter of all such fraud losses) (FFA 2014).

In general there have been two common patterns of technical response against both cyberdependent and cyberenabled threats. The first centres upon preventing threats ever reaching a network/computer at all, with firewalls, passwords and filters being obvious examples of such a strategy.[3] For, if connectivity is central to cybercrime, then reducing this would seem to provide an ideal crime control option. For example, keeping a network sealed off from the internet by use of intranet or locking-down operating systems—as with Mac computers—has had demonstrable success in relation to virus control. More extreme controls—such as the decision by Chinese and other administrations to impose wholesale limits on internet traffic in and out of their jurisdictions—has also been very effective, though at an obvious ethical cost. A key problem with blocking techniques is sensitivity. Too many controls may mean that much of what we want to access from the internet is unavailable or that major civil liberties end up being abused. Thus, the drastic restriction of internet access might 'work', but at the price of also restricting all the benefits connectivity brings. And, of course, such controls are no use against the 55 % of all cyberattacks which now issue from individuals like disgruntled or incompetent employees—the so-called, 'insider threat' (IBM 2015).

The second pattern of technical response has centred upon detecting and dealing with a problem once it has reached the computer (e.g. antivirus, AV, protection, techniques for collecting digital evidence etc.).

---

[3] 'Whitelisting' of favoured sites, or creating a 'sinkhole' which diverts malicious traffic to a spoof site where it can be analysed (Bruneau 2010) offer other examples.

Though antivirus protection has been the most commonly used of these its effectiveness has been increasingly questioned. Claims that antivirus is 'dead' (Krebs 2014) have been supported by recent experiments indicating that only about 5 % of viruses are taken down by existing AV (Perlroth 2012). And because antivirus is a predominantly commercial product, there are obvious worries that there may be vested interests in 'having a problem'. However, suspicions that cybersecurity firms may even lie behind some strains of virus remain unproved, though there is certainly evidence that states have been involved in such activity. For example, some of the most powerful malware ever created—virus strains like Stuxnet, Duqu Flame and Equation Family—appear to have been created by the US and Israeli authorities to compromise targets like Iran's nuclear programme or to spy on Russian cybersecurity (McElroy 2012; Galperin and Quintin 2015).

Evaluation of antivirus is better handled within the wider package of measures that might simply be called cyber or internet security. For, aside from AV and filtering, this will also incorporate relatively straightforward measures, such as: keeping proper records of all hardware and software used on a network; effective management of the way ports, protocols and services are used on networked devices; or simply restricting administrative access. Or, at the network level, measures such as enhanced ISP controls, interventions by Computer Emergency or Computer Security Incident Response Teams (CERT/CSIRT) and advanced encryption (cf. CPNI 2015). Since no one is offering us very much data about the scope of these activities, their effectiveness is very hard to evaluate, though, as the Snowden revelations have revealed, misuses of them to spy on ordinary citizens (often illegally) may make them more of a public threat than cybercrime itself. Huge amounts are now spent on cybersecurity, with one recent study indicating that antivirus alone costs the UK in the vicinity of $170 m per annum, and in excess of $3400 m at the global level (Anderson et al. 2012).[4] However the research also suggests that returns on this investment have not met expectations—especially given that cybercrime security costs tend to be in excess of cybercrime criminal profits. And so,

---

[4] If other costs, such as cleaning up an infection are incorporated, Anderson et al. estimate this figure could rise to over $25,000 m globally—around $1200 m for the UK.

The straightforward conclusion to draw on the basis of the comparative figures collected in this study is that we should perhaps spend less in anticipation of computer crime (on antivirus, firewalls etc.) but we should certainly spend an awful lot more on catching and punishing the perpetrators. (ibid p. 26)

Such a conclusion is unexpected given the widespread presumption that, without a technical cybersecurity response, cybercrime is likely to get significantly worse. Yet quantifying the protection it does bring is far from clear. Such reflections raise important questions about how far our faith in technical solutions to cybercrime is well placed. For the tendency noted earlier—to view cybercrime simplistically, as a technology crime—inevitably reinforces the technological fetishism behind cybersecurity solutions, no matter how much lip service is paid to the human factors in cybercrime. A more rounded, socially grounded interpretation of cybercrime (see McGuire 2007 for example) offers an alternative to these fixations, one which has not yet been properly tested for its crime-control impacts.

What then of more orthodox, human-based forms of response, such as those offered by our traditional criminal justice system? In policing terms, the development of specialised cyber provision aimed at enhancing the skills required for more effective detection, apprehension and prosecution of cybercriminals has been a very common response, with around 90 % of countries who responded to a recent UN survey (UNODC 2013) stating that they had—or were going to put—in place specialised structures for cyberpolicing. More than 75 % said that existing law enforcement now have a cyber-focused unit, and around 15 % reported specialised agencies (ibid.). However, disparities in resourcing within less-developed nations means that this figure is less reassuring than it sounds—especially given the obvious attractions of cybercrime within such jurisdictions.

A recurring problem for specialised cyberpolicing provision has been a lack of stability and continuity. In the UK, for example, the extensive expertise that had been built up by the National Hi-Tech Crime Unit (NHTCU) was effectively lost when its functions were replaced by the new Serious and Organised Crime Agency (SOCA). In turn, SOCA has now been absorbed into the new National Crime Agency (NCA) which has also incorporated other specialised cyber-policing agencies such as CEOP, one of the pioneers of online child protection. It has also taken over responsibility for countering cyberfraud from the, now defunct, National Fraud Authority. Overly centralised agencies like these raise questions about the level of responsibility placed in one body, though too many units tasked with a cybercrime policing function, as in the USA, can produce their own problems around communication, data sharing or task duplication. Thus, though the FBI has a clear cyber-brief at the federal level it also shares this responsibility with partnership agencies, such as the National Cyber Investigative Joint Task Force, the National Cyber-Forensics and Training Alliance, the Computer Crime and Intellectual Property Section (based in the Department of Justice) and the Homeland Security Electronic Crimes Task Forces (situated within the Secret Service). State level cyberpolicing further complicates this picture with agencies such as the New York State Troopers Computer Crime Unit, the Minnesota Internet Crimes Against Children Task Force and even an Alaska Cyber Crimes Working Group. Whilst this proliferation of specialised units benefits politicians who want to look like they are doing something, the police themselves often privately confess to feeling an element of coercion in creating them and a resulting lack of confidence in their effectiveness (McGuire 2015). Commentators have also suggested that an enhanced cyberpolicing presence may be little more than 'reassurance policing' (Wall 2013). But, no matter how sophisticated national forces may become, the lack of any effective capacity to combat cybercrime at the transnational level will always prove counterproductive. For, aside from a few transnational-facing agencies such as the Virtual Global Task force, specialist cyberpolicing at the international level remains very limited. Although agencies like European Union Cybercrime Task Force (EUCTF) and the United Nations office on Drug and Crime (UNODC) have a transnational cyber-brief they have few powers, and national police forces are required to pursue internal co-operation through traditional means such as Interpol, Europol or other international agencies.

Arrest and prosecution prevalence measures have also been used as a method for assessing the success of cyberpolicing. For example, the FBI regularly issues announcements about the latest cybercriminals it has apprehended—most recently the 12 arrests which followed the recent takedown of the Darkode hacking form (DoJ 2015). Similarly, the Metropolitan Police Central e-Crime Unit (PCeU) pointed to the successful conviction of 89 cybercriminals and the disruption of 26 organised cybercrime groups (in the UK and abroad) between 2011 and 2013 as evidence that their interventions were working (Met Police 2013). However, the indications are that, within most jurisdictions, the level of proactive detections of cybercrime incidents through police investigation remains low. Indeed, the majority of cybercrimes are still brought to the attention of the police via victim reports, rather than police action (UNODC 2013, p. 118) Thus, in addition to arrest rates, police often fall back upon cost effectiveness metrics to demonstrate success—for example the $115 m the FBI claimed to have saved the US in 2010 as a result of their interventions against cybercrime (Snow 2011), or the PCeU's claim that their actions reduced financial harm and created up to £1.1 billion worth of savings to the UK economy between 2011 and 2013 (Met Police 2013). However, like all cost metrics such claims are challenged by various conceptual and methodological ambiguities—what is harm, what level of reduction, how was the sum calculated, etc. etc.? Thus, whilst the need for a cyberpolicing presence is self-evident, there is a need for far more research and far better elucidation of concepts and definitions if there is to be any certainty about the extent to which it is working

Even more spectacular than the development of specialised cyberpolicing has been the growth in cyber-related legislation. Many of the early complaints about tackling cybercrime centred upon the inadequate legal frameworks for pursuing it (cf. Scholberg 2014) and it is clear that the rapid development of 2.0 left many jurisdictions unprepared for the novelty of tools used within the digital environment. For example, criminal innovations like the illicit use of identification, the development of spam and the distribution of illicit online imagery could not be prosecuted under existing laws because of their digital character (ibid.). The sheer scale (and speed) of the legislation which followed is not just unusual in terms of how law has been used to regulate technology, it is probably unprecedented in legal history. The notoriously legislative bent of the USA means that it has led the way in passing a succession of cyberspecific laws—at both federal and state levels. For example, with state level attempts to criminalise online gambling,[5] or laws against sexting. Their necessity has often been unclear. For example, even though persuading minors to engage in an (unlawful) sex act could be prosecuted under existing legislation, many US states felt the need to introduce laws which specifically criminalised the use of a computer to do this (Brenner 2001). It is interesting then that the most distinctively cyberspecific laws—the (federal) Computer Fraud and Abuse Act (CFAA) and in the UK the Computer Misuse Act (1990)[6]—were enacted before the advent of the internet proper. In general though, the UK has preferred to use existing legislative tools against cyberoffending, such as the Fraud Act (2006) or the Sexual Offences Act (2003). Equally important as cyber-specific legislation has been the task of developing systems for the collection of electronic evidence and most jurisdictions report at least some capacity for collecting computer forensic material, such as encrypted files or browser patterns (UNODC 2013, p. 162). However, many also report difficulties in resourcing this or in being able to access individuals with sufficient expertise to extract it.

One more complex metric for assessing the effectiveness of legal (and policing) responses has been to look at suspect to offence ratios for particular cyberoffences (i.e. the number of individuals brought into contact with law enforcement in relation to the offences) and to then compare these to ratios for more standard offences. This metric confirms suspicions that ratios for typical cybercrime offences, like hacking or computer fraud, remain far lower than conventional crime—c. 40 suspects for every 100 offences, compared to around 90 for rape or homicide (UN 2013, p. 171). In fact, only very high-profile offences—like the making or distributing child pornography—are comparable. Take, for example, convictions under the UK Misuse of Computer Act. Between 2007 and 2012, a time when hacking, malware and other forms of computer misuse were (purportedly) skyrocketing, only around 80 individuals were found guilty. As suggested, this might be because such offences have been prosecuted under different laws (such as the Fraud Act), but it is equally possible that the prevalence of these offences is lower than imagined.

---

[5] In Louisiana LA. REV. STAT. ANN. § 14:90.3 (West 1997).
[6] 18 U.S.C. 1030. Both have been subject to ongoing revision and amendment—for example via other legislation such as the Police and Justice Act 2006.

At least three critical questions have arisen in relation to the legal response to cybercrime. One very significant problem has been the failure to develop any very satisfactory regulatory framework at the international level. This is in spite of the fact that transjurisdictionality—the way that cyberoffences can by committed by criminals in foreign jurisdictions—is viewed as one of the key problems of cybercrime. At least half of cybercrime acts are reported to have some transnational elements (UNODC, p. 54), but only agreements like the Budapest Convention or the Protocol to the United Nations Convention on the Rights of the Child (2010) have any international dimension. However, none of these have any legal force, and major international players such as Russia, China and India have refused to ratify the former. Not only has the Convention been subject to critique (see, for example, Marion 2010) there are few indications of how successful it has been in reducing cybercrime. Of course, other forms of international co-operation exist, such as collusion in the extradition of cybercriminals—for example in the recent extradition of Ercan Findikoglu from Germany to the USA on suspicion of ATM frauds (Strohm 2015). However, extradition tends to be a very one-way affair (almost invariably to the USA) and only happens where there are existing extradition agreements.

A second problem relates to the possibility of over-legislation, since too much law can clearly *create* cybercriminality where none previously existed. Worse, it can undermine public trust by criminalising too widely. This concern is reflected in a third problem, the disproportionate use of law against cybercriminals. At a time when those responsible for the large scale financial frauds which pushed the world economy into recession remain almost entirely unpunished, cyberoffenders have faced draconian sanctions. Thus, Aaron Swartz (a hacktivist who used illegal methods to force universities to make their research more freely accessible) was threatened with a 30-year sentence (he subsequently committed suicide), whilst Ross Ulbricht, who created the Silk Road online market was handed a life sentence, even though website hosts (e.g. an online newspaper forum) are not generally held accountable for illegal actions which occur as a result. These and many other examples force us to ask whether this legal excess actually helps reduce cybercrime or merely augments the feeding frenzy around it.

Finally, how effective have preventative responses to cybercrime been, especially those which centre upon directly engaging the public or the private sector? Reductions in offending are not the only objective here. More intangible outcomes, such as public reassurance or enhanced confidence in using the net, are also significant. But though engagement and education have often been highlighted as essential ingredients of any counter-cybercrime strategy, results have been mixed. One widely discussed problem has been the attitudes of the private sector—especially banks and financial services—which have been notoriously reluctant to share data about attacks or compromises to their systems. Equally well, the public have often been slow to engage more actively in fighting cybercrime, whether by reporting crimes more regularly and effectively, or simply by engaging in more security-conscious uses of ICT. It is surprising just how deep-seated this problem remains. In 2014 around 37 % of UK laptop owners were still admitting that they did not have a password or PIN number for their device and more than half of UK mobile phone (54 %) and PC (59 %) users and as many as two-thirds (67 %) of tablet owners also confessed to a lack of security (GSO/Vision Critical 2014). Similar problems beset the attempt to improve the reporting of cybercrime, in spite of the development of dedicated reporting platforms across many jurisdictions, such as IC3 in the USA, Pointe de Contacte in France and the Action Fraud hotline in the UK. Lack of awareness has been one problem here, with just 2 % of UK internet users saying that they knew of the Action Fraud hotline (Ipsos Mori 2013). Though this can be partly attributed to the hotline having just been rolled out when the survey was conducted, two years later over half of users were still saying that they had no idea where to report cybercrime (GSO/Vision Critical 2014). More worryingly, less than a third of the public said that they reported cybercrime events at all (ibid.). Over-excitable reporting of cybercrime has not helped public confidence in online security and has often persuaded them that the threat is more significant than it is or—worse—that nothing can be done. One result has been to create crime—for example in the emergence of online vigilantism by individuals seeking to crack down on popular hate figures like the 'online paedophile' (cf. Booth 2013). The conclusion has to be that, though there have been improved provisions for public and private responses to cybercrime over the last few years, they have clearly not yet resulted in the feeling that we are anything like on top of the problem.

The Challenge of Cybercrime 4.0?

To what extent might any of these previous successes (or indeed failures) be instructive within the, as yet untested, context of Cybercrime 4.0 and its refiguring of the offending landscape? Will its enhanced connectivities, its reshaping of service delivery and the increasingly intelligent interactivity available prove too testing a cocktail for existing responses? Or is our fear of the threat likely to be disproportionate to the actuality?

Its first defining factor—enhanced network multiplication—seems, prima facie, to be no more than a continuation of what went before 4.0 and so would not imply anything radically new to deal with. But the real challenge here lies in the *scale* of connectivity and the significantly enhanced range of criminal opportunities this offers. Recent research suggests that devices connected by active wireless grew by 20 % between 2013 and 2014 alone, with the total number of connected devices more than doubling (ABI Research 2014). And with over 55 % of UK mobile users using smartphones to maintain friendships on social networking sites and over 30 % saying they buy things via their phone (vs. 23 % in 2012) it is clear that simply conducting everyday life will require increasing connectivity. Network multiplication will be further accelerated by the, much vaunted Internet of Things scenario—where everything from household appliances to utility meters are now being connected together. For example, some projections (Press 2014) suggest that, over the next five years connected refrigerators will have been adopted by over 35 % of consumers, smart thermostats by over 30 % and 'self-driving' vacuum cleaners by around 18 %. Over 100 million connected wireless light bulbs and lamps will be in use globally by 2020 (ibid.). More intimate forms of immersion into an 'always on' environment—in particular from the increasing use of wearable devices such as watches, fitness monitors, clothing or data-enabled glasses—creates another set of risks from network multiplication (cf. Park and Jayaraman 2003; Wasik 2013). Recent data suggest that the wearables market doubled between 2013 and 2014 (Press 2014), with API's alone (data requests from wearable fitness devices) rising by over 500 % in the six months from the end of 2015 to June 2013 (Meeker 2013). Devices located *within*, as well as without, the body (cf. Cellan-Jones 2015) further extend this relationship. Network-enabled chips inserted under the skin offer one more familiar version of the 'connected body' scenario, as do medical devices like pacemakers or artificial organs (Pentland 2005).

It is this diversity of enhanced connectivity which will inevitably produce new risks. Cybercriminals are already using enhanced connectivity to disable AV protection, for example in the phenomenon of 'crypting' (cf. Krebs 2014), where new malware is 'product tested' by online groups against existing AV protections. But the increasing number of threat assessments centred upon the Internet of Things (see for example Europol 2014; Home Office 2015) emphasise that it is not just the number, but the *variety* of things which are connected that is fundamental to the new threat landscape. On the one hand such connections will open up a new spectrum of unsecured entry points to our networks. But equally worrying is the way that many objects in this network may serve as an enabler for other crimes. Suppose, for example, that a hacked meter reveals that power usage has dropped. Thieves could use this to conclude that homeowners are away, thereby enhancing the capacity of burglars to better evaluate possible targets. Or what of the new connectivities provided by near field communication (NFC), as used in contactless payment systems? Banks insist that card data can only be read at distances of five centimetres, but cybersecurity researchers have demonstrated how very inconspicuous machinery can be used to intercept contactless payments much further away—up to 80 cms (Dyson 2013). Worse, other researchers, using easily obtainable scanners, were able to obtain personal data that was meant to be hidden on contactless debit/credit cards. They then used this data to purchase other far more valuable items—including a £3000 TV (Bachelor 2015). At the more exotic end of the risk spectrum are the criminal opportunities presented by internal bodily devices. One example is the notorious pace-maker hack concept which, in theory, could enable internal medical devices to be manipulated or disrupted remotely. The fact that high-ranking politicians like Dick

Cheney (who wore a pacemaker during his latter period in office) have been thought to be vulnerable as a result (Peterson 2013) suggests that is not just a fantasy. And whilst Europol's prediction of the first murder via hacked internet-connected device by the end of 2014 (cf. Europol 2014) did not come to pass, but this does not rule it out in the near future.

The second key factor within the 4.0 threat landscape centres upon shifts in the delivery of computing services, in particular the development of cloud-based provision. From being a resource which was predominantly user driven and owned—the traditional box on the desktop—computing provision has increasingly become something remote. And this means that it is controlled centrally by large providers who operate with the kind of service delivery model more commonly seen with utilities like gas and electricity. At first glance, no special criminal risks appear to be posed by this—indeed the opposite. For surely, it might be argued, if the responsibility for computing provision (and therefore its security) is taken away from (fallible) individuals and placed in the hands of better informed and better resourced providers, criminal threats will decrease rather than increase? Unfortunately, when information rather than power is the commodity in question, utility metaphors—however useful—become somewhat strained. A first and most obvious difference relates to ownership. We do not think of water or electricity as something which is 'owned' by us, but rather that it is supplied to us. By contrast, our personal data *does* in a sense belong to us (in spite of the best efforts of data brokers to obscure this) and therefore can be stolen. Where computing power is centralised so, too, is much of the information which used to reside primarily upon personal computing devices, and an inevitable result is the creation of vast new honeypots of data. Prima facie, the new superdata honeypots created by the cloud come with considerable security attached, but equally well, nothing is absolutely secure and, once inside Cloud security, criminals have an almost unlimited opportunity to access sensitive material. A key weakness lies with hypervisors (cf. Vaugn-Nichols 2014), tools essential to running cloud services which—in a nutshell—can create and run virtual machines (VMs). These are software devices which share the same physical hardware with other VMs (like a server), but which have their own operating system. Given that many VMs may share the same hypervisor it is evident that if the hypervisor can be hacked it is, in a sense, game over for the other VMs. Up to 35 % of vulnerabilities attached to virtual machines have been connected to the hypervisor (IBM 2010).

Even though cloud provision is at a relatively early stage, there have already been some instances of the problems it is likely to generate. Take for example AWS, the Amazon cloud which, given Amazon's extensive resources, should be one of the more secure services. But AWS has been linked to a number of cybersecurity incidents, notably the 2014 attack on the company Code Spaces, when someone acquired an entry to their control panel on AWS (Venezia 2014). A classic extortion attack followed, which involved demands for money in return for ceding control back to Code Spaces. When Code Spaces refused to give in to the demands and attempted to take control back, the hacker began to delete many of their key resources—including the backups which were accessible via the same panel (ibid.). The consequences of this attack were serious for the company—it was effectively forced to cease operations—and emphasises how easily 'insider' attacks, via the cloud, can be more destructive than traditional 'outside-in' hacks.

Amazon is not the only major cloud provider to experience security issues. In another notorious recent attack the Apple iCloud was comprised when a series of personal celebrity photos were accessed and then posted on websites like 4chan (cf. Arthur 2014). One accusation is that Apple's security around the Find My iPhone service did not prevent 'brute force'[7] attacks and it was this weakness that may have been exploited for the hack (ibid.). Alternatively, a cloud-based Dropbox account where some of these photos were stored may have been accessed—again emphasising the danger of internal cloud attacks. More worryingly, the attack may have been human centred, with access secured by obtaining passwords, or by an ex-employee gaining access to one account then chaining to others, or by some variation upon phishing, where a user was fooled into handing over log-in details. Either way, once inside, access rapidly multiplied through address books linked to other address books. The hack provides a perfect example of how responses to 4.0

---

[7] These occur where there is no attempt to decrypt but simply to check through every permutation or candidate for a code or password.

criminality will need to be sophisticated enough to incorporate more than purely technical measures.

It is not just the novel way in which cloud architectures function which is likely to present new criminal opportunities. A second worry is the immense computing power which the cloud offers, power which can be hired easily and cheaply. In most cases this is a positive development, providing smaller companies and individuals with access to the kind of computing power and software previously available only to large organisations. But this wider access can inevitably also be exploited by those with less noble objectives—for example, for password cracking. Whereas encrypted passwords might once have taken many years to crack (if they could be at all), cloud computing power can help unlock them in a matter of days—and often at a very low cost. Research from Germany has demonstrated how Amazon cloud services could be used to break in to various wi-fi networks in around 20 minutes—and at a cost of less than $2 (Goodin 2011). There are worrying implications here, not least, evidence that such a method was used in the serious breach of Sony's PlayStation systems in 2010. This compromised over 100 million customer accounts, resulting in one of the largest data breaches in the USA in recent years (Galante 2011). The power of cloud computing has been equally useful in creating botnets—chains of computers under a central control which can be used for DDoS and other attacks. A proof of concept example of this was demonstrated at the 2014 Black Hat conference in Las Vegas, when a cloud-based botnet of over a thousand computers was constructed. This used only free trials and cloud accounts in combination with an automated system to generate unique email addresses which signed up for these accounts in huge numbers. (Greenberg 2014).

A second set of options for exploiting the different patterns of service delivery which are emerging centre more on functionality and the, so-called, app. The shift from an internet serviced primarily by websites to one which increasingly functions in terms of applications/apps has been fairly subtle, but appification has become a major trend within computing service delivery. For example, in January of 2014, 47 % of internet traffic was made up of apps (O'Toole 2014), whilst a recent survey of over 6000 web developers (VisionMobile 2015) suggested that over 23 %

of HTML5 mobile developers already have a predominant focus upon developing web apps—increasingly close to the 38 % who are developing mobile websites. Available evidence remains somewhat limited, but what we do know suggests that apps are becoming important new criminal resources to be exploited. The fact that apps have to be downloaded and stored on a device—one of the most dangerous things that can be done in terms of computing security—creates some obvious loopholes. Research by IBM indicates that web application vulnerabilities have become the most prevalent vulnerability affecting servers and were responsible for over 55 % of all disclosures in 2010 (IBM 2010). Similarly, in 2011/12 around 10 % of data-breach incidents could be linked to web-based app attacks—a figure which rose to 35 % of all data-breach incidents by 2014 (Verizon 2014).[8] Unlike traditional websites, the way many apps function also means that they often store sensitive personal data or information. For example, accessing many games or shopping apps requires users to hand over postcode, debit and credit card data. This results in further obvious vulnerabilities—especially given that this access is often by mobile phone. Like the cloud, apps raise testing questions about ownership and its negative implications. For, although there are plenty of free apps—most are 'owned' in ways not typical of websites—invariably by large app-store owners, such as Apple and Google. This results in an undue influence over the kinds of app which are permitted to exist and how they are built. Indeed, entire classes of apps can be rejected without transparent justification—for example, Apple has refused all apps related to Bitcoin. This does not just impede the kind of experimentation that was possible with the early internet but turns the tools used by the large providers for creating apps into targets themselves. For example, researchers have uncovered a substantial number of vulnerabilities in the Google app maker, some of which potentially allow server privileges within the cloud to be exploited for the kinds of internal attacks discussed above (Constantin 2014).

In all of this nothing has yet been said about the implications of the third ingredient of the 4.0 landscape, the proliferation of artificially intelligent agents across the web. It is not just that space precludes detailed

---

[8] Based on an analysis of over 1300 data-breach incidents investigated by Verizon.

consideration of this, but also that the implication of AI for cybercriminality remains a major unknown in terms of criminal opportunity. The possibility that driverless cars could be subject to cyberattacks which hand over key functions like braking and steering to third parties has already been demonstrated (Harris 2014; Versprille 2015) But otherwise, whether it is more intelligent botnets, phishing frauds conducted by artificial agents, or criminal conspiracies taking guidance from Siri or other online 'companions' (Goodman 2015), the risks posed by synthetic minds connected to the internet can only be partially evaluated at present. From Frankenstein to the Forbidden Planet, artificial agency has always stoked irrational fears within us. The key challenge will be to separate out such fears from the genuine criminal liabilities likely to be posed by this aspect of the 4.0 landscape (cf, Hallevy 2010).

The predominance of technical solutions in addressing cybercrime 1–3.0 is likely to be maintained in the response to cloud and app based criminalities—in spite of the doubts raised earlier. Criminal justice based responses will clearly also remain indispensable—even though 4.0 is likely to significantly augment the problems posed by 'traditional' cybercrime. Take as just one example the increased availability of anonymous communication channels and the ease in setting up (and closing down) anonymous accounts provided by the cloud. Not only will this make it more difficult for authorities to detect and apprehend cybercriminals, it will also make it far more challenging to obtain the forensic evidence needed to convict them. The 'traditional' cybercrime problem of transjurisdictionality can therefore only get worse, since many providers of cloud services also make it possible to locate their virtual machines within distinct physical locations. As a result, it will be entirely possible for a virtual machine created in, say, Asia to be used to mount attacks on locations in the USA or UK. One very recent example of these difficulties can be seen in the decision of the notorious file-sharing website Pirate Bay to shift its operations to cloud providers around the world. The result has been that providers host the Pirate Bay, without knowing that they are doing so and that the service can shift from country to country as necessary. And this means that there has been scarcely any take-down time for the site in the two years since it was created (BBC 2012).

Conclusions: 4.0 and Beyond...

The risks posed by cybercrime have nearly always been characterised as 'constantly' evolving. But evidence for our success in managing these risks is, so far, mixed. On the one hand it is clear that, after a slight delay in appreciating the significance of this form of crime, responses have become more comprehensive and targeted and there is now greater collaboration in managing them across most jurisdictions. And, whether it is technical responses, criminal justice interventions or a more informed and engaged public, real obstacles have been put in the way of unfettered cybercriminality which should not be overlooked. Yet, just when we might have thought it was becoming safer to enter the online waters, a new game appears to be coming to town. A massively connected, increasingly intelligent network, where services are provided by third parties over whom we have little control and even less knowledge. If cybercrime really is as technology dependent as we are told, these ever-shifting permutations may be something we will simply have to adjust to. But it is certainly hard to conclude anything other than existing provisions will be inadequate for the new risks of the 4.0 landscape. However, we should also remember that in a world where boundaries between our online or offline lives have become so eroded, cybersecurity can no longer be a matter of simple faith in technology to fix technology's (criminal) woes. Instead, effective responses must embrace what has always been the case, how best to respond to those humans who will use any available means to do bad things to other humans.

References

ABI Research. (2014, August 20). Internet of Everything market tracker.

Anderson, R., et al. (2012). *Measuring the cost of cybercrime.* Available at: http://weis2012.econinfosec.org/papers/Anderson_WEIS2012.pdf

Arthur. (2014, September 1). Naked celebrity hack: Security experts focus on iCloud backup theory. *Guardian.*

Bachelor, L. (2015, July 23). Contactless card fraud is too easy, says Which? *Guardian.*

BBC. (2012, October 17). The Pirate Bay moves to the cloud to avoid shutdown. *BBC.*

Bequai, A. (1986). Techno-Crimes: The computerization of crime and terrorism. D.C. Heath and Company.

Booth, R. (2013, October 25). Vigilante paedophile hunters ruining lives with internet stings. *Guardian.*

Bruneau, G. (2010). DNS Sinkhole' SANS Institute Reading Room, *White Paper.*

Cabinet Office. (2011). The UK cyber security strategy. *HMSO, 201.*

Cellan-Jones. (2015, January 29). Office puts chips under staff's skin. *BBC.*

Constantin, L. (2014b, December 9). More than 30 vulnerabilities found in Google App Engine. *Computerworld.*

Cowley, S. (2012, March 2). FBI Director: Cybercrime will eclipse terrorism. *CNN-Money.*

CPNI. (2015). Critical Security Controls guidance, Centre for Protection of National Infrastructure guidelines.

CSIS/McAfee. (2014, June). Net losses: Estimating the global cost of cybercrime. *Centre for Strategic and International Studies.*

CTIA. (2013, May 22). Wireless consumers aware of cyberthreats and know they should protect themselves, yet many don't. *Press Release.*

DoJ. (2015, July 15). Major computer hacking forum dismantled, Department of Justice Press Re lease.

Dyson, R. (2013, October 31). Engineers claim to prove risks of 'contactless' bank cards. *Daily Telegraph.*

Europol. (2014). Internet Organised Crime Threat Assessment 2014.

FFA. (2014). *Fraud, the facts,* Financial Fraud Action Annual Report.

Fortinet. (2013). Happy birthday, Mobile Malware! *White paper.*

Galante, J. (2011, May 16). Sony network breach shows Amazon cloud's appeal for hackers, Bloomberg.

Galperin, E., & Quintin, C. (2015, February 19). Russian researchers uncover sophisticated NSA malware *EFF.*

Goodin, D. (2011, January 11). Researcher cracks Wi-Fi passwords with Amazon cloud. *Register.*

Goodman, M. (2015). *Future crimes.* New York: Doubleday.

Greenberg, A. (2014, July 24). How hackers hid a money-mining botnet in the clouds of amazon and others. *Wired.*

GSMA. (2014). Mobile economy report, 2014, GSMA Intelligence.

GSO/Vision Critical. (2014). Survey on Internet security, summary at https://www.gov.uk/government/news/top-10-online-enabled-frauds-hitting-british-wallets-to-the-tune-of-670-million-with-high-emotional-cost

Hallevy, G. (2010). The Criminal Liability of Artificial Intelligence Entities. http://papers.ssrn.com/sol3/papers.cfm?abstract_id=1564096

Harris, M. (2014, July 16). FBI warns driverless cars could be used as 'lethal weapons'. *Guardian*.

Home Office. (2015, March 10). Internet of things: Potential risk of crime and how to prevent it. HO.

IBM. (2010). X-Force Mid-year Trend Report.

IBM. (2015). Cyber Security Security Intelligence Index.

Internet Watch Foundation. (2012). Internet Watch Foundation Annual and Charity Report 2012.

Ipsos Mori. (2013). Public attitudes to internet security, Details in McGuire and Dowling.

Krebs, C. (2014, May). Antivirus is dead: Long live antivirus! Krebs on Security.

Krishnan, A. (2009). *Killer robots: Legality and ethicality of autonomous weapons*. Farnham: Ashgate.

Maass, P., & Rajagopalan, M. (2012, March 1). Does cybercrime really cost $1 Trillion? *Propublica*.

Marion, N. (2010). The council of Europe's cyber crime treaty: An exercise in symbolic legislation. *International Journal of Cyber Criminology, 4*(1&2), 699–712.

McElroy, D. (2012, May 28). Flame: world's most complex computer virus exposed. *Daily Telegraph*.

McGuire, M. (2005). *Hypercrime: The new geometry of harm.* Abingdon: Routledge.

McGuire, M. (2013). *Policing responses to Cybercrime,* Unpublished interview research.

McGuire, M., & Dowling, S. (2013). *Cybercrime: A review of the evidence.*

Meeker, M. (2013, May 29). Internet Trends Report, KPCB.

Met Police. (2013, September 27). Cyber investigations save UK £1.01 billion, Press Release.

Norton. (2014). Annual report.

O'Toole, J. (2014, March 28). Mobile apps overtake PC Internet usage in U.S. CNN Money.

Ofcom. (2007). *The Communications Market 2007.*

Ofcom. (2014). Adult media use & attitudes report.

Ofcom. (2015). Adult media use & attitudes report.

Pagallo. (2013). *The laws of robots: Crimes, contracts, and torts*. Dordrecht: Springer.

Park, S., & Jayaraman, S. (2003). Enhancing the quality of life through wearable technology. *IEEE Engineering in Medicine and Biology Magazine, 22*(3), 41–48.

Parker, D. (1976). Crime by computer. New York: Charles Scribner's Sons.

Pentland, A. (2005). Healthwear: Medical technology becomes wearable. *Studies in Health Technology and Informatics, 118*, 55–65.

Perez, S. (2014, April 1). Mobile app usage increases in 2014, as mobile web surfing declines. *Tech Crunch*.

Perlroth, N. (2012, December 31). Outmaneuvered at their own game, antivirus makers struggle to adapt. *New York Times*.

Peterson, A. (2013, October 21). Yes, terrorists could have hacked Dick Cheney's heart. *Washington Post*.

Ponemon. (2010–2014). Cost of data breach reports, Ponemon Institute.

Press, G. (2014, August 22). Internet of things by the numbers. Forbes.

Sanger, D. (2013, May 6). U.S. blames China's military directly for cyberattacks. *New York Times*.

Schmidt, et al. (2009). Smartphone malware evolution revisited: Android next target? In *MALWARE, 2009 4th International Conference*.

Scholberg, S. (2014) The history of cybercrime: 1976–2014, Cybercrime Research Institute.

Snow, G. (2011, April 12). Statement before the Senate Judiciary Committee.

Spencer, L. (2015, February 13). 16 million mobile devices hit by malware in 2014. *ZDnet*.

Strohm, C. (2015, June 23). Most-wanted cybercriminal extradited to U.S. from Germany. Bloomberg.

Tuomi, A. (2002). The lives and death of Moores Law. *First Monday, 7*(11), 4.

UNODC. (2013). Comprehensive study on cybercrime. Available at: http://www.unodc.org/documents/organizedcrime/UNODC_CCPCJ_EG.4_2013/CYBERCRIME_STUDY_210213.pdf

Vaughn-Nichols, S. (2014, March 29). Hypervisors: The cloud's potential security Achilles heel. *ZDNet*.

Venezia, P. (2014, June 23). Murder in the Amazon cloud. *Infoworld*.

Verizon. (2015). Data Breach Investigations Report.

Versprille, A. (2015). Researchers hack into driverless car system, take control of vehicle. *National Defense Magazine*, May.

VisionMobile. (2014). Developer economics Q1 2015: State of the developer nation. Available at: https://www.developereconomics.com/reports/developer-economics-q1-2015/#key-insights

Wall, D. (2013). *Cybercrime and the culture of fear: Policing the reassurance gap in cybersecurity*. Berlin: Springer.

Wasik. (2013, December 17). Why wearable tech will be as the smartphone. *Wired*.

11

Addressing Prostitution: The Nordic Model and Beyond

Helen Johnson and Roger Matthews

Introduction

There are few social issues on which opinion is more deeply divided than that of prostitution. On one side is the liberal pro-prostitution lobby who believe that people enter prostitution out of choice. These liberals and fellow libertarians seek to normalise prostitution and call for a free market in the sale and purchase of sexual services and either the removal of sanctions altogether or, alternatively, favour the provision of some form of state licensing and approval. On the other side are abolitionists, who see prostitution as a form of violence against women and an expression of male power and exploitation. For these abolitionists the objective is to decrease the trade in commercialised sexual services and limit as far as possible the various forms of exploitation and coercion that they see as being associated with prostitution.

There is a clear and identifiable link between the way in which prostitution is conceived and the type of policy response advocated. Thus it is

H. Johnson (✉) • R. Matthews
University of Kent, Canterbury, UK

necessary at the outset to position oneself in this debate and clarify the normative vantage point from which we begin. Our main concerns with prostitution centre on exploitation, coercion and suffering. Therefore, we gravitate towards an abolitionist approach and reject the liberal claims that prostitution involves a free exchange between equal parties. As Carole Pateman (1988) has argued, the act of prostitution is qualitatively different from the provision of other forms of (service) labour, because in the act of prostitution the identity of the person is bound up with the purchase of the body of the seller and the level of intimacy involved. Just as the act of rape is seen as being qualitatively different from other forms of violence, so prostitution is seen to be different from other forms of labour.

Nor do we believe that women routinely enter prostitution out of free choice. In fact, it is often the case that women enter prostitution when they run out of choices. Paradoxically, although liberals claim to be defending the women involved in prostitution by emphasising the notion of choice, this emphasis places responsibility and, by implication, the culpability on the women involved. Moreover, the notion of choice tends to individualise what is essentially a class condition (Jeffreys 1997).

One immediate point of identification and difference between liberals and abolitionists is to be found in the use of terminology. While abolitionists normally use the word prostitution to identify the provision of intimate commercialised sexual services in exchange for money or goods, liberals prefer to use the euphemism sex work. The significance of the term sex work is that it lumps together a wide range of activities, ranging from lap dancing and telephone sex to sexual penetration. This has the effect of obscuring and sanitising the often dangerous and demeaning aspects of prostitution. In addition, the use of the vague term sex work provides an obstacle to the development of policy since different aspects of the sex trade necessarily require different responses. This use of this form of terminology also tends to present pimps and brothel owners as boyfriends, partners or managers, rather than exploiters and coercers.

An instructive example of the different approaches adopted by abolitionists and liberals is their respective responses to the five women involved in prostitution who were murdered in Ipswich in 2006. While abolitionists, and indeed the local authority, called for support to help the women leave prostitution, the main intervention from the liberal pro-prostitution lobby was to chastise the media for describing the murdered women as prostitutes and insisting that they be called sex workers. This term, it was claimed, was less stigmatising and less essentialising. However, referring to someone as a sex worker is no less essentialising than calling him or her a prostitute.

The liberal and libertarian pro-prostitution lobby tend to favour either a policy of state licensing (legalisation) or a free market in the exchange of commercialised sexual services (decriminalisation). Both of these approaches have been tried in different countries with little success (Raymond 2003). Although their introduction was justified on the basis of cleaning up the sex trade and improving the conditions for those involved, the outcome has been an increasing involvement of organised criminal networks, widespread exploitation and the growth of sex trafficking (Jeffreys 2004; Raymond 2013; Matthews 2008). The limitations of these approaches have been well documented and we will not rehearse them here. Instead, we will focus on what has become known as The Nordic Model, which essentially involves the criminalisation of the purchase of sex and the decriminalisation of the sale of sex. This approach is attracting considerable international interest and offers a radical and arguably progressive approach to the challenging issue of regulating prostitution (Skilbrei and Holstrom 2011).

The Nordic Model

In contrast to the legalisation and decriminalisation approaches that have been adopted in the Netherlands, New Zealand and elsewhere, an alternative approach, often referred to as the Nordic Model, is gaining support in various countries as politicians and policy makers are searching for a more viable and coherent approach to deal with prostitution. Although there are variations in the nature and implementation of the Nordic Model in different countries it has gained considerable ground internationally over the last two decades (Bucken-Knapp and Schaffer 2010). In many of the counties concerned, criminalising the purchase of sexual services and decriminalising the sale has reversed the victim-offender relationship that had previously existed for hundreds of years. The Nordic Model has been adopted by a number of countries in the recent period, including Sweden, Norway, Iceland, Finland, Canada, France and Ireland. There are other countries, such as, Lithuania and the UK, which appear to be moving in this direction (Home Office 2014). The arguments in support of the Nordic Model are varied and appeal to different audiences. Some of the justifications for the adoption of this approach are principled and normative, while others are pragmatic (Scarhed 2010).

One of the main arguments in favour of criminalising the purchase of sexual services is associated with what is sometimes referred to as the 'myth of mutuality' (Plumridge et al. 1997). In opposition to the claim that prostitution involves a free and open exchange between equal partners it is argued that the prostitute–client relationship involves an asymmetrical power relation. That is, the relationship is ultimately controlled by the purchaser who is able to orchestrate the transaction through the power of money. It is the client's sexual desires and interests that are being catered for, while the sexual desires of the prostitute are strategically irrelevant. Second, that policy makers have begun to distinguish between the individual prostitute and the business of prostitution. In this way, they have been able to maintain what was formally seen as a contradictory position, which involves adopting a more sympathetic approach to those who sell sex, on the one hand, while opposing the commercial and exploitative aspects of the trade on the other.

Third, and relatedly, women and young men involved in prostitution have become widely seen as victims rather than offenders. Many of those involved in prostitution have been found to enter the trade at a young age and, in a considerable number of cases, before the age of consent. Others have been found to have been groomed, induced or coerced into prostitution, while a significant proportion of those involved in street prostitution are identified as problematic drug users whose engagement in prostitution is mainly motivated by drug dependency. A great deal has been written in recent years about the different forms of victimisation that those involved in prostitution experience and it has become increasingly clear that they are amongst the most victimised social groups (Matthews 2011).

Fourth, the image of the client or buyer has changed. The establishment of internet sites, such as Punternet, provides some insight into the attitudes and interests of those who purchase sex. Overall, the frank exchanges and evaluations of the 'performances' of the women whose services they have purchased involve a disturbing combination of contempt, aggression and objectification (Sharpe and Earle 2003). It has been widely acknowledged for some time that women involved in prostitution experience a certain level of violence and abuse, mostly at the hands of their clients. The liberals, while recognising that prostitution is a risky business, have tended to play down the level of everyday violence and suggest that there are a few 'bad apples' and that these exceptional perpetrators of violence can be dealt with by organising 'ugly mugs' campaigns (Sanders 2005; Kinnell 2013). In this way it is assumed that by circulating images of known abusers locally women can be made safe and the level of violence significantly reduced or eradicated. However, the widespread incidence of violence experienced by women involved in both on and off street prostitution suggests that it is considerably more endemic than is often recognised and is associated with the vulnerability of the women involved and the perpetrators' sense of impunity (Sparks 1981).

There is also a growing body of research on men that purchase sex. What this research shows very clearly is that a buyer's motivation is much more superficial and transient than is often suggested and that they are relatively easily deterred. Three recent surveys that have asked purchasers what would deter them from paying for sex have found that almost anything that makes this transaction problematic would be enough to dissuade them. While all these surveys found that over 80 per cent of purchasers in England, Scotland and Canada would be deterred by the introduction of legislation criminalising the purchase of sex, almost the same percentage said that they would be deterred by forms of shaming and stigmatisation (Durchslag and Goswani 2008; Farley et al. 2009; McLeod et al. 2008).

The preference for the use of formal legal sanctions rather than relying on informal controls lies in part in the objective of increasing general, rather than specific, deterrence. That is, to change attitudes towards buying sex amongst the general population. The evidence from both Sweden and Norway suggests that criminalising the purchase of sex had precisely this effect, particularly amongst the young (Jacobsen and Kotsadam 2010).

One issue that has been raised but not fully addressed in recent research is how many and what percentage of men pay for sex. Some research suggests that purchase of sex is widespread amongst men of all social groups, while other research suggests that it is a particular group of men—mostly older, single, disabled or lonely men—who pay for sexual services (Coy et al. 2007; Sanders 2008). The limited available evidence suggests that neither of these positions are accurate and that the truth lies somewhere between these extremes. A recent survey carried out in the UK, for example, suggests that while the number of purchasers may be increasing the proportion of men who have ever paid for sex is in the region of four per cent and many of these will have done so less than five times in the past (Ward et al. 2005).

The Liberal Critique of the Nordic Model

The Nordic Model has been in place since 1999 in Sweden and since 2008 in Norway (Bucken-Knapp and Schaffer 2010). During this period various assessments have been made of its effects and, while the assessment is generally positive in terms of reducing prostitution and sex trafficking, liberal critics have identified what they see as the limitations and undesirable consequences of the legislation. These critiques can be summarised as follows:

- That it infringes sex workers' rights to liberty and security of the person
- Although the legislation may have reduced the visibility of prostitution it has merely moved indoors and online
- It has undermined sex workers' access to HIV prevention initiatives and other forms of health care
- Client numbers have been reduced and those that remain are more likely to be drunk, abusive or request unprotected sex
- The competition for the reduced number of clients has lowered prices and decreased sex workers' bargaining power
- Because transactions have to be completed quickly it is difficult for the seller to assess whether the client may be dangerous
- Because women operate from more isolated locations they are more vulnerable
- Sex workers are subject to aggressive policing and continued surveillance
- Sex workers cannot employ others to assist them and provide security

In sum, it is argued that although the intention of the Nordic Model is to eliminate exploitation and protect women involved in prostitution, the impact of the legislation serves to reduce women's control over their situation and thereby decrease their level of personal safety (Chu and Glass 2013). Some of the negative consequences of the Nordic Model identified by liberal critics, such as increased isolation, decreasing demand and decreased earnings are, to some extent, an inevitable consequence of reducing demand. The question, as always, is whether the claimed negative effects of the intervention outweigh the gains.

The claim that decreasing demand will increase the level of violence is unconvincing. As noted above, violence is endemic rather than peripheral to prostitution (Church et al. 2001). Moreover, violence is often inflicted not when women are advertising for custom but when they are alone with the client, particularly behind closed doors or in an isolated location. The important point is that all of the women who have exited prostitution because of the decline in demand are spared this threat of violence from buyers, pimps and third party controllers.

The argument that prostitution in Sweden has moved from the street to indoor premises is without credible empirical support. Many of the women involved in street prostitution in Sweden and elsewhere are not competent or reliable enough to be employed by profit-seeking entrepreneurs and not organised enough to operate effectively from their own premises. The high prevalence of drug addiction amongst those involved in street prostitution makes it difficult for many of these women to meet the demands of operating off street.

Those women who remain involved in prostitution in Sweden and other countries that operate with a version of the Nordic Model do receive considerable attention and support from the relevant agencies in addressing their health problems. The provision of such support is seen is part of the strategy of caring for deserving victims and also partly as a strategy to help women overcome the dependencies that might be keeping them involved in prostitution. Considerable emphasis is also placed on reducing exploitation and the activities of those third parties who pressure or coerce women to remain in prostitution (MJP 2004; Waltman 2011).

In countries in which the adoption of the Nordic Model involves the decriminalising of the sale of sex or soliciting, the argument that it involves a reduction of the rights of liberty and security makes little sense.

In countries in which the sale of sexual services was already decriminalised before the introduction of the Nordic Model, there is little change in the ability of women to exercise their right to rent out their bodies. However, the 1949 United Nations Convention on the Suppression of the Trafficking in Persons and the Exploitation of the Prostitution of Others states: 'That prostitution and the accompanying evil of the traffic in persons for the purpose of prostitution are incompatible with the dignity and worth of the human person and endanger the welfare of the individual, the family and the community.' This convention therefore defines prostitution as incompatible with the UN Declaration of Human Rights 1948, which guarantees human dignity and integrity to all. Additionally, feminist abolitionists contend that prostitution constitutes a form of violence against women and hence a violation of their human rights.

Overall, the critiques of the Nordic Model are weak and to some extent disingenuous since the liberal pro-prostitution lobby objects to the very notion of addressing demand, while their general aim is to defend and perpetuate prostitution. Liberals seem to be driven by the misguided belief that prostitution is an expression of sexual freedom and an assumption that freedom involves either a lack of state interference or the formal licensing of prostitution by the state.

Beyond the Nordic Model

Although the Nordic Model represents a major step forward in the regulation of prostitution it is not a panacea. Passing legislation alone is rarely enough to effect meaningful social change and, while in countries like Britain it would undoubtedly go a long way towards reducing the trade in commercialised sexual services, there are a number of considerations that require attention if a comprehensive response to prostitution is to be developed. Therefore, in this section our aim is to identify some of these outstanding issues and suggest some ways in which the essential components of the Nordic Model could be better adapted to the British context. These include developing an effective exiting strategy, providing appropriate forms of drug treatment, changing public attitudes in relation to demand, developing strategies to prevent new entrants into prostitution, dealing with sex trafficking, instigating consistent policing strategies and considering the impact of the internet on the sex trade.

Exiting

A key feature of the Nordic Model is placing emphasis on the need to help women exit prostitution. The significance of this aspect of the approach is that women involved in prostitution are no longer viewed as offenders, or even as passive victims, but as agents capable of making decisions about the quality and direction of their own lives. Although we know quite a bit about how women enter prostitution we know much less about how they leave. However, a growing body of research has found that the vast majority of women involved in prostitution would like to leave given the opportunity (Hester and Westmarland 2004; Mayhew and Mossman 2007; Johnson 2015).

Arguably, one of the limitations of the implementation of the Nordic Model in Sweden and elsewhere is that it tends to rely on psychotherapeutic approaches developed by writers such as Judith Herman (1992). These approaches are limited inasmuch as they are mainly backward looking, aimed at the most damaged women and often involve years of counselling and therapy. Recent research carried out in the UK, however, has found that the majority of women do not need years of counselling to exit and that many can leave prostitution relatively quickly given appropriate levels of support and motivation (Matthews et al. 2014; Matthews and Easton 2010). Research on exiting has shown that it requires the development of new roles and the adoption of a non-prostitute identity and that this involves not only dealing with past deficits but also having a sense of hope and a vision of an alternative future (Ebaugh 1988; Mansson and Hedin 1999; Maruna 2001).

Inasmuch as prostitution support groups have engaged with the issue of exiting in the UK they have largely adopted a reactive approach. This is in part a consequence of operating with a harm minimisation agenda that aims to respond to the women's needs and problems. However, an effective exiting policy, it is suggested, needs to move from a reactive stance to a more proactive approach that is able to encourage and facilitate the exiting process. The adoption of a proactive approach in Ipswich, following the murders in 2006 of five women involved in prostitution, proved successful in removing the majority of women from the streets and helping them to exit (Poland et al. 2008). One of the most important aspects of this proactive approach was to create a context in which exit is possible and where their lives can be reimagined without waiting for the women themselves to reach rock bottom (Johnson 2015; Matthews et al. 2014; Mossman and Mayhew 2007).

However, the lack of interest in exiting has meant that existing strategies are not well developed and there is a lack of funding for developing exiting programmes. Clearly, any effective exiting strategy needs to consider both agency and structure and develop sensitive interventions that are able to provide targeted support and identify the women's capacity to change. Previous research suggests that, despite years of abuse and exposure to violence, many of the women undergoing the process of exiting are remarkably resilient and able to block off their past and re-establish a new sense of self (Rumgay 2004). For many women who decide to exit it is necessary to address a number of needs. The most common issues are drug addiction and providing a response that allows women to reduce their dependency on the income from prostitution. Once these issues are addressed women are in a better position to make clear and constructive decisions.

Providing an Appropriate Response to Drug Addiction

The association between drug use and prostitution has largely focused to date on the consumption of crack cocaine and heroin by women involved in street prostitution. Estimates vary, but the available research suggests that somewhere between 70 and 90 per cent of those involved in street prostitution in the UK are problematic drug users. However, research on women involved in off street prostitution has also found that many have a drug habit, although their drugs of choice may be different (May and Hunter 2006; Matthews et al. 2014).

For 'problematic' intravenous drug users, the preferred method of treatment has been the use of methadone. This has been widely hailed as an effective treatment, which is seen to stabilise heroin addiction. However, it has been argued that methadone maintenance simply replaces one form of addiction with another (Bourgois and Schonberg 2009). In addition, it is claimed by some critics that methadone is far more pharmacologically addictive than heroin and that withdrawal symptoms can be more severe and prolonged. Research indicates that between five and ten per cent of people addicted to heroin fail to respond to methadone, while some continue to use heroin alongside methadone (Doran 2008). The choice of methadone over other treatments seems to be governed by two considerations—cost and the desire to maintain some form of dependency. The cost of placing someone on methadone is estimated to be in the region of £3000 per year (Gossop et al. 2001). There are in excess of 170,000 people in the UK given regular doses of methadone and there was a 60 per cent increase in methadone prescriptions between 2003 and 2007 (Byford et al. 2013). As an alternative a 12-week detoxification programme costs between £6000 and £12,000, whereas residential rehabilitation costs between £600 and £700 per week. In general however, only better-off addicts tend to receive residential rehabilitation.

Thus, if the aim is to achieve abstinence rather than long-term dependency some form of detox and/or residential treatment may be necessary. The implication of this argument is that the frequent calls for the implementation of fast-track methadone treatment programmes is not likely to solve the problem. In addition, there are issues about the availability of drug treatment programmes not only for opiate users but also for those addicted to cocaine, cannabis and many polydrug users.

We should also be cautious about seeing the removal drug dependency as a solution to involvement in prostitution. Research indicates that a significant percentage of women who radically reduce their drug use or give up heroin or crack cocaine continue to be involved in prostitution. For women to successfully exit tends to require other forms of intervention, including formal and informal support (Buchanan 2004; Hedin and Mansson 2003; Matthews et al. 2014).

Addressing Demand

One of the notable features of countries like Sweden and Norway is that prior to the introduction of the Nordic Model there was a body of public opinion that felt purchasing sex was either undesirable or unacceptable. In this context passing legislation to criminalise the purchase of sex is more straightforward and more likely to be effective. However, in countries like Britain public opinion is more ambivalent on this issue at the present time. In line with most European countries and America, the purchase of sex has been widely accepted for many years and it remains a non-problematic theme in the popular media. Films such as *Pretty Woman*, *Klute*, *Last Exit to Brooklyn*, and *Secret Diary of a Call Girl* amongst others continue to present the purchase of sex as an acceptable and legitimate activity.

As became clear in recent anti-smoking campaigns their effectiveness relied on a combination of both formal and informal sanctions. Changing public opinion on the desirability of smoking played a significant role in making the legal sanctions stick (Reid 2005). In addition, decreasing the visibility of cigarette packets and emphasising the risks played no small part in the effectiveness of this campaign. The implication of this approach in countries like Britain that are moving towards the Nordic Model is that there is a need to increase public awareness of the motivations of buyers and the impact of their actions, both in relation to the women concerned and to society in general. At the same time every effort should be made to raise awareness amongst the buyers themselves.

There has in the past been a small number of local awareness raising campaigns. Probably best-known was the poster campaign carried out in Westminster and Nottingham in 2008, which read 'Walk in a Punter, Walk out a Rapist'. This campaign was designed to sensitise buyers to the possibility that the woman had been trafficked. This poster campaign was linked to an online initiative that included a web page dispelling common myths about trafficking and exploitation.

Campaigns have also been organised in conjunction with major sporting events to address the issue of sex tourism. The Campaign Against Trafficking in Women (CATW) sponsored an international campaign around the slogan 'Buying Sex is Not a Sport'. In addition there has been the 'I'm Not Buying it' campaign and during the Super Bowl 2011 there was a publicity campaign centred around the slogan 'Real Men Don't Buy Sex' (Marcovich 2006). These campaigns serve not only to sensitise the general public but also to responsibilise the buyers (Durchslag and Goswani 2008). Although these initiatives are important in influencing public perceptions many campaigns are short-lived or under-funded. Such campaigns need to be more widely distributed, not only in the form of leaflets and posters but by becoming part of the school curriculum and of a wider social debate in the way that domestic violence and bullying have done. In addition to addressing demand it is also necessary to reduce supply.

Developing Prevention Strategies

There is a considerable amount of literature on how people become involved in prostitution. This literature clearly indicates that it is predominantly poor women and girls from dysfunctional families, who have been abused or neglected, or those who have been in local authority care. Alternatively, they have been referred to as 'throwaways' who for some reason find themselves homeless or destitute (Flowers 2001). In conventional terms this involves identifying the 'at risk' group who become marginalised and vulnerable at an early age and are susceptible to involvement in the sex trade.

Despite the relative ease with which this at risk group can be identified girls and young women continue to be recruited from the same sources. We know a great deal about the risk factors associated with entry into prostitution but we have been slow to act on this information. The risk factors that have been identified include substance misuse, sexual victimisation, being in care, school exclusion, self-harming or attempted suicide, runaways and homelessness. These factors tend to make young people vulnerable to coercion, grooming or persuasion (see Matthews 2008).

In the UK there are a number of agencies engaging in some form of preventative work with vulnerable young people, including the NSPCC, the Local Area Child Protection Committees, Barnardo's, youth offending teams and social workers (Swann and Balding 2002). Their activities are commendable but they tend to be uncoordinated and under-funded. A recent report on how local partnerships respond to child prostitution, for example, found that only a quarter of the Local Safeguarding Children's Boards (LSCBs) were implementing the 2009 government guidance on safeguarding children and young people from sexual exploitation and that the prosecution of abusers is rare (Jago et al. 2011). LSCBs were found not to be proactive in implementing the guidance and only ten per cent work together with the police. In general, it was found that current thresholds of intervention are too high and many of the LSCB's did not record data on child exploitation and were unable to provide intelligence to inform strategic preventative interventions (CEOP 2011).

There are, of course, some examples of good preventative work going on with young people in certain parts of the country, but it is clear that preventative work with young people at risk remains patchy and inconsistent (Matthews and Easton 2010). In a period of growing inequality and child poverty in Britain there is an urgent need to provide a coordinated and comprehensive response to young people at risk of sexual exploitation.

The Problem of Sex Trafficking

Although the implementation of the Nordic Model in countries like Sweden has served to reduce sex trafficking, there remain ongoing issues about how women who have been trafficked should be treated, and indeed how the problem of trafficking is conceived and defined. There are two related issues that need to be addressed. The first is the problem of definition and, by implication, the meaning of coercion. The second is the nature of the response that the appropriate authorities take towards those who are deemed to have been trafficked.

Following the ratification of the Council of Europe Convention Against Trafficking in Human Beings in December 2009 the Anti-Trafficking Monitoring Group was set up to monitor the implementation and compliance in the UK with the Convention. Their research found that the government misunderstood the key provisions of the Convention, employed largely unaccountable officials and overlooked the necessary safeguards for child victims of trafficking (Anti-Trafficking Monitoring Group 2010). The use of untrained officials, accompanied by flawed legal guidance relating to who should be identified as victims of trafficking, results, it is suggested, in the failure to consistently identify and assist legitimate victims. Adopting a relatively narrow definition and interpretation of trafficked persons results, it is suggested, in victims being wrongly identified. This can have serious consequences for the individuals concerned. The Anti-Trafficking Monitoring Group report concludes:

> The existing system is neither satisfying the provisions of the Convention nor key principles of the Rule of Law itself. Pockets of good practice contrast with the centralised system that lacks any formal coordination and seems to be failing to refer trafficked persons to assistance and protection ... The system has so far failed to contribute significantly to either an increase in prosecution or a wider knowledge of trafficking (Anti-Trafficking Monitoring Group 2010: 13).

Although there have been attempts to provide a positive response to victims of sex trafficking in a number of European countries following the ratification of the Council of Europe Convention on Action Against Trafficking in Human Beings in December 2008, responses have been uneven and inconsistent. Trafficking has been defined as a crime and anyone who has been subject to trafficking should be recognised as a victim. However, a series of difficulties have been identified which involve: (a) a misunderstanding of key roles of the Convention; (b) not addressing the entirety of the Convention; (c) delegating considerable authority on identification through a flawed mechanism staffed by substantially unaccountable officials; and (d) overlooking the necessary safeguards for child victims of trafficking contained in the implementation of the Convention. Some of these deficiencies may be the result of familiar bureaucratic and implementation issues, but it is also probable that such inefficiencies also arise from the lack of priority given to victims of trafficking. At the heart of the difficulties in implementing the provisions of the Convention was a flawed identification process that consistently failed to identify and assist people who had been trafficked (Anti-Trafficking Monitoring Group 2010).

The report by the Anti-Trafficking Monitoring Group (2010), which focused mainly on the situation in the UK, found that letters sent to applicants by the relevant authorities were inconsistent and contradictory. For example, one such letter reads: 'Your account is consistent with that of a person who has been trafficked ... but you have not reached the threshold of reasonable grounds to believe that you are a victim of trafficking for the purposes of the Convention. Even if it was accepted that you had been trafficked from ... to the UK and held against your will and forced to ... it is not accepted that you currently qualify as a victim of trafficking for the purpose of the Convention' (p. 39). However, the Convention clearly states that anyone who has been trafficked, regardless of their current immigration status or whether they are under the control of the trafficker when identified as a potential victim of trafficking, should be considered to be a victim of trafficking. A policy that restricts the definition of victim to those who when identified fall under certain categories is not consistent with the aims of the Convention. So the policy and the practice in the UK of making negative decisions in cases in which the trafficked person has already escaped the influence of the trafficker does in fact violate the provisions of the Convention. In addition, a number of researchers have pointed out that many trafficked persons are detained mainly for the purpose of gathering information about traffickers, after which the women themselves are likely to be deported and not offered any of the support that the Convention is designed to provide.

In a subsequent review of the National Referral Mechanism for Victims of Human Trafficking (Home Office 2014a) it was reported that the system of referral was disjointed with a low awareness. Decision-making was found to be poor with limited information sharing amongst the relevant personnel. The report expressed concern about the level of support given to victims and states that 'the current data collected and provision does not support the effective identification of victims'.

These issues were evident in an Association of Chief Police Officers (ACPO) report that attempted to classify migrant women involved in prostitution in England and Wales. The 17,000 women identified by the police were divided into three categories, trafficked, vulnerable and independent economic migrants. The report claims that 2600 were trafficked, 9200 were vulnerable and 5500 were neither trafficked nor vulnerable (see Jackson et al. 2010). Whereas those defined as trafficked clearly met the criteria of abuse, vulnerability and coercion, those defined as vulnerable but not trafficked were, in many cases, subject to abuse at the point of recruitment and at the destination and experienced 'exploitative conditions of work'. However, these women, according to the police definition, fall short of the threshold of being trafficked. Again, this is at odds with the definition and guidelines provided by the European Convention.

The net result of these deficiencies is that many people who have been trafficked are treated as illegal immigrants and are subsequently deported, or are detained by the police as either offenders or witnesses. Moreover, the tendency to define trafficking down does mean that the formal number of trafficked persons in any period is significantly reduced and this lends weight to the arguments of those liberal commentators who want to deny the reality of trafficking and redefine trafficked persons as economic migrants (Agustin 2006; Mai 2009; Weitzer 2005).

The Police and Law Enforcement

It is one thing to pass legislation designed to regulate prostitution, but it is another for this legislation to be effectively enforced. The evidence from Sweden is that the police enforce the current legislation consistently and effectively. However, in countries like the UK, enforcing laws relating to prostitution has historically been a low priority for the police. Many of the 'vice squads' that were set up in the 1970s and 1980s have been dismantled and the police tend to act increasingly as a referral agency. The reality is that working in 'vice' has always been seen as low-level police work in the UK and the police's main interest in the past has been to see prostitution as a source of information gathering about activities and actors in the 'underworld' (Matthews 2005).

There has been some enforcement of kerb-crawling over the past two decades, mainly as a result of public and political pressure, but police activity in this regard has been uneven and patchy (ACPO 2011). However, if we look at the police generated data on recorded crime in England and Wales we can see that over the last few years the main focus remains on women 'soliciting for the purpose of prostitution' which, although decreasing in 2010–2012, remains in the region of 1000 cases per annum. The number of crimes recorded for the exploitation of prostitution has remained consistently low, at around 150 per year since 2009–2010, while the numbers of trafficking and grooming offences

Table 11.1 Police recorded crime by offence in England and Wales 2009–2015

	2009–10	2010–11	2011–12	2012–13	2013–14	2014–15
Female soliciting	1190	626	707	883	750	868
Exploitation of prostitution	148	153	111	120	124	152
Trafficking for exploitation	58	66	59	70	123	193
Sexual grooming	303	309	371	370	460	693

Source: Home Office 2015

have increased, mainly as a result of growing political and media pressure (see Table 11.1).

In relation to those proceeded against in magistrates' courts in England and Wales between 2010 and 2013, we find that the number of male kerb-crawlers was 96 in 2010, of which 79 were found guilty (Ministry of Justice 2015). In 2013 the number proceeded against was 515, of which 321 were found guilty. In the same year the number of women proceeded against for soliciting was 419 of which 340 were found guilty. Thus, there has been an increase in the number of males prosecuted and convicted for kerb-crawling and a decrease in the number of women processed through the courts for soliciting in recent years.

However, if we compare these figures to the previous ten years, we find that the number of men convicted for kerb-crawling in 2002, for example, was 1993, while the number of women found guilty at magistrates' courts in England and Wales in 2002 was 2678 (Home Office 2004). Overall, this suggests that either there has been a significant decrease in the number of women involved in street prostitution and the number of kerb-crawlers over the past decade or, alternatively, that the police have been less actively involved in making arrests and prosecuting those involved. The available evidence suggests that both of these developments have occurred simultaneously.

One police initiative in the UK in recent years that has gained a considerable amount of attention has been 'Operation Pentameter', which ran from 2005 to 2006 in two phases. Its primary aim was to recover women trafficked for sexual exploitation (Avenell 2008). The operation resulted in 85 female victims of trafficking being rescued, but there were major problems in coordinating and implementing this initiative. The police officers involved in the operation, it transpired, had little knowledge and experience of women trafficked for sexual exploitation and little knowledge of the scale of off street prostitution. There were also major problems in the identification of victims, while the vast majority of officers were found to have a limited knowledge of victim support measures.

According to a report by Nick Davies (2009) in the Guardian newspaper, ten of the 55 police forces involved in the operation never found anyone to arrest, while 122 of the 528 arrests made by the police were wrongly recorded. Among the 406 arrests that did take place most of those arrested (230) were women and some were never implicated in trafficking at all. Although the police describe the operation as 'the culmination of months of planning and intelligence gathering', the reality was that during six months of concerted effort they found only 96 people to arrest for trafficking, of whom 67 were charged. Of these, 22 people were finally prosecuted for trafficking, seven were acquitted, and only 15 men and women were finally convicted.

Another example of ineffective policing of prostitution in England and Wales is the licensing of premises used for prostitution. Although Britain is formally an abolitionist country, which has a long history of outlawing brothels, it remains the case that brothels are regularly licensed as massage parlours or saunas, although it is widely known that they are in fact brothels. Not only are these premises licensed with limited safeguards but they are also allowed to operate largely undisturbed, unless there is a complaint or a report of underage girls being present. Monitoring the sites in which two or more women operate from the same premises is a relatively straightforward task, but one which the police in Britain, in general, seem reluctant to undertake. This example underlines the point that passing legislation to remove brothels is only one part of the process, the other part is enforcing the legislation.

There have, however, been some positive moves by the police recently in the UK and the USA involving the seizing of the proceeds of commercial sexual exploitation. Utilising the Proceeds of Crime Act (2002) in the UK has facilitated financial investigations of illicit activities and provided the capacity not only to create opportunities for prosecution but also to confiscate the considerable profits being made by third parties

(ACPO 2011). The assets seized from these operations could potentially be used to fund support and exiting programmes for women involved in prostitution.

The clear message from this example of policing prostitution and trafficking in the UK is that the capacity of legislation to better regulate prostitution—no matter how progressive it might be—requires consistent and dedicated policing and enforcement. It also requires a change in police culture and the tolerance of buyers' needs to be challenged, while at the same time women involved in prostitution should be seen as requiring supportive rather than punitive interventions. However, the task of policing prostitution has to some extent become more challenging with the growth of internet sites.

Regulating the Internet

The expansion of the internet has provided a major stimulus to the growth of the sex trade in general and prostitution in particular. Although some liberal commentators have argued that it has given women involved in prostitution greater freedom and independence the reality appears to be the opposite. The evidence, to date, indicates that not only has it increased the level of child prostitution but also that the vast majority of internet providers are subject to third party controllers and facilitators (Wells et al. 2012). As Donna Hughes has argued:

> The technological innovations and unregulated use of the internet have created a global medium for men's sexual exploitation and abuse of women and children. The sex industry has aggressively adopted every new information technology to increase men's sexual access to women and children. A mutually beneficial relationship exists between prostitution and related activities, such as online strip shows, sex shows and commercial voyeurism. The global communications forums have increased the visibility and exposure of women and children being exploited and abused, while conversely increasing the privacy and communication of men who exploit and abuse them. These forums normalize men's exploitive and abusive behaviour. Violence and humiliation are eroticized. (Hughes 2004: 1)

Hughes argues that there has been a blurring of the boundary between prostitution and pornography with acts of prostitution being filmed and later sold on the web. At the same time internet technologies have shifted the balance of power towards the pimps and commercial exploiters. It has been argued that saturating the internet with pornography and increasingly explicit advertisements for the sale of sexual services is having the effect of changing social and sexual relations as well as individual beliefs and identities.

While buyers remain hidden they are able to trawl the internet and access websites that provide endless details of the women whose services they aim to purchase, including their ratings and the range of services they offer. For the women involved there is a sense of over-exposure and the increased likelihood that they will be recognised in public. Most importantly, this form of sexual exploitation serves to normalise prostitution and the sex industry (Castle and Lee 2008).

Although the sale of sexual services on the internet has no doubt increased the profits and control of pimps and sex entrepreneurs, they have, however, been subject to certain controls and restrictions. Most notably the Craigslist section on 'erotic services' was closed down after a protracted legal battle (Stone 2009; Lundenberger 2010). In addition, there have been a number of legal actions, particularly in America, against websites advertising children. Facebook has also removed dozens of pages of explicit photographs with descriptions of specific sex acts alongside phone numbers, addresses and prices, following an investigation by *The Times* newspaper (Hamilton et al. 2013). However, for the most part the authorities see internet prostitution as a victimless crime and are reluctant to intervene unless there is a complaint or evidence of underage children being involved.

There have, however, been a few cases in which those involved in advertising the sexual services of others have been successfully prosecuted and many countries do have an existing body of legislation that could significantly reduce, if not end, internet prostitution. In America, for example, it is suggested that internet buyers could potentially be prosecuted under pandering, pimping and prostitution laws (Green 2001). Pimping, according to the Californian Penal Code prohibits 'any person from living or deriving support or maintenance ... in the earnings or proceeds of the person's prostitution'. Pandering is a felony offence punishable by up to six years in prison for persuading or encouraging another to engage in prostitution. There are also statutes prohibiting the use or renting of premises for prostitution. The webcasting of prostitution could constitute a violation of this statute. Most states in America have statutes criminalising the promotion of prostitution, while in Texas, for example, it is an offence to knowingly own, invest in, finance, control, supervise or manage a business for prostitution involving two or more people.

In Canada recent legislation criminalised 'anyone who receives material benefit from the crime of purchasing sexual services' and introduced a sweeping ban on advertising the sale of sexual services (Woolley 2014). In the UK it remains an offence for 'a man knowingly to live wholly or in part on the earnings of prostitution'. This offence falls under the Sexual Offences Act 1956 and carries a sentence of up to seven years' imprisonment. This legislation is largely directed at pimps but has been applied to landlords charging exorbitant rents. Under the legislation there needs to be proof that the perpetrator 'exercised control, direction or influence' over her movements in such a way as to show him to be 'aiding and abetting' her in prostitution. Those running escort agencies that advertise women for prostitution on the internet could conceivably be considered for prosecution under the legislation.

In addition, Lord McColl of Dulwich presented a Private Member's Bill to the House of Lords in June 2015 entitled 'Advertising of Prostitution (Prohibition) Bill', which states that:

> A person who publishes or causes to be published or distributed an advertisement which advertises a brothel or the services of a prostitute or any premises or service in terms, circumstances or manner which give rise to the reasonable inference that the premises is a brothel or that the service is one shall be guilty of an offence.

For the purposes of this proposed legislation the term advertisement includes every form of advertising or promotion including the use of the internet. The presentation of the Bill, whatever its outcome, indicates that there is an appetite for controlling the trade in sexual services over the internet and it may well be followed by more wide-ranging legislation designed to control the operation of the internet in general.

Paradoxically, however, one significant feature of the internet is that it has promoted the availability of 'free sex', with individuals advertising independently or through agency or dating websites. The fact that such services are readily available through the internet raises questions about the motivation of people who still want to pay for sexual services. It suggests that the purchasing of sexual services of those involved in prostitution is, as we have always suspected, not so much about sex as about power. It also undermines the frequently articulated rationale by buyers that they pay for sex because they are frustrated and cannot gain access to a social partner.

Examples of policing extreme forms of pornography and juvenile prostitution on the internet demonstrate that the advantage of this situation for regulatory agencies is that buyers can be identified and traced in a way that, previously, was difficult. Although buyers may believe that they have privacy and immunity the reality is that if internet prostitution was seriously policed with the cooperation of internet providers it would be relatively easy to identify buyers.

Conclusion

It has been argued in this chapter that the Nordic Model represents a potentially progressive strategy for regulating prostitution by criminalising the demand for sexual services and treating the women involved in prostitution as either victims or agents. The overall effect of the Nordic Model has been shown to reduce the number of commercial transactions and to provide a disincentive to sex trafficking. In this way it has the capacity to reduce exploitation and suffering. However, the Nordic Model in itself does not provide a total solution to the issue of prostitution and sex trafficking. In countries like the UK that are moving towards the adoption of the Nordic model there are a number of associated issues that need to be addressed either to help facilitate its introduction or to make its implementation more successful (All Party Parliamentary Group 2014).

Taking the UK as an example, it is suggested that an effective and comprehensive interventionist strategy has to include a radical rethink of the exiting process and a focus on general social attitudes towards the purchase of sex, which may involve developing publicity and educational campaigns. The growth of the internet and its impact on the sex trade raises challenging issues of regulation, while the international issue of sex trafficking requires a serious re-conceptualisation of the meanings of coercion and consent, together with the development of a more positive and coordinated response. There is evidence that in the UK and other European Countries a fundamental shift is taking place in social attitudes and that the purchase of sex is becoming less acceptable, while the women involved in prostitution are increasingly seen as being capable—with the appropriate support—of exiting prostitution and moving away from a life of abuse, exploitation and coercion.

As we learnt from anti-smoking campaigns an effective strategy needs to engage with the issue at a number of different levels. There is a requirement to develop formal legal responses alongside more informal strategies that connect with the hearts and minds of the general public. Introducing the Nordic model in countries like the UK would no doubt be a very positive step, but for this legislation to be effective a number of other related changes in policy and practice need to take place.

References

ACPO. (2011). *ACPO strategy and supporting operational guidance for policing prostitution and sexual exploitation*. Association of Chief Police Officers.

Agustin, L. (2006). The conundrum of women's agency: Migration and the sex industry. In R. Campbell & M. O'Neill (Eds.), *Sex work now*. Cullompton: Willan.

All Party Parliamentary Group. (2014). *Shifting the burden: Inquiry to assess the operation of the current legal settlement on prostitution in England and Wales*. London: HMSO.

Anti-Trafficking Monitoring Group. (2010). *Wrong kind of victim? One year on: An analysis of UK measures to protect trafficked persons*. ATMG.

Avenell, J. (2008). *Trafficking for sexual exploitation: A process review of operation pentameter*. Research report. London: Home Office.

Bourgois, P., & Schonberg, J. (2009). *Righteous dopefiend*. Berkeley: University of California Press.

Buchanan, J. (2004). Missing links? Problem drug use and social exclusion. *Journal of Community and Criminal Justice, 5*(4), 390–404.

Burken-Knapp, G., & Schaffer, J. (2010). Why Norway banned the purchase of sexual services—Ideas in prostitution policy. *Paper presented at the Swedish Political Science Association Annual Meeting.* Gothenburg.

Castle, T., & Lee, J. (2008). Ordering sex in cyberspace: A content analysis of escort websites. *International Journal of Cultural Studies, 11*(1), 107–121.

CEOP (2011). *Out of mind, out of sight: Breaking down the barriers to understanding child sexual exploitation.* London: Child Exploitation and Online Protection Centre.

Chu, S., & Glass, R. (2013). Sex work law reform in Canada: Considering problems with the Nordic model. *Alberta Law Review, 51*, 101–124.

Church, S., Henderson, M., Barnerd, M., & Hart, K. (2001). Violence by clients towards female prostitutes in different work settings. *British Medical Journal, 332*, 524–525.

Coy, M., Horrath, L., & Kelly, L. (2007). *Its just like going to the supermarket: Men buying sex in East London.* London: London Metropolitan University.

Davies, N. (2009). Inquiry fails to find a single trafficker who forced anybody into prostitution. *The Guardian*, October 20.

Doran, M. (2008). Economic evaluations of interventions to treat opiate dependence. *PharmacoEconomics, 26*(5), 371–393.

Durchlag, R., & Goswani, S. (2008). *Deconstructing the demand for prostitution: Preliminary insights from interviews with Chicago men who purchase sex.* Chicago Alliance Against Sexual Exploitation.

Ebaugh, H. (1988). *Becoming an Ex: The process of role exit.* Chicago: Chicago University Press

Farley, M., Bindel, J., & Golding, J. (2009). *Men who buy sex: Who they buy and what they know.* London/San Francisco: Eaves/Prostitution Research and Education.

Flowers, R. (2001). *Runaway kids and teenage prostitution.* Westport Connecticut: Praeger.

Gossop, M., Marsden, J., Stewart, D., & Treacy, S. (2001). Outcomes after methadone maintenance and methadone reduction treatments. *Drug and Alcohol Dependence, 62*(3), 255–264.

Green, M. (2001). Sex on the internet: A legal click or an illicit trick? *California Western Law Review, 38*(2), 527–546.

Hamilton, F., Ahmed, M., & Kenber, B. (2013). Children are at risk as prostitutes use Facebook to sell their wares. *The Times*, January 30.

Hedin, U.-C., & Mansson, S.-V. (2003). The importance of supportive relationships among women leaving prostitution. In M. Farley (Ed.), *Prostitution, trafficking and traumatic stress*. New York: Haworth Press.

Herman, J. (1992). *Trauma and recovery*. New York: Basic Books.

Hester, M., & Wetmarland, N. (2004). *Tackling street prostitution: Towards a holistic approach*. In *Home Office Research Study 279*. London: Home Office.

Home Office (2004). Paying the Price: a consultation paper on prostitution. London: Home Office.

Home Office (2014). *Shifting the burden: Inquiry to assess the operation of the current legal settlement on prostitution in England and Wales*. London: HMSO.

Home Office (2014a). *Review of the national referral mechanism for victims of human trafficking*. London: HMSO.

Home Office (2015). *Crime in England and Whales*. London: Home Office.

Hughes, D. (2004). Prostitution online. *Journal of Trauma Practice, 2*(3–4), 113–131.

Jackson, K., Jeffrey, J., & Adamson, G. (2010). *Setting the record: The trafficking of migrant women in the England and Wales off-street prostitution sector*. London: Project Acumen, ACPO.

Jago, S., Arosha, L., Brodie, I., Melrose, M., Pearce, J., & Warrington, C. (2011). *What's going on to safeguard children and young people from sexual exploitation?* Luton: University of Bedfordshire.

Jakobsson, N., & Kotsadam, A. (2010). *Do laws affect attitudes? An assessment of the Norwegian prostitution law using longitudinal data* (Working Paper 457). Department of Economics, University of Gothenburg.

Jeffreys, S. (1997). *The idea of prostitution*. Melbourne: Spinifex Press.

Jeffreys, S. (2004). The legalisation of prostitution: A failed social experiment. *Women's Health Watch Newsletter, 64*, 8–11.

Johnson, H. (2015). *The emotional trajectories of women's desistance: A repertory grid study on women exiting prostitution*. PhD Thesis, University of Kent.

Kinnell, H. (2013). *Violence and sex work in Britain*. Routledge.

Lindenberger, M. (2010). Craiglist comes clean: No more 'Adult Services' Ever?' *Time Magazine*, September 16.

Mai, N. (2009). *Migrant sex workers in the UK sex industry*. London: London Metropolitan University.

Mansson, S.-V., & Hedin, U.-C. (1999). Breaking the Mathew effect—On women leaving prostitution. *British Journal of Social Welfare, 8*, 67–77.

Marcovich, M. (2006). *Report of the CATW campaign: 'Buying sex is not a sport'*. Campaign Against Trafficking in Women.

Maruna, S. (2001). *Making good: How ex-convicts reform and rebuild their lives.* Washington, DC: American Psychological Association.

Matthews, R. (2005). Policing prostitution: Ten years on. *British Journal of Criminology, 45,* 1–20.

Matthews, R. (2008). *Prostitution, politics and policy.* London: Routledge.

Matthews, R., & Easton, H. (2010). *Prostitution in Glasgow: A strategic review: Glasgow community safety services. www.saferglasgow.com.*

Matthews, R. (2011). 'Female Prostitution and Victimization: A Realist Analysis' *International review of victimology.* 21(1), 85-100.

Matthews, R., Easton, H., Young, L., & Bindel, J. (2014). *Exiting prostitution: A study in female desistance.* Basingstoke: Palgrave Macmillan.

May, T., & Hunter, G. (2006). Sex work and the problem of drug use in the UK: The links, problems and possible solutions. In R. Campbell & M. O'Neill (Eds.), *Sex work now.* Cullompton: Willan.

McColl, L. (2015). Advertising of Prostitution (Prohibition) Bill 2015–16. http://services.parliament.uk/bills/2015-16/advertisingofprostitution.html. London: HMSO.

McLeod, J., Farley, M., Anderson, L., & Golding, J. (2008). *Challenging men's demand for prostitution in Scotland.* Glasgow: Women's Support Project.

Ministry of Justice. (2015). *Justice statistics.* London: HMSO.

MJP. (2004). Purchasing sexual services in Sweden and the Netherlands. Norway: Ministry of Justice and the Police. Available at http://www.regjeringen.no/en/dep/jd/Documents-and-publications/Reports/Reports/2004/Purchasing-Sexual-Services.html?id=106214

Mossman, S., & Mayhew, P. (2007). *Key informant interviews: Review of the prostitution reform act 2003* (Report for the Ministry of Justice). Wellington: Ministry of Justice.

Pateman, S. (1988). *The sexual contract.* Cambridge: Polity Press.

Plumridge, E. W., Chetwynd, S. J., Reed, A., & Gifford, S. J. (1997). Discourses of emotionality in commercial sex: The missing client voice. *Feminism & Psychology, 7*(2), 165–181.

Poland, F., Boswell, G., & Killett, A. (2008). *Evaluation research report for Ipswich Street Prostitution Strategy 2007–08.* University of East Anglia.

Raymond, J. G. (2003). Ten reasons for not legalizing prostitution and a legal response to the demand for prostitution. *Journal of Trauma Practice, 2,* 315–332.

Raymond, J. (2013). *Not a choice, not a job: Exposing the myths about prostitution and the global sex trade.* Nebraska: Potomac Books.

Reid, R. (2005). *Globalizing tobacco control.* Bloomington: Indiana University Press.

Rumgay, J. (2004). Scripts for safer survival: Pathways out of female crime. *The Howard Journal, 43*(4), 405–419.

Sanders, T. (2005). *Sex work: A risky business.* Cullompton: Willan.

Sanders, T. (2008). *Paying for pleasure: Men who buy sex.* Cullompton: Willan.

Scarhed, A. (2010). *Evaluation of the prohibition of the purchase of sexual services.* Government Offices of Sweden.

Sharpe, K., & Earle, S. (2003). Cyberpunters and cyberwhores: Prostitution on the internet. In Y. Jewkes (Ed.), *Dot cons, crime, deviance and identity on the internet.* Willan: Cullompton.

Skilbrei, M.-L., & Holmstrom, C. (2011). Is there a Nordic regime? *Crime and Justice, 40*(1), 479–517.

Sparks, R. (1981). Multiple victimisation: Evidence, theory and future research. *Journal of Criminal Law and Criminology, 72*(2), 762–778.

Stone, B. (2009). Under pressure: Craiglist to remove erotic Ads. *The New York Times*, May 13.

Swann, S., & Balding, V. (2002). Safeguarding children involved in prostitution. Guidance Review. London: Department of Health.

Waltman, M. (2011). Sweden's prohibition of the purchase of sex: The law's reasons, impact and potential. *Women's Studies International Forum, 34*(5), 449–474.

Ward, H., Mercer, C., Wellings, K., Fenton K., Erens, B., Copas, A., & Johnson, A. (2005). Who pays for sex? An analysis of the increasing prevalence of female sex contacts among men in Britain. *Sexually Transmitted Infections.* http://sti.bmj.com/cgi/content/abstract/81/6/467

Weitzer, R. (2005). The growing moral panic over prostitution and sex trafficking. *The Criminologist, 5*(September/October), 2–5.

Wells, M., Mitchell, K., & Ji, K. (2012). Exploring the role of the internet in Juvenile prostitution cases coming to the attention of law enforcement. *Journal of Child Sexual Abuse, 21*, 327–342.

Index

Note: Page numbers with "n" denote notes.